THE BEST KEPT SE
(

AMERICA WON THE VIETNAM WAR!

OR

HOW THE LEFT SNATCHED DEFEAT FROM THE JAWS OF VICTORY

Dr. Robert Owens,

America Won the Vietnam War!
by Robert R. Owens, Ph.D.

Printed in the United States of America

ISBN-13:
978-1544252742

ISBN-10:
1544252749

Contents

THE DELIBERATE DELUSION

PREFACE

"Knowledge" Versus "Common Knowledge"

In the summer of 2003, I had the occasion to spend some quality time with some relatives. As the conversation waxed and waned, one brother-in-law made it a point to steer the conversation to a reflection on the Vietnam War. Neither of us are veterans but both of us have well staked-out political opinions. My brother-in-law is a Left Coast Liberal of the New Age School and I am what I like to think of as a "Classical Liberal" of the Theodore Roosevelt School or what modern parlance has termed a "Conservative."

As one of America's greatest heroes, Yogi Berra once said, "It was like déjà vu all over again."[1]

In a moment's time, our conversation flashed back thirty years. My brother-in-law religiously rehearsed the stock platitudes and "common knowledge" first created by the Democratic Republic of Vietnam (once known as North Vietnam) and their sympathizers and later perfected by the leftist media. According to this cacophony of woe, The Vietnam War represented at best, "America's worst defeat," and at worst, "An immoral war waged by Capitalists to exploit the vast resources of Vietnam." These philosophical broadsides sent my mind back to review how we as a society had arrived at the place where such politically charged assumptions had become, "Common Knowledge."

I remembered that, thirty years ago, the daily drone of this type of bombast had prevailed on the campuses, on the nightly news broadcasts, and in the newspapers. Day after day, week after week until, as each source quoted the other they built a seamless wall of subjective opinion offered up as objective fact. I recalled how the intervening years had seen the rise of the former protestors into leading positions within our society, in publishing, in academia, and in politics. Then I thought about how during the intervening years America's anti-American social elite had squandered and depreciated the valiant service of our troops in Vietnam.

To say a vocal and powerful minority had accomplished a change in perception is one thing but to look at a united Communist Vietnam today and say, "America Won the Vietnam War" takes some explaining. How could this have possibly come about IF America won?

Like the self-fulfilling prophecy of a Marxist fever-dream, the United States Congress finally affirmed the hyperbolic self-depreciating propaganda of the left. They codified it through legislation and they reaffirmed it through their rhetoric. Of course we must remember, this was a Congress which, following its successful ouster of President Nixon was firmly in the grasp of the far-left McGovern (Born:1922)[2] fringe of the Democrat Party.

Being an Historian who teaches (among other things) Military History at the college level, I tried to shed some reason into the harangue. I tried to point out the difference between victory and defeat on the battlefield, between achieving goals, achieving total victory, and winning the peace. I tried to cite some sources and to see if my relative had anything to back up his vehemently expressed opinions besides an emotional investment in "Being Right!" However, just as thirty years ago when the fanatical followers of "Free Speech" began their campaign to drive free speech from the campuses of our universities replacing it with a "Political Correctness" that allows no deviation and penalizes everything except the Liberal Party Line, the "conversation" soon degenerated into the frenzy and heat of a personal attack.

This highly unpleasant experience made me realize that when the methodology of self-induced hysteria and verbal bombast does not allow any space for the methodology of referencing documented sources and reality it is not worth the effort. It is most especially not worth the effort within the context of a family reunion with nothing of substance to gain and a relationship to lose.

Nevertheless, this encounter pointed out to me the vast sea of emotions still attached to the war in Vietnam.

I certainly don't fault my brother-in-law for his passionately held hatred of any thought which disagrees with his historical ideology. He has a lifetime of self-image invested in his beliefs. He was a courageous conscientious observer who after turning in his draft card served his sentence of community service while I am merely a person with a high draft number that the Army would not accept as a volunteer. However, I accepted the now much-maligned "Domino Theory." In addition, I believed, at the time, as I believe today that we really were engaged in a war against the forces of Totalitarian International Communism, known as "The Cold War."

Many pundits tell us the speedy victory of Gulf War I with its VJ-Day style celebrations brought closure to America's Vietnam angst. However I believe the continuing emotional attachment of the Bridgers who planned and the Boomers who executed both the war and the protest tell us differently.

As we look back through the lens of time, the Vietnam War has sufficiently entered our "History" for a reevaluation, for a search for knowledge. This is a reevaluation of what has become, through the ever-present drumbeat of the media and the incessant preaching of educators, "Common Knowledge."

---

[1] Berra, Yogi, The Yogi Book: "I Didn't Really Say Everything I Said!" Workman Publishing: New York, NY, 1998, p. 30.

[2] http://gi.grolier.com/presidents/ea/side/mcgovern.html (11-25-03) Informational

Dedicated with appreciation and admiration to those who sacrificed so much: America's Vietnam Veterans.

Robert R. Owens, Ph.D.
12-31-03

Introduction

This study must begin with a question and a definition:

What is victory?

Defined in many ways by many people, often in ways specifically designed to suit their own purpose we might say, "Victory is in the eye of the beholder."

In this work, I define victory in two basic ways:

1. Prevailing on the field of battle.

2. Achieving the goals set for the military by the political leadership.

It is within the context of these twin definitions that I will present the case for my conclusion that **America WON the Vietnam War**. I realize that I will face the attack of the well-entrenched establishment. An establishment that has a stake in perpetuating the "Common Knowledge" that America was defeated on the battlefield. I realize that as an Historian I risk the (almost inevitable) accusation of "Historical Revisionism." However, my purpose is to correct the "Hysterical Revisionism" which in a scant 30 years has changed the heroic self-sacrificing victory of America's Vietnam soldiers into the rout of a defeated army. A rout which is etched in the minds of millions as represented by the oft replayed pictures of frantic, terrified people clinging to the undercarriages of helicopters as they leave an American Embassy about to be over-run. Pictures, which even the true believers among the historical ideologues should not hesitate to admit, are not part of the military record but of the political. Actually, they are pictures of events, which occurred two years AFTER the end of the war.[3]

This book does not attempt to present a detailed examination of the day-today field operations. Suffice it to say I believe that the forces of the United States won the war on the battlefield as evidenced in Hanoi's eventual decision to sign the Paris Peace Accords. If the Communists had not perceived that they would not and could not win on the field of battle, they never would have signed that agreement.

No point-by-point analysis is made of the Paris Peace Accords. Instead, this work shows that the goals and aims of the United States, as represented in the public pronouncements and official statements of its political leaders over a period of approximately 40 years, found fulfillment in and through this document. A document solemnly signed by all parties and solemnly observed by none.

Throughout this work many excerpts from long quotations (mainly speeches and documents), form a contiguous and integral component within the text. In challenging the long held quasi-religious positions of the Left, I know that the veracity of this work and the validity of the scholarship presented will face immediate assault by the purveyors of the established interpretation of the Vietnam War. Therefore, the full text of these pivotal quotations appears in the Appendix so that the actors and events of history may speak with their own voices within their own context. Where deemed necessary to the flow of the presentation of supporting evidence or for the development of a contextual understanding certain long quotes have been included within the text. In addition, to provide the reader with a source for further study the addresses of many websites have been included in the footnotes, which do not reflect direct references but are instead for information only. These references are marked "Informational."

It is my belief that this work is not only necessary for historical accuracy but is imperative in the cause of justice for the brave men and women who fought and won the war, our Vietnam Veterans.

To you, the brave and unappreciated veterans of
Vietnam I say:

You may not have received a parade when you came home. The major media may continue to malign your name. However, beginning here, it is my hope that you will finally see the record of your courageous achievements corrected and the history of your self-less service acknowledged as I work to reveal the best kept secret of the twentieth century,

"America Won the Vietnam War!"

[3] Herrington, Stuart A.. Peace With Honor?. Presido: Novato, CA., 1983, pp.173-187, passim.

HISTORICAL CONTEXT

CHAPTER ONE

The Early History of Indochina

Indochina is the eastern most peninsula of Southern Asia. Politically, in the nineteenth and early twentieth century major divisions included: Upper and Lower Burma, ruled by Britain; the Malay Peninsula, which England shared with Siam; the Empire of Siam, and French Indochina. French Indochina included the Colony of Cochin China, the vassal kingdoms of Cambodia and Annam, the Tong-King and the Laotian Protectorates. The peninsula stretches for about 1200 miles from the Chinese frontier on the north to the Cambodian coast on the south. At its widest point from the Gulf of Tong-king on the east to the Bay of Bengal on the west its width is approximately 1000 miles. Its approximate area is 735,000 square miles, or about one-fourth the area of the United States. Its population during the later colonial period stood at approximately 34,000,000.[4]

French Indochina had an area almost four times the size of France. This area has a productive soil suitable to intense agriculture. Several large rivers generally flowing from north to south water the land. There are rich deposits of minerals and other resources. Several spacious natural harbors, especially along the eastern coast inspired an early interest in international trade. Located between India and the Far East the area has always benefited from its location as a natural crossroads of traders.

The lofty mountain ranges located between the major river basins acted as a barrier to the growth of a regional national unity among the tribes occupying the northern area. In a similar fashion, the rapid change of climate acted as a hindrance to north-south tribal growth. This growth occurred primarily through migration and trade along the courses of the major rivers. Both of these facts acted as natural buffers to a wider unity. They also acted as an incubator of independent national development on a smaller local scale. Consequently from the earliest times, there has been a marked difference between the people of North and South Vietnam.

During the colonial period, the people of Indochina represented every degree of civilization. The original inhabitants were of Malay origin, migrating from the islands of the Pacific. Known by various names during the colonial period, the survivors of these original inhabitants included the Moïs in Vietnam, Pnongs in Cambodia, Khas in Laos.[5]

At a very early period, several waves of invasion swept over Indochina. Coming from northern India the first of these floods consisted of various tribes of Aryans. These Aryans drove the earlier inhabitants into the remote areas and mountains. The invaders possessed themselves of the lush lowlands. The Aryans founded the Khmer Empire, which came to possess all the territories under study.

Although the actual history of the Khmer Empire is still lost the vast and widespread remains of the Khmer Empire bare stark evidence of the far-reaching impact and influence of the Khmer people in the day of their power. The evidence of their remains speaks of a people secure and free from the fear of either internal disruption or external invasion. The currently known remains indicate a culture possibly without peer in the area.

Peoples of the far-conquering Mongol race constituted a second great wave of early invasion. They came down through Southern China. They established themselves as conquerors founding the Annamite Empire. The Annamites gradually absorbed the earlier inhabitants. The first rulers claimed descent from the royal house of China. This Chinese dynasty ruled until 257 BC. Two native dynasties, governed from 257 to 110 BC the Annamite empire as vassals of the Chinese Empire. Then in 110 BC a resurgent Chinese Empire cast aside the devise of ruling through proxies as they conquered, occupied, and formally annexed Annam. For the next thousand years from 110 BC until 930 AD, Chinese governors administered Annam as the southern most province of the Celestial Empire.

For a long, silent period of more than nine hundred years, the region labored under Chinese domination and there is little independent historical information concerning Indochina. Then in the beginning of the tenth century, the Annamite chiefs revolted. They successfully broke free of Chinese domination, and established a new dynasty. China never recognized the legality or permanence of this separation and continued to claim a titular sovereignty over Indochina until the intervention of the French.

At the beginning of this period of independence Annamite influence extended only over what today is northern Vietnam. However, they soon concentrated all its forces against the Ciampas. This invasion faced serious and sustained opposition. The fact that Hue remained the capital of the Ciampese Kingdom as well into the fifteenth century in the face of almost constant warfare shows that Ciampas fought long and well. Eventually the Annamite pressure forced the Ciampese to retire towards the south.

Due to almost constant attack by the Annamites by the end of the seventeenth century, they had completely absorbed the kingdom of Ciampas. The same period witnessed the final ruin of the Khmer Empire. In 1658, the now united Annamites and Ciampas defeated the King of Cambodia, forcing him to acknowledge the hegemony of Annam. In 1675, when civil war broke out in the territories of the King of Cambodia, Annam interfered conquering the southern territories of that kingdom. The Annamites then set up vassal kings to administer the area. When a new revolution broke out in Cambodia in 1689, Annam quickly moved in to profit from the continued destabilization of Cambodia to colonize various districts with their own people.

By the end of the seventeenth century, the empire of Annam included either directly or as vassals all the territories of Indochina. It is from this time that the Nguyen family rose to prominence as imperial governors.

A great insurrection against the Annamite Empire marked the last decades of the eighteenth century.[6] Two brothers of the western branch of the Nguyen family, Nguyen van Nhac (1777-1792)[7] and Nguyen van Hue (1952-1792)[8] led this revolt. The brothers forced the last member of the royal family to flee to China. After this another member of the Nguyen clan, Nguyen-an, sought out French assistance and in 1789, he seized Saigon and Hue in 1801. In 1802, Nguyen-an felt secure enough to declare himself emperor and taking the name of Gialong (1761-1820).[9]

Once in possession of nearly all the territories which would eventually become colonial French Indochina, Gialong worked at the reconstruction and reorganization of a country devastated by years of internecine war. He spent years developing a vast system of transportation consisting of both canals and roads. To integrate and administer his new empire Gialong built a long and impressive royal road. This road started at Saigon and terminated at the Chinese frontier. It passed through Hue and Hanoi thus uniting the north and the south, then as now the two main divisions of the region.

Gialong owed his empire to the assistance of Europeans.

Throughout his reign, he lavished favor and privileges on them. However, after his death his son and successor, Minh Mang (1820-41), [10] hated westerners and began imposing restrictions on their activities. These anti-western policies initiated by, Minh Mang especially his vicious persecution of Christian missionaries eventually provided the justification for French intervention.[11]

French Indochina

Napoleon III (1808-1873)[12] looking to expand his French Empire and using the excuse that Christians were being persecuted made the decision to invade Indochina in July 1857.[13] In August 1858; he sent a fleet of 14 ships and an army of 5,000 men to conquer the country. They landed at the port of Da Nang. Due to their superior weapons, the French were able to capture the city in a one-day assault. However, they did not have the necessary shallow-draft boats to move up the river and assault the Vietnamese capital of Hue. At this time, the Second Opium War broke out in China. The French joined the other western powers in attacking the Chinese in an effort to open-up the opium traffic to their control. Due to this drain on their resources in the area, there were no reinforcements available for the attack in Indochina. In addition, The French had expected that massive anti-government uprisings by Vietnamese Catholics would coincide with their assault. These uprisings failed to materialize. Then the climate began to work against the Europeans as French casualties from tropical diseases soon exceeded their casualties from battle. Then, when the rainy season, came in October French army hunkered down to wait for the spring.

Leaving an open Da Nang in his rear, Admiral Rigault Genouilly (1807-1873)[14], the French commander decided turned his attention to the south. He managed to capture

Saigon, and the rice-growing Mekong delta region. The more numerous Vietnamese forces now laid siege to the French in Saigon. Throughout 1861, the battle see-sawed back and forth until reinforcements and some Spanish troops from Manila relieved the weary French garrison. Taking the offensive the Franco-Spanish forces soon conquered approximately half of the Mekong delta.[15]

The Vietnamese were not able to resist the more advanced military technology of the Europeans. Finally forced to surrender the Vietnamese signed a treaty that that gave up the provinces captured by the French. Having enough to handle in the Philippines he Spanish soon left Vietnam to the French. In 1863, the King of Cambodia gave in to French pressure and signed a treaty that transferred Cambodia's vassalage from Siam to France. In an effort to prevent Vietnamese interference in Cambodian affairs, the governor of Saigon annexed the rest of the Mekong delta for France in 1867.

After ten years of colonial government, the Third French Republic decided it was time to expand their holdings through the seizure of more colonies. Captain Henri Riviere (1827-1883) led a force of 250 men in April 1882 to Hanoi with orders to suppress the Black Flags. This group had become dominate in most of Tonkin. Riviere was defeated and then the French became determined to impose French control over Tonkin.[16]

The assault began in August 1883, when a great army moved north accompanied by a large French fleet, which carried out a merciless bombardment of the city of Hue. It was then learned that the Vietnamese Emperor Tu Duc (1848-1883)[17] had died just a few weeks before the new invasion. With the Imperial court in turmoil the court officials did not feel strong enough politically or militarily to resist and so they surrendered the whole country to the French.[18]

The French moved quickly to take complete control of

their new colony. However, as they neared the border with China a new war broke out between France and China, which still claimed an ancient right of suzerainty over Vietnam. At first, the Chinese made advances on land but in 1885 the French fleet occupied several seaports on the Chinese coast. This compelled China to get out of Vietnam as the only way to dislodge the French from their home territories. [19]

Eventually French Indochina embraced the whole of the eastern, and a large portion of the northern and southern sections of the peninsula. On the north and northeast, the Chinese provinces of Yunan and Kwang-si formed its boundary. The Gulf of Tong-king and the Sea of China bounded it on the east and the southeast. A treaty line drawn between Siam and Cambodia was the border on the west. The Right Bank of the Mekong separated the colony from Siam and Burma. This region included an area estimated at 262,000 square miles.

The Colonial Government of French Indo-China

An appointed governor-general ruled the colony in the name of the French government. In typical colonial fashion he had the sole right to correspond with the French Government. He had complete control of the land and sea forces in Indo-China. Two councils, the Superior Counsel of Indo-China, and the Counsel of Defense assisted the governor-general both of which, were appointed either by the governor-general or the French government. All effective authority was in the hands of the French colonialists. However, the native sovereigns exercised certain severely proscribed powers in matters of purely local interest.[20]

This short history of Indochina before the Vietnam War serves to show a region long under foreign domination, a region ripe for the twentieth-century winds of self-determination.

[4] http://www.newadvent.org/cathen/07765a.htm (11-6-03).

[5] Ibid.

[6] http://art-hanoi.com/toda/19.html (11-26-03).

[7] Ibid.

[8] http://www.geocities.com/olmightykhan/Vietnamese.html (11-26-03).

[9] http://www.geocities.com/imperialvietnam/gialong.html (11-26-03).

[10] http://www.richmond.edu/~ebolt/history398/EmperorMinhMang.html (11-26-03).

[11] Ibid.; Karnow, Stanley. Vietnam: A History. The Viking Press: New York, 1983, Pages 66-67.

[12] http://www.newadvent.org/cathen/10699a.htm (11-26-03).

[13] Ibid, Pages 71-73.

[14] http://www.britannica.com/eb/article?eu=65304 (11-17-03). Informational.

[15] Karnow, pages 72-78, 107.

[16] http://www.onwar.com/aced/data/india/indochina1882.htm (11-17-03).

[17] http://www.geocities.com/imperialvietnam/tuduc.html (11-17-03). Informational.

[18] Karnow, pages79-86.

[19] Hayes, Carlton, J. H. Contemporary Europe Since 1870. The Macmillian Company: New York, 1958, pages 94-97.

[20] Clifford, John H. (Managing Ed.). The Standard History of the World. The University Society: New York, 1914, Volume 6: page 3349, 3635-3636; Volume 7: page 3844-3845, 3851-3854; Volume 8: Pages 4636-4637; Volume 10: page 132-138.; Johnson, Rossiter (Editor-in-Chief). Kenway, Sir Robert Douglas. "France In Annam." The Great Events by Famous Historians. (Volume 19: pages 120-132) by. The National Alumni: New York, 1905..; http://www.guidetothailand.com/thailand-history/indochina.htm (11-5-03); http://reference.allrefer.com/encyclopedia/I/Indochin.html (11-5-03); http://www.zum.de/whkmla/region/seasia/xfrindochina.html (11-5-03); http://en.wikipedia.org/wiki/French_Indochina (11-5-03).

CHAPTER TWO

World War II

The great shock of World War I caused the European colonial powers to draw heavily upon their subject peoples for resources of men and material. During the long war the natives, many of which, fighting alongside their masters, who had always worked hard to project an image of unassailable superiority, saw that these foreign interlopers came close to defeat. These factors combined with the propaganda efforts of the western powers in claiming to fight for "democracy" and "self-determination"[21] ushered in a new era of restiveness and discontent among the people of Southeast Asia with the status quo.

In the aftermath of the Great War and especially during the society shaking domestic economic problems caused by the Great Depression, the Western Powers seemed to lose their resolve for empire. After centuries of almost uninterrupted military dominance, the ever-intrusive "Big Brothers" suddenly appeared distracted and vulnerable. In the colonies this ushered in an era marked by shifting diplomatic alignments, faltering loyalties, and raised hopes.

Then, during the late 1930s and the early 1940s the self-imposed colonial masters seemed more interested in defending against the advancing Nazi advances in Europe then they were about their Asian colonies. The Europeans took their superiority for granted. Feeling so secure as the ruling class that they could not only drain their Asian provinces of military personnel and supplies they could also recruit their subjects to both guard themselves and fight for them in far-flung theaters. This created a situation, which not only starkly revealed their new weakness to the subject people but also at the same time trained and armed those same people.

The inattention to support and the need for help on the part of the Europeans opened opportunities for many Southeast Asian nationalists to assert leadership. The repercussions of this fluid situation can be can be seen in the following Vietnamese examples. The founding of the Vietminh, (the Vietnamese abbreviation for "League of the Revolution and Independence of Vietnam"[22]) resistance in 1941. In 1943 Nguyen Ai Quoc changed his name to Ho Chi Minh (1890-1969)[23] and assumed the leadership of Vietminh resistance.[24] Beginning in 1944, Vo Nguyen Giap (b. 1912)[25] reformed the rag-tag Vietminh militia into the Vietnam Liberation Army.[26]

However, the Westerners firmly ensconced in their cultural and racial bigotry and preoccupied with weathering the onslaught of the European fascists did not take the Asiatic fascists of Japan seriously as a threat. They imagined that they would remain impervious to defeat at the hands of people from an inferior race. These deep-seated convictions of invulnerability persisted although by that time the Empire of the Rising Sun had successfully copied and in many ways improved the technological and organizational edge, which had given the Europeans their military superiority for so long.

The cause for the eruption that would become known as, the Franco-Japanese Border War, which lasted from Sept.

22, 1940 to Sept. 24, 1940,[27] was that Japan demanded the right of passage for her troops through French Indochina. Japan desired this right in order to attack the Nationalist Chinese[28] forces. The French colonial bureaucrats in Hanoi still secure in their tropical fastness and their imagined western superiority refused out of hand. This in turn prompted Japan, with its vast legions of battle hardened troops to launch a massive ground attack on the French. Their attack commenced at the supposedly impregnable border forts located at Dong-Dang and Long-Son. Haiphong became the next target as the Japanese air force launched an indiscriminate bombing attack while the Imperial Japanese navy landed marines at the port cutting off the city. Two days of intense fighting left hundreds of French troops dead and a Colonial Government inclined to compromise.[29]

In January of 1941, Thailand acting as an ally of Japan, invaded French Indochina.[30] This invasion flowed as the prearranged result of almost continual border skirmishes instigated by Japan and initiated by the Thai military. In the first few days of the war, the Thais were generally successful against light resistance. Nevertheless, the French hastily gathered reinforcements from the far-flung outposts of Indochina and soon forced the Thais to fall back with heavy casualties. At this time the only available French Navy vessel in Southeast Asian waters was an old cruiser. However, on Jan. 17, in a stunning victory the French ship was able to destroy a large portion of the Thai navy.[31] A Japanese brokered cease-fire on Jan. 28 did not reflect the actual outcome of the fighting but did reflect the overwhelming power of the Japanese in what had become for them a new sphere of influence.

The Japanese brought both parties to the negotiations in Tokyo and while using, the niceties of diplomacy imposed a peace that suited its purposes. This peace formally recognized that French Indochina was now a part of the Japanese sphere of influence. The inclusion of such statements as: "It is my firm belief that the establishment of **a sphere of common prosperity throughout Greater East Asia** (emphasis added) is not only Japan's policy, but indeed a historical necessity in the event of world history,"[32] and "The Japanese Government considered that it would be undesirable in the interests of the whole East Asia if this state of affairs were allowed to last long, and therefore **we have decided to mediate** (emphasis added) between the two countries"[33] accentuated the new relative status of the two powers in the area.[34]

According to the treaty signed on March 11, the victors surrendered large areas of both Cambodia and Laos to Thailand thus ending the Franco-Thai Border War.[35] Explicit within the agreement was the admission by France that this agreement stood upon the guarantee of the Japanese government. "In signing the above-mentioned terms of mediation, letters were exchanged between France and Japan and between Japan and Thailand which have clarified to the effect **that Japan guarantees** (emphasis added) the definitive nature of the settlement of the dispute by the aforementioned terms of mediation and that agreements will subsequently be made with respect to the maintenance of peace in Greater East Asia and the establishment and promotion of the specially closer relations between Japan and Thailand and between Japan and French Indo-China."[36] In the accepted diplomatic language of the day, this statement in and of itself implicitly recognized the over-riding influence and power of Japan as the hegemonic power within the region.[37]

While the defeated French government in Vichy[38] labored under the occupation of Germany the French colonial government, feeling and responding to the pressure of Japan did more than succumb to the advances of Japan and its ally. Once they saw which way the wind was blowing the French began actively collaborating with the fascist military expansionists of Tokyo.[39] This is clearly seen in the statements made in an exchange of letters between the Japanese Foreign Minister and the French Ambassador. When the Japanese Foreign Minister stated, "The Japanese Government, on the other hand, entertain no doubt that the Government of France, on their part, will endeavor for the maintenance of peace in Greater East Asia and especially for the establishment of good neighborly and amicable relations between Japan and French Indo-China, as well as for the promotion of closer economic relations between Japan and French Indo-China, and that **they will declare to the Japanese Government that they will not enter into any agreement or understanding with a third Power or Powers regarding French Indo-China envisaging economic or military cooperation aimed either directly or indirectly against Japan** (emphasis added)."[40]

This new spirit of accommodation on the part of the Europeans is also evident in the response of the French Ambassador, "**On the basis of that spirit and being desirous of avoiding all kinds of a conflict between Third Powers, the Government of France hereby declare that they have no intention of entering into any agreement or understanding with a third Power or Powers regarding French Indo-China envisaging political economic or military cooperation aimed either directly or indirectly against Japan** (emphasis added)."[41]

This coerced collaboration of the French with the Japanese is acknowledged and commented on by the official of the United States charged with oversight in this area of foreign policy when he stated, "**The present unfortunate situation in which the French Government of Vichy and the French Government of Indochina find themselves is, of course, well known. It is only too clear that they are in no position to resist the pressure exercised upon them** (emphasis added)."[42] The French responding to the relative weakness of their position vis-à-vis the Japanese in the new order of things in Southeast Asia entered a formal agreement, which called for military cooperation.

The provisions of this agreement implicitly acknowledged Japan as the dominant power when the Japanese pledged "to respect the rights and interests of France in East Asia, especially the territorial integrity of French Indo-China and the French sovereignty over the whole of the Union of French Indo-China."[43] The French as the junior partner agreed "not to conclude with any third Power or Powers any agreement or understanding regarding Indo-China envisaging political, economic or military co-operation which is directly or indirectly aimed against Japan."[44]

As outlined above on August 30 1940, representatives of Vichy-France and Japan signed the Matsuoka-Henry-Pact. This pact permitted the Japanese to station troops in French Indo-china.[45] This concession gave them what they sought all along, the opportunity to open another front against the Nationalist Chinese.[46] It is obvious that the Japanese did not see the French as equal partners and the colonial administration that the Japanese allowed it to continue was merely a matter of convenience.[47] Early in 1941 (as outlined above) the French were forced to cede territory in western Laos and Cambodia to Thailand. Then in 1941, the Japanese persuaded the French to sign the Franco-Laotian Treaty of Protectorate, which greatly enlarged the territory of the Kingdom of Luang Prabang in Laos.[48]

One of the stated goals of the Japanese Empire in World War II was to drive the Western Powers out of Asia thus ending colonialism and creating an "Asia for Asians." For the xenophobic Japanese of the later colonial era this translated into the creation of the "Greater East Asia Co-Prosperity Sphere," which in turn translated into "Asia for the Japanese."[49]

As part of the coordinated attacks, which served as

Japan's declaration of war upon the Western Powers the Imperial Japanese forces carried out many brilliant and bodacious assaults upon the Asiatic outposts of Western colonialism. The Japanese chose those targets, which it considered within either its natural sphere of influence or necessary to the establishment of its line of defense. All of the sites were also close enough for previously established Japanese forces to overpower. These attacks centered around a strategy designed to seize natural resources and secure sea lanes as a means of establishing a great oceanic fortress from the mid Pacific to their Imperial homeland.[50]

As the Japanese were extending their military power and economic influence, south through China and into Southeast Asia their propaganda proclaimed that Asia should be ruled by Asians and promised independence from the hated colonialism of the West.[51] At first some Southeast Asians admired and welcomed the Japanese.[52] They saw them as Asians who had been able to beat the Westerners at their own game in building a modern industrial nation and what appeared at the time as a superior military.

However when the proffered independence did not materialize, many of the Southeast Asian nationalists who had spearheaded the long resistance to Western colonialism soon converted those movements to the new cause of driving the new Japanese colonialists out.[53]

In Thailand, which was officially in alliance with Japan the underground Free Thai operated several divisions. Some of these divisions operated underground in Thailand mounting mainly small-scale irritation sabotage against the large Japanese force that remained as a "guest" of the Thai government. Some of these guerrilla divisions operated from outside the nation, raiding across the borders.[54]

Resistance groups throughout Southeast Asia were from beginning to end more nationalist than anything else. Their main goal always remained freeing their various nations from foreign domination. They didn't care if this meant freedom from the long endured colonialism of the West or the newer homegrown colonialism of the expanding Japanese Empire. One of the most significant developments of World War II in Southeast Asia was that these self-chosen and highly motivated nationalists used the turmoil as an opportunity to advance their individual causes.[55]

On June 6 1944, when allied forces landed in Normandy, which soon brought about the liberation of France from Nazi domination, the Japanese felt that they could no longer count on the collaboration of the French. On March 9 1945, the Japanese officially took control of Indochina from the powerless French.[56]

Immediately following this, at the prompting of the Japanese, Emperor Bao Dai (1913-1997)[57] declared Vietnam independent,[58] King Norodom Sihanouk (B. 1922)[59] declared Cambodia independent,[60] and King Sisavang Vong (1885-1959)[61] of Luang Prabang declared Laos independent.[62] After centuries of foreign domination, all three of these states theoretically regained their independence. In reality all three were merely were Japanese puppet states.

In Vietnam, by the end of the war the Vietminh,[63] composed of both nationalists and communists under the leadership of Ho Chi Minh and General Vo Nguyen Giap had gained almost complete control of the Northern section of Vietnam. The Vietminh made no secret of their intention to fight for full independence from both Japan and France and in 1945 as the war, wanes Ho Chi Minh also declares the independence of Vietnam.[64] This independence is at first encouraged and then spurned by the victorious Western Allies. The French wanted their empire back and the allies, for various reasons supported them.

In 1946 after months of delays and stalling tactics on the part of the French, negotiations with the Vietminh for "free state" status of Vietnam within the French Union broke down. Then the freshly reinvigorated French supplied with massive doses of American aid announced their intention to reassert complete control over Indochina. This unilateral action initiated the beginning of the First Indochina War, the War for Independence from France.

The French cast about for a way to legitimize their foreign control looking for a way to pacify the restive native populations who longed for freedom. Finally, using bribes as well as threats in 1947, the former Emperor of Vietnam Bao Dai who was still in exile, agreed to deal with France. The French then granted limited independence as the Vietminh failed in an attempt to raise a successful a revolution across all of Vietnam.

Hoping for an early extension of International Communism into the resource rich area of Southeast Asia, the Soviet Union and Red China recognized Ho Chi Minh's Communist government as the legitimate government of Vietnam in 1950. As a predictable counter-balance, the United States and Britain recognized Bao Dai's government. At this time, the U.S. also granted military aid to support the French efforts at defeating the Communists thus, with the Cold War as a backdrop began a long involvement in the wars of Indochina.

---

[21] Karnow, page121.

[22] http://www.historyguy.com/wars_of_vietnam.htm (11-25-03). Informational.

[23] http://www.vietquoc.com/0006vq.htm (11-17-03). Informational.

[24] Karnow, page 97.

[25] http://reference.allrefer.com/encyclopedia/G/Giap-VoN.html (11-17-03). Informational.

[26] http://www.cosmicbaseball.com/giap7.html (11-5-03).; http://www.cnn.com/SPECIALS/cold.war/episodes/11/interviews/giap/ (11-5-03).

[27] http://www.netcomuk.co.uk/~dpohara/thai.htm (11-25-03). Infor-

mational.

[28] http://www.bartleby.com/59/10/nationalistc.html (11-25-03). Informational.

[29] http://www.historyguy.com/wars_of_vietnam.htm (11-5-03).

[30] Bemis, Samuel Flagg. A Diplomatic History of the United States. Holt, Rinehart and Winston, Inc. : New York, 1965, p. 869.

[31] http://www.netcomuk.co.uk/~dpohara/thai.htm (11-25-03). Informational.

[32] http://www.ibiblio.org/pha/policy/1941/410207a.html (11-20-03). Yosuke Matsuoka Japan's Foreign Minister's address at opening of Thai-French indo-china border dispute, Mediation Conference. Tokyo Gazette, Vol. IV, no. 9, pp. 384-5.

[33] Ibid

[34] For the full text of Yosuke Matsuoka Japan's Foreign Minister's address at opening of Thai-French Indo-China border dispute, mediation conference, see appendix.

[35] http://www.historyguy.com/wars_of_vietnam.htm (11-5-03)

[36] http://www.ibiblio.org/pha/policy/1941/410311b.html (11-20-03). Mediation terms of the Thai-French Indo-china border dispute. Tokyo Gazette, IV, p. 417, 422 ff.

[37] For the full text of mediation terms of the Thai-French Indo-China border dispute, see Appendix.

[38] http://www.spartacus.schoolnet.co.uk/2WWvichy.htm (11-25-03). Informational.

[39] Weinberg, Gerhard L. A World at War. Cambridge University Press, 1994, p168.

[40] For the complete text of an Exchange of letters between the French Ambassador, Charles Arsène-Henry and Yosuke Matsuoka, Japanese Foreign Minister, see Appendix.

[41] Ibid.

[42] For the full text of Acting Secretary of State Sumner Welles' statement on Japanese-French collaboration in Indochina, see Appendix.

[43] For the full text of the Agreement between Japan and France pledging military co-operation in defense of Indo-China, see appendix.

[44] Ibid.

[45] http://www.zum.de/whkmla/region/seasia/wwiifrindoch.html (11-5-03).

[46] Weinberg, p.166.

[47] Karnow, 140.

[48] http://www.zum.de/whkmla/region/seasia/wwiifrindoch.html (11-5-03).

[49] http://wgordon.web.wesleyan.edu/papers/coprospr.htm (11-5-03).; Keegan, John. The Second World War. Penquin Books:New York, 1989, pages 248-249.

[50] http://www.euronet.nl/users/wilfried/ww2/japan-1.htm (11-5-03).

[51] http://www.msu.edu/~navarro6/srop.html (11-5-03); Fernández-Armesto, Felipe. Millenium. Scribner: New York, 1995, pages 549-550.

[52] Cooper, Chester. The Last Crusade. Dodd, Mead & Co.: New York, 1970, p.21.

[53] Karnow, pages 126-127.

[54] http://www.zum.de/whkmla/region/seasia/wwiithai.html (11-25-03). Informational.

[55] Weinberg, pages 534, 875.

[56] Ibid. p. 875.

[57] http://www.geocities.com/imperialvietnam/baodai.html (11-20-03). Informational.

[58] http://www.vietquoc.com/0007vq.htm (11-7-03).

[59] http://www.norodomsihanouk.info/biography/king-cv.htm (11-17-03). Informational.

[60] http://travel.yahoo.com/p-travelguide-826566-cambodia_independence-i (11-7-03).

[61] http://www.nationmaster.com/encyclopedia/Sisavang-Vong (11-25-03). Informational.

[62] http://www.4dw.net/royalark/Laos/laos.htm (11-7-03).

[63] http://www.bartleby.com/65/vi/VietMinh.html (11-5-03).

[64] Karnow, page 135.

CHAPTER THREE

The Cold War: From World War II through the Korean War

Only a context gives us any possibility to understand an event or a series of events. Just imagine seeing a picture of someone with no background and trying to guess the location of the picture. The Cold War[65] as a whole is a subject too vast for this arena and so certain limitations will guide this circumscribed presentation. Believing that a text without a context is a pretext, this chapter presents information regarding the Cold War as the means of providing information on the larger context in which the Vietnam War raged. This need for a context is key to understanding the Vietnam War.

The Cold War might almost be termed World War III. After defeating the forces of Totalitarianism in its Fascist incarnation in World War II, the liberal democracies of the West next faced a titanic struggle against the even stronger forces of Totalitarianism in its equally virulent Communist expression. This massive international conflict raged for almost fifty years and ranged over every continent of the world. It was a war with many shifts from hot to cold from détente to fiery battle. Today as we gaze backwards through the fog of time, we see the dying embers of ideological dreams reflected only in the wisdom we have gained and the insights we can pass along.

The Cold War is Recognized and Acknowledged

A famous speech by Sir Winston Churchill (1874-1965),[66] one of the greatest speakers and possibly the most adroit user of the English language contains certain phrases, **"the special relationship,"** and **"the sinews of peace, "** which became the accepted terminology of the age. It is the phrase **"the iron curtain"** however, which immediately attracted international attention. The imagery and the intellectual impact of this classically Churchwellian turn-of-phrase had a deep and lasting impact on the cultural psyche as well as public opinion in the West. It is a well-established practice among historians to date the beginning of the Cold War from this speech. This is the most important speech that Churchill delivered while he was the leader of the Loyal Opposition. In addition, experts in both English and in Speech Communication regard it as one of the preeminent examples of public speaking in the Twentieth Century.

The most famous paragraph in this speech, the one so often quoted as the opening round of the West's admission that they had embarked upon another crusade and a fundamental statement necessary for the understanding of the Cold War expressly says,

> **From Stettin in the Baltic to Trieste in the Adriatic, an iron curtain has descended across the Continent.** (Emphasis added.) Behind that line lie all the capitals of the ancient states of Central and Eastern Europe.

> Warsaw, Berlin, Prague, Vienna, Budapest, Belgrade, Bucharest and Sofia, all these famous cities and the populations around them lie in what I must call the Soviet sphere, and all are subject in one form or another, not only to Soviet influence but to a very high and, in many cases, increasing measure of control from Moscow. Athens alone-Greece with its immortal glories-is free to decide its future at an election under British, American and French observation. The Russian-dominated Polish Government has been encouraged to make enormous and wrongful inroads upon Germany, and mass expulsions of millions of Germans on a scale grievous and undreamed-of are now taking place. The Communist parties, which were very small in all these Eastern States of Europe, have been raised to pre-eminence and power far beyond their numbers and are seeking everywhere to obtain totalitarian control. Police governments are prevailing in nearly every case, and so far, except in Czechoslovakia, there is no true democracy."[67]

Churchill also referred to his experience between the First and the Second World Wars when he tried to raise the alarm concerning the need to stand up to the Totalitarian Nazis. He compared this speech to his wilderness experience as in the same vein he attempted to call the West to stand firm before the second great onslaught of Totalitarianism through the forces of International Communism.

> Last time I saw it all coming and cried aloud to my own fellow-countrymen and to the

> world, but no one paid any attention. Up till the year 1933 or even 1935, Germany might have been saved from the awful fate which has overtaken her and we might all have been spared the miseries Hitler let loose upon mankind. There never was a war in all history easier to prevent by timely action than the one which has just desolated such great areas of the globe. It could have been prevented in my belief without the firing of a single shot, and Germany might be powerful, prosperous and honoured (sic.) to-day; but no one would listen and one by one we were all sucked into the awful whirlpool. We surely must not let that happen again. This can only be achieved by reaching now, in 1946, a good understanding on all points with Russia under the general authority of the United Nations Organisation (sic.) and by the maintenance of that good understanding through many peaceful years, by the world instrument, supported by the whole strength of the English-speaking world and all its connections. There is the solution which I respectfully offer to you in this Address to which I have given the title "The Sinews of Peace."[68]

The Truman Doctrine

Struggling with a poor economy and the evaporation of their empire on February 21, 1947, the British government announced that it would withdraw aid to Greece and Turkey.[69] Simultaneously with its public announcement, the British Embassy in Washington informed the U.S. State

Department of this fact. The leaders of America had been monitoring the situation as Greece's economic and political conditions worsened. The United States viewed with alarm the precipitous rise of a Communist-led insurgency known as the National Liberation Front, or the EAM/ELAS,[70] which had the support of the Soviet Union.[71]

Concurrently the United States followed contemporaneous events in Turkey. That country still labored through the economic and social turmoil resulting from the loss of its empire after World War I. The Soviet imperialists had replaced the Russian imperialists as a Great Power seeking to force the Turks into an access-control-sharing agreement regarding the strategic Dardanelle Straits.[72] With Britain's summary announcement the English withdrew from its traditional role of balancing powers so that no one power came to dominate this gateway to the Mediterranean the United States stepped forward accepting the responsibility.

In America while attending a meeting of legislative officials, the Undersecretary of State, Dean Acheson (1893-1971)[73] revealed a theory of international interaction that would later gain currency as **the domino theory**.[74] He stated that if Greece and Turkey fell to the forces of Totalitarianism as represented in International Communism the conquest would soon spread to adjoining countries.

Using the lessons of history Acheson pointed out that the West faced a struggle for power and dominance every bit as deadly as that, which had once raged between Carthage and Rome. Initially shocked by the directness of the diplomat's language the legislators quickly grasped the significance of the situation. They proposed a program tailored to give support to not only the governments of Greece and Turkey but to any government, which might subsequently find itself under attack.

Looking to the political consequences, these elected officials of America's two major parties did not believe that they should to bear the political burden alone. Therefore, they insisted that if President Truman (1884-1972)[75] would do two things they would support this plan of action in a bipartisan fashion. First, they wanted him to address a joint session of Congress, which outlined the dangers of the Greek and Turkish crisis. Secondly, they wanted the President to appeal directly to the American people through a nation-wide radio broadcast. Agreeing to both of these requests President Truman led the nation into what would become a decade's long struggle as Congress voted to implement a program of defense against International Communism.

President Harry S. Truman addressed a joint session of Congress on March 12, 1947. In this address, he also made it clear that the forces of freedom must remain continually vigilant to the encroachment of the forces of Totalitarian International Communism on the world's stage. Not only speaking in broad generalities the President directly referenced the immediacy of current events specifically by asking Congress for hundreds of millions in assistance for Greece and Turkey. In this speech, the President declared that America would forever miss the achievement of it destiny unless it stood up for freedom. "We shall not realize our objectives unless we are willing to help free people maintain their institutions and their national integrity against aggressive movements that seek **to impose upon the totalitarian regimes** (emphasis added)."[76] Following this identification of the enemy, the President uttered a sentence that would enter history as **the Truman Doctrine**.[77]

Boldly declaring, **"It must be the policy of the United States to support free peoples who are resisting attempted subjugation by armed minorities or by outside pressures"** (emphasis added). Thus, President Truman stood up to defend the freedom of the world against the gathering Totalitarian onslaught of International Communism. This doctrine became the foundation of American international action for the next four decades as the Cold War bubbled and boiled around the globe.

After President Truman had fulfilled his part of this political bargain the Republican controlled Congress approved massive aid to Greece and Turkey. This quid-pro-quo arrangement between the executive and legislative branches began what became a long if sometimes boisterously debated bipartisan prosecution of the Cold War. Historians have raised and continue to raise questions concerning the Truman Doctrine. They have studied its long-term consequences; they have looked into its relationship to domestic politics, as well as its origins. The Truman Doctrine proved to be the last nail in the coffin of America's generations-long love affair with its traditional policy of isolationism[78] while at the same time heralding its acceptance of global leadership.

The following series of events brought muscle and sinew to the bare bones of Churchill's prophetic remarks.

As World War II ended and the Axis powers withdrew the Stalinist leader of the Communist National Liberation Army Enver Hoxha (1908-1985)[79] supported by the advancing Soviet Army took control in Albania. He and his secret police locked an independent and highly isolated variant brand of Totalitarianism on this hapless country, officially proclaiming the Albania Communist in 1944.

Josip Tito (1892-1980)[80] the leader of the Partisan Fighters who had organized resistance to the Nazi occupiers gained power after the war and brought his country into the Communist bloc.

The democracies opposed the forces of International Communism in the United Nations.[81] This new international body, which replaced the League of Nations[82], offered a hope for uniting the world in the pursuit of peace. However, the East and the West remained suspicious of each other. In 1946, the United States offered a proposal for the creation of an international agency designed to regulate the research and production of nuclear energy. The Soviet Union as the unquestioned leader of International Communism fought this proposal saying that since only the United States had nuclear weapons at that time it would use the new organization to keep other countries from gaining them. As the outlines of the Cold War developed the Soviets sought to advance itself as the defender of oppressed peoples against the rapacious capitalists.

In 1946, continuing its subjugation of the very nations the world had waged the Second World War to liberate the Soviets imposed Communist governments in Bulgaria and Romania. In 1947, they seized power in Hungary and Poland. In 1948, Czechoslovakia joined the other nations of Eastern Europe behind the lengthening Iron Curtain. As the Soviets integrated these governments and economies into their centralized system, they effectively became satellites of the Soviet Union.[83]

Then in 1949, China fell to the Communists under Mao and the West saw a triumphant Totalitarianism on the march. The democracies of the West perceived this new manifestation of Totalitarianism by the Communists to be just as diabolical as the variant by the Fascists they had just defeated in World War II. This Communist menace vocally proclaimed its belief that it was inevitable that they should eventually rule the world, just as the Fascists before them had done. There seemed to be an unbroken string of conquests as Communism grew from a minor movement in a defeated country in 1917 to a self-righteous crusading juggernaut that had swallowed Russia, all of eastern Europe and China. Pointing to the pseudo-scientific historical and social theories of Karl Marx (1818-1883)[84] the Soviet Communist Totalitarians took every opportunity to announce that the law of history itself moved inexorably towards their ultimate victory. Then came Korea.

The Korean War[85]

During World War II, the major allied leaders Churchill, Roosevelt (1882-1945)[86], and Stalin (1879-1953)[87] held several "Summit" meetings to decide how to prosecute the war. They also used these meetings to decide the shape of the post-war world. In Asia as the once proud Japanese Empire tottered towards defeat the Allies tried to bribe the Soviets to fulfill their promise to declare war on Japan once the war in Europe ended. As part of this strategy, they decided to divide the Japanese colony of Korea (1910-1945).[88] Instead of remaining united, they divided it by an artificial line drawn at the 38th parallel followed by occupation by the Soviet Union in the north and the United States in the south.

The Communists under Joseph Stalin brought in, Kim Il-sung (1912-1994)[89] as the dictator of the North. They also provided the North Korean Peoples' Army with vast amounts of surplus Russian arms. Hundreds of tanks and thousands of artillery pieces soon swelled the North Korean Army into a formidable fighting force. The Soviet Communists sent a large number of personnel to advise and train this rapidly growing client army. At this time in South Korea, the United States as the occupying power sponsored the first free elections in the country's history. The winner in this contest turned out to be President Syngman Rhee (1875-1965).[90] Rhee was a nationalist with a long history of resisting the Japanese occupation. He had argued against the division of Korea and he advocated the restoration of national unity, by any means necessary. Rhee lost the support of the Americans because of his fiery rhetoric and his authoritarian domestic policies. Due to these differences the Americans quickly withdrew the majority of troops to Japan and did not give the South Koreans much in the way of equipment or training.

In June of 1950, the North Koreans invaded South Korea. Many border incidents and several small force attacks that in reality proved to have been probing actions foreshadowed this action. Still this massive invasion caught the unprepared South Koreans, the United States and the free world off guard. The North Korean Communists behind a fast moving wall of tanks soon rolled up the South Korean resistance as they quickly headed south.

In this, the next hot phase of the Cold War (after Greece and Turkey), the United States turned to the newly created United Nations. As a permanent member of the Security Council,[91] the U. S. offered a resolution calling on the world body to condemn the North Korean aggression. Due to a Soviet boycott the motion passed.[92] This American-sponsored joint resolution called on all members of the international organization to aid in the defense of South Korea.

By mid-1951, after successive changes of offensive advantage the land battle reached a terrible and deadly equilibrium where western firepower like a meat-grinder[93] held the masses of invading Communists at bay. However, the Communists, caring little for human life proved that they would sacrifice any amount of men to remain in the war. The two sides remained locked in mortal combat. The allies had overwhelming firepower as well as absolute air and naval supremacy, nonetheless they lacked the ability to deliver a knock-out punch to force the Communists out of the war. Conversely, the Communists could not break through the entrenched western army. Day after day, the casualties mounted, until finally the two sides agreed to meet for peace talks.

These talks dragged on for more than two years until on July 27 1953, more from exhaustion than from the resolution of any problems both sides finally agreed to a cease-fire.[94] This armistice agreement called for a Demilitarized Zone along the border, which was in approximately the same place the border had been before the North invaded. Both sides were supposed to withdraw from the border. A United Nations' commission still oversees the provisions of this agreement.

The best way to understand the Korean War is as a civil war fought with foreign intervention analogous to the Spanish Civil War[95] of the 1930s. This first direct "war" between the two sides of the Cold War was a harbinger of many of the attributes which would one day surface in Vietnam.

After the Korean War, the Cold War became increasingly tense. Throughout the 1950s, both sides accused each other of seeking to dominate the world. Both sides believed religiously in the superiority of its political and economic system. Each side asked for sacrifices from their people as they strained their societies to support a massive arms race. Both sides used every avenue of propaganda to project the image of the Cold War as an epochal battle between good and evil, between right and wrong both claiming to be the good and the right. Every local war, every palace revolt, and every incident on the international scene became a new beachhead in the Cold War. This highly polarized and highly charged atmosphere made it extremely difficult to settle any of the complex international problems of the day in a peaceable manner. The extreme ideological and political outlooks of the two sides constantly railed against compromise, which is the hallmark of international cooperation. This mighty battle triggered a constant fear among the people of the world that the next small local conflict might turn into a world-destroying nuclear conflagration. Whole generations grew to adulthood in fear of World War III.

It is this atmosphere of bitterly contested ideologies and of war both hot and cold raging on a global stage that serves as the context within which any serious student of history must consider the Vietnam War. For this confusing milieu of advancing East, and defending West next encountered the First Indo-China War. The outcome of that war and the decisions based upon Cold War assumptions led directly to America's involvement in the Vietnam War.

---

65 http://www.coldwar.org (11-14-03). Informational.

66 http://www.winstonchurchill.org/i4a/pages/index.cfm?pageid=1 (11-14-03). Informational.

67 For the full text of Sir Winston Churchill's speech at Westminster College, Fulton, Missouri March 5 1946, see the Appendix.

68 Ibid.

69 http://www.eh.net/bookreviews/library/0635.shtml (11-25-03). Informational.

70 http://www.britannica.com/eb/article?eu=32248 (12-17-03). Informational.

71 http://www.geocities.com/gunsnroseswillreunite/ (11-25-03) Informational.

72 http://www.pamun.org/Position-Paper-Example-2.php (11-25-03). Informational.

73 http://www.trumanlibrary.org/oralhist/acheson.htm (11-14-03). Informational.

74 http://en.wikipedia.org/wiki/Domino_Theory (12-17-03). Informational

75 Ibid. (11-14-03). Informational.

76 Cooper, p. 13.

77 For the full text of the Truman Doctrine. see the Appendix.; Truman, Harry S. Memoirs: 1946-1952. Signet Books: New York, 1956, p.p. 134-135; McCullough, David. Truman. Simon & Schuster: New York, 1992, pp.382-383; Truman, Margeret. Harry S. Truman. William Morrow & Co. Inc., 1972, pp.343-344; Commager, Henry Steele. Documents of American History. Appelton – Century – Crofts: New York, 1963, pp. 524-526.

78 Mann, Robert. A Grand Delusion. Basic Books: New York, 2001, p. 9, 13-17, 51-53.

79 http://www.albanian.com/main/history/hoxha.html (11-14-03).

Informational.

80 http://www.spartacus.schoolnet.co.uk/2WWtito.htm (11-14-03). Informational.

81 http://www.un.org/aboutun/history.htm (12-17-03). Informational.

82 http://www.yale.edu/lawweb/avalon/league/league.htm (11-25-03). Informational.

83 Bemis, pp. 921-923; McCullough, pp. 382-383..

84 http://www.philosophypages.com/ph/marx.htm (11-26-03). Informational.

85 http://www.centurychina.com/history/krwarfaq.html (11-14-03); Matloff, Maurice (Ed.) Army Historical Series: American Military History: Office of the Chief of Military History, U. S. Army: Washington, D.C. 1973, pp. 545-571. Informational

86 http://www.fdrlibrary.marist.edu (11-14-03). Informational.

87 http://www.marxists.org/reference/archive/stalin (11-14-03). Informational.

88 Truman, H., p349, 422-423; Matloff, pp. 534-535. http://times.hankooki.com/lpage/opinion/200306/kt2003061614450111410.htm (11-26-03). Informational.

89 http://clinton.cnn.com/SPECIALS/cold.war/kbank/profiles/kim (11-14-03). Informational.

90 http://www.spartacus.schoolnet.co.uk/COLDsyngman.htm (11-14-03). Informational

91 http://en2.wikipedia.org/wiki/United_Nations_Security_Council (12-17-03). Informational.

92 Matloff, p. 545.

93 http://www.tv.cbc.ca/national/pgminfo/korea/korea2.html (12-3-03).

94 http://news.findlaw.com/hdocs/docs/korea/kwarmagr072753.html (11-26-03). Informational.

95 http://www.sispain.org/english/history/civil.html (11-14-03). Informational.

CHAPTER FOUR

The Cold War: The First Indochina War

The Cold War was without a doubt the defining characteristic of the post-World War II world. However, immediately following the War and for the first two decades afterwards the international socio-political system underwent another massive change. This was the passing of Europe's vast colonial empires. As result of this change more than one hundred new sovereign states were (re)born and the two Superpowers quickly saw these new states as pawns to be played and squares to be taken.[96]

Following their devastating experience in World War II, the French were unable immediately to reestablish their unquestioned authority in Indochina. Ho Chi Minh, and his Vietminh, proclaimed the independence of the Democratic Republic of Vietnam although they only had actual power in the northern section of the country. The weakened France quickly agreed to recognize Vietnam as an independent nation within the context of the French Union, with the details of this independence to be worked out later.

The French did not really want to lose this jewel of their

colonial empire and so the negotiations hit one snag after another as they droned on interminably.[97] Finally n December 1946, Ho Chi Minh tired of this game and his Vietminh forces staged surprise attacks against French garrisons throughout the country. The French responded with indiscriminant reprisals and large campaigns against a guerrilla force that always seemed to melt into the population. Completely disavowing any further allegiance to the continued authority of the French colonial authorities, Ho Chi Minh and his Communist Vietminh began attacking French outposts along the border with China. They did this with military aid and logistical support from the Communist Chinese and the Soviet Union as the war dragged on the guerrilla actions spread through the country.

As previously stated, the French colonial masters imposed a provisional government in 1949 which the United States recognized in 1950. The Emperor Bao Dai served as the ceremonial head of this government.[98] In 1951, the Vietminh allied themselves with Communist groups in Laos and Cambodia thus creating a common front throughout the entire area of French Indochina. The military arm of the Vietminh was ably led by General Vo Nguyen Giap. As the war dragged on the United States continued to support the French seeing this as one more battle in the Cold War[99] as is shown by the following excerpt from a joint Franco-American Communiqué dated September 30, 1953:

> The forces of France and the Associated States in Indochina have for 8 years been engaged in a bitter struggle to prevent the engulfment (sic.) of Southeast Asia **by the forces of international communism** (emphasis added). The heroic efforts and sacrifices of these French Union allies in assuring the liberty of the new and independent states of

> Cambodia, Laos and Vietnam has earned the admiration and support of the free world. In recognition of the French Union effort the United States Government has in the past furnished aid of various kinds to the Governments of France and the Associated States to assist in bringing the long struggle to an early and victorious conclusion.
>
> The French Government is firmly resolved to carry out in full its declaration of July 3, 1953,[100] by which is announced its intention of perfecting the independence of the three Associated States in Indochina, through negotiations with the Associated States.
>
> The Governments of France and the United States have now agreed that, in support of plans of the French Government for the intensified prosecution of the war against the Viet Minh, the United States will make available to the French Government prior to December 31, 1954 additional financial resources not to exceed $385 million. This aid is in addition to funds already earmarked by the United States for aid to France and the Associated States.[101]

Giap searched for the opportunity to fight a decisive battle. Believing that he saw the opportunity for such a battle, he launched an attack against a strategically important French position located at Dienbienphu[102] in northwestern Vietnam on March 13, 1954. For 56 days, the French were under siege. The battle-hardened Vietminh troops located on surrounding ridges maintained a continuous barrage with artillery and mortar. Until finally on May 7 1954, the beleaguered French soldiers who were running short of supplies surrendered. The Vietnamese victory over the French at Dienbienphu compares to America's victory at Yorktown. While it did not immediately end the war, militarily it broke the will of the colonial power to commit the men and material necessary to launch another major campaign.

While this great victory demonstrated the military prowess of the Vietminh, they still had direct control only in the north. Having tasted defeat and mired in domestic political descent concerning the war France reluctantly entered an international conference in Geneva to hammer out an agreement for a cease-fire and the withdrawal of the French colonial forces. Supported by the French the non-Communists set up a government south of the demarcation line, while Ho Chi Minh set up a government north of the 17th parallel. The war to re-impose empire had never been popular in France and as the losses mounted it became very unpopular. Despite the loss of prestige, most of the citizens of France felt were relief when on July 21 1954, the "Final Declaration of the Geneva Conference On Restoring Peace in Indochina," ended the First Indochina War.[103]

Thus in July 1954, Vietnam was formally divided into the Communist dominated Democratic Republic of Vietnam (North Vietnam) and the Republic of Vietnam (South Vietnam) which was firmly aligned with the West. The United States was not a signatory to the Geneva Declarations and the Eisenhower Administration was not averse to making their intentions concerning the situation in Indochina known. The following excerpt from the official American response to the Geneva Declarations, while calling for free elections supervised by the United Nations to re-unite Vietnam also make it clear America stood ready to support the new states in efforts to resist the imposition of any settlement detrimental to their freedom.[104]

The American Response to the Geneva Declarations, 3 July 21, 1954.
Declaration

The Government of the United States being resolved to devote its efforts to the strengthening of peace in accordance with the principles and purposes of the United Nations takes note of the agreements concluded at Geneva on July 20 and 21, 1954 between … it will refrain from the threat or the use of force to disturb them … it would view any renewal of the aggression in violation of the aforesaid agreements with grave concern and as seriously threatening international peace and security.

In connection with the statement in the declaration concerning free elections in Viet-Nam (sic.) my Government wishes to make clear its position which it has expressed in a declaration made in Washington on June 29, 1954, as follows:

In the case of nations now divided against their will, we shall continue to seek to achieve unity through free elections supervised by the United Nations to insure that they are conducted fairly (emphasis added).

With respect to the statement made by the representative of the State of Viet-Nam (sic.), the United States reiterates **its *traditional*** (emphasis added) **position that peoples are entitled to determine their own future**

> (emphasis added) and that it will not join in an arrangement which would hinder this. Nothing in its declaration just made is intended to or does indicate any departure from **this traditional position** (emphasis added).
>
> We share the hope that the agreements will permit Cambodia, Laos and Viet-Nam (sic.) to play their part, in full independence and sovereignty, in the peaceful community of nations, and will enable the peoples of that area to determine their own future.[105]

The stunning Communist victory in the Chinese Civil War[106] in 1949 caught America by surprise. Accusations of "Who lost China" filled the air as the previous commitment to a bipartisan Cold War strategy descended into partisan wrangling.[107] The subsequent massive Chinese intervention in Korea further exasperated American feelings of imminent danger and crisis. These events transformed America's traditional anti-colonialist foreign policy into support for the reassertion of French colonialism as a means to stop the spread of Communist Totalitarianism into Indochina.[108]

When the French lost their war in Indochina, the United States stepped into the breach.[109] Following and attempting to fulfill its "traditional" role of supporting the self-determination of nations. The United States, accepting the fiat accompli of French defeat and withdrawal sought to do this by providing diplomatic, economic, and military aid for the non-Communist successor states of South Vietnam, Cambodia, and Laos.

In the following chapters, we turn our examination to America's direct involvement in the great conflict known as either the Second Indochina War or the Vietnam War. If we seek to maintain any claim to that most elusive of all commodities, historical objectivity we must leave this war in its proper context. American political and military leaders consistently, from the beginning to the end viewed the Vietnam War as the next "Hot" phase of the continuing Cold War. As will be shown these leaders made this view abundantly clear through repeated public pronouncements. Moreover, it is only in this perhaps myopic, perhaps synoptic view that the ensuing American involvement can be understood unless of course the intention is not to understand but to interpret, not to record but to revise.

---

[96] Bemis, pp. 907-935; Bernstein, Barton J. & Allen J Matusow (eds.) The Truman Administration: A Documentary History. Harper & Row Publishers: New York, 1966, pp. 158-298. Informational.

[97] Karnow, pp. 148-157; Herring, George C. America's Longest War. Alfred A. Knopf: New York, 1986, pp. 5-9.

[98] Ibid., pp. 15-17.

[99] Adams, Sherman. Firsthand Report. Popular Library: New York, 1961, p 123-4; Mann, pp.73-76, 80-82, 84-85, 89-91, 106-114; Herring, pp 10-12.

[100] http://www.yale.edu/lawweb/avalon/intdip/indoch/inch017.htm (11-20-03). Documents on American Foreign Relations, 1958 (New York, 1954), pp. 347-348. Indochina - Additional United States Aid for France and Indochina: Joint Franco-American Communiqué, September 30, 1953. The Avalon Project at Yale Law School. Informational.

[101] For the full text of the Indochina - Additional United States Aid for France and Indochina: Joint Franco-American Communiqué, September 30 1953, see the Appendix.

[102] http://www.dienbienphu.org/english (11-14-03); Herring, pp. 30-38. Informational

[103] For the full text of The Final Declaration of The Geneva Conference: On Restoring Peace in Indochina, July 21 1954, see Appendix; Adams, p. 127-128.

[104] Bemis, pp. 958-959; Herring, pp. 29-30; 35; 37-40, 44; Mann, pp.

166-167, 172-175.

[105] For the full text of The American Response to the Geneva Declarations, July 21 1954, see appendix.

[106] http://cityhonors.buffalo.k12.ny.us/city/aca/hist/ibhist/ibhiststud/histiur.html (11-14-03). Informational.

[107] Donovan, Robert J. Nemesis. St. Martin's: New York, 1984, p. 37; McCullough, p. 744; Truman, M. p.409.

[108] http://www.time.com/time/time100/leaders/profile/hochiminh.html (11-5-03). Informational.

[109] Adams, p. 128; Herring, p. 57; Karnow, pp.219-220

AMERICA'S WAR

CHAPTER FIVE

Eisenhower

Initial U.S. political and military involvement in Vietnam appeared to American leaders as a natural outgrowth of America's strategic position vis-a-vis the military and political onslaught of Totalitarianism as expressed in International Communism.

World War II had left the United States the preeminent power in the free world. However, this preeminence did not bring peace. Just as the threat of Fascism dominated the world scene of the 1930s and 1940s, from 1946 until 1991 the free nations of the world faced what they perceived as a monolithic International Communism dedicated to world domination.[110] Believing that those who do not learn from history face the repetition of it, the Truman administration sought to profit from the shameful example of appeasement by the Western Democracies of the Fascist dictators before World War II.[111] Consequently, they developed a policy known as containment.[112] This policy dictated that the West would counter Communist aggression no matter where it occurred through direct intervention by the Western allies.

After World War II, President Truman had no sympathy for the re-establishment of European colonialism. In

Indochina, he favored Vietnamese independence. However, Ho Chi Minh, his principle supporters, and the Vietminh front they created had strong political and logistical connections to International Communism. In addition, the rapid and brutal expansion of Communist control throughout Eastern Europe, the victory of the Communists in China, and the recent experience of the Korean War all worked to make France's war against Ho Chi Minh and his Vietminh appear more as a battle against International Communism than as a battle to re-conquer a recalcitrant colony. America's historical opposition to colonialism[113] was appeased when France organized Vietnam under Emperor Bao Dai as an autonomous state within the French Union. Using this action as diplomatic cover, the United States began actively to support the French against the "Communists."

As the American involvement evolved, the military and governmental leaders repeatedly recognized the First Indochina War as an engagement of the Cold War.[114] As such, it seemed a logical reaction on the part of the West following the stunning Communist victory in China, the aggression of the Korean War, and the obvious links of the Vietminh to International Communism. To understand American involvement in Vietnam and in the interest of objectivity students of history should view this policy as the Asian expression of Truman's Containment Policy.

The Domino Theory

By 1954, it became obvious that the French effort to defeat the Communist forces in Indochina had failed. In March, the French faced the loss of an entire army at Dien Bien Phu. The France appealed to the United States to intervene through massive and sustained military involvement. However, President Eisenhower (1890-1969)[115] decided this would not serve American interests and therefore he did not send the requested aid to the beleaguered French army which subsequently surrendered in early May. Although he did not come to France's aid,[116] Eisenhower saw that the French defeat if not somehow countered could ultimately result in the triumph of International Communism in Indochina. The President spelled out his view of the importance of the region in geo-political terms through many channels as shown in the following excerpts from a news interview:

> **Question by Robert Richards, Copley Press: Mr. President, would you mind commenting on the strategic importance of Indochina for the free world** (emphasis added)? I think there has been, across the country, some lack of understanding on just what it means to us.
>
> **The President.** You have, of course, both the specific and the general when you talk about such things. First of all, you have the specific value of a locality in its production of materials that the world needs. …
>
> **Finally, you have broader considerations that might follow what you would call the "falling domino" principle. You have a row of dominoes set up, you knock over the first one, and what will happen to the last one is the certainty that it will go over very quickly. So you could have a beginning of a disintegration that would have the most profound influences** (emphasis added). …

> But **when we come to the possible sequence of events, the loss of Indochina, of Burma, of Thailand, of the Peninsula, and Indonesia following** (emphasis added), …
>
> Finally, the geographical position achieved thereby does many things. It turns the so-called island defensive chain of Japan, Formosa, of the Philippines and to the southward; it moves in to threaten Australia and New Zealand.
>
> It takes away, in its economic aspects, that region that Japan must have as a trading area or Japan, in turn, will have only one place in the world to go—that is, toward the Communist areas in order to live.
>
> So, **the possible consequences of the loss are just incalculable to the free world** (emphasis added).[117]

Although the United States paid approximately 80% of French costs,[118] Eisenhower refused to send troops to support the French. However, after they surrendered he did choose to support the newly re-organized South Vietnamese government as the best available means to hold the line against the advancing forces of International Communism.[119] President Eisenhower fervently believed that the American people could only understand the on-going conflict in Vietnam and America's involvement within the broader context of the Cold War.[120] He clearly stated his purpose for America's continuing aid to the government in South Vietnam. The tenor of his statements is evident in the following excerpt from a letter to President Diem (1901-1963)[121] of Vietnam dated October 23, 1954. "The purpose of this offer is to assist the Government of Viet-Nam (sic.) in developing and maintaining a strong, viable state, capable of resisting attempted subversion or aggression through military means."[122]

The following is a condensed history touching only the highlights of American involvement in Vietnam under President Eisenhower.

1955:

After the defeat of France in the First Indochina War and believing that the forces of International Communism are surging south from the newly conquered China through North Vietnam into the rest of Indochina the United States begins a program of direct military and economic aid to South Vietnam, Cambodia, and Laos. Although mandated by the Geneva Declaration President Diem refuses to hold a nationwide reunification election supervised by the United Nations. Instead of the mandated nationwide election, Diem holds a referendum in South Vietnam only. This referendum asks the people if they want to continue under the constitutional monarchy headed by Emperor Bao Dai or do they want to renounce the monarchy and form a republic. Diem and his forces win the referendum and subsequently proclaim the Republic of [South] Vietnam with Diem as President. The United States supports Diem in these actions.[123]

1956:

Besides sending military and economic assistance, the United States begins sending military advisors to train South Vietnamese troops. Using the newly trained troops, accompanied by American advisors, Diem attacks suspected Communists and other groups who oppose him throughout South Vietnam.[124]

1957:

Diem makes a well-publicized state visit to the United States. President Eisenhower pledges continued support while Communist espionage, subversion, and covert military activity grows throughout South Vietnam. The Communist government in North Vietnam directly organizes, supplies, and directs this insurgency, aimed at destabilizing the government of South Vietnam.

1959:

To counter increased levels of infiltration of both men and material through the Ho Chi Minh Trail, which the Communists had recently built through supposedly neutral Laos and Cambodia the United States begins covert operations in throughout South East Asia.

1960:

The National Liberation Front for South Vietnam (NLF),[125] commonly known as the "Viet Cong," is formed by North Vietnamese leaders

Now with the Cold War won and the peace dividend spent gazing into the gathering mist of half a century, it is easy to suffer from the twenty-twenty vision of hindsight. As we look at the decisions of the American leaders who led us into and out of Vietnam, it is easy to dismiss their vision of Vietnam as the "Next" battleground of the Cold War as overly simplistic. Today, it may be easy to write off their conduct as the knee-jerk reaction of the almost paranoid veterans of World War II. Today it is equally easy to say this vision totally discounted an already decades long struggle for national independence. It is also easy to accuse the American administrations of those days of having a myopic vision, which focused in inordinate amount of attention on Europe and on an Asia consisting only of Japan and China. It is easy to assign American aid to France in Indochina as merely a way of paying for French cooperation with America's plans for the defense of Europe through the North Atlantic Treaty Organization (NATO).[126] All these assumptions are easy to make when looking back from the security of a victorious America and a vanquished International Communism. However, generations of Americans grew to maturity under the constant threat of political, economic, social, and military annihilation, a threat constantly proclaimed by the leaders of an aggressive and advancing International Communism. While that threat existed, the luxury of these "easy" assumptions did not.

After the Communists conquered China in 1949, the United States saw the continued existence of a free Japan as the number one objective of America's Asian policy. The newly democratized Japan was the lynchpin of America's concept of an island defensive chain stretching from Japan, through Formosa, south to the Philippines. In addition, just as before World War II the continued health and development of the Japanese economy required access to the markets and raw materials of Southeast Asia. The Communist onslaught in Korea in 1950 served to convince the Cold Warriors of Washington that the continued aggression of what they perceived as a monolithic International Communism meant an immediate threat to America's defensive line in Asia.[127]

This American policy led to a steady escalation of U.S. involvement. Inheriting a policy of supporting the French in Indochina from President Truman, President Eisenhower while continuing to avoid direct military intervention, increased the level of aid until the disastrous defeat at Dien Bien Phu in 1954. The Geneva Declaration, which ended French involvement and to which the United States was not a party provided for a North-South partition of Vietnam until elections could be held. The United States immediately began to support the creation of an independent Vietnamese regime in South Vietnam to counter-balance to the Communist regime of Ho Chi Minh in the North. Eisenhower adhering to the "domino theory" expressed the belief that if the forces of International Communism succeeded in conquering Vietnam, they would soon conquer all of Southeast Asia.

The war in Vietnam was hardly a blip on the screen of the candidates, the pundits, or the voters during the hotly contested presidential race of 1960.[128] What were the major concerns? "The Missile-gap"[129] "Who 'LOST' Cuba?"[130] and the survival of America's economy in the face of this mounting worldwide challenge that was the Cold War.[131]

---

[110] Adams, p. 127.

[111] Mann, p. 99.

[112] http://www.indyflicks.com/danielle/papers/paper04.htm (12-5-03).

[113] Holbo, Paul S. and Robert W. Sellen (eds.). The Eisenhower Era. The Dryden Press: Hinsdale, IL., 1974, p. 152

[114] Adams, p. 129.

[115] http://www.eisenhower.archives.gov (11-14-03). Informational.

[116] Adams, p. 127.

[117] For the full text of Presidential Press Conference April 7 1954, see Appendix.

[118] Holbo, pp. 151-152.

[119] Ibid. p. 155.

[120] Adams, p. 123.

[121] http://hungngo.web1000.com/NgoDinhDiem.html (11-17-03). Informational.

[122] For the full text of Eisenhower's Letter of Support to Ngo Dinh Diem, October 23 1954, see the Appendix.

[123] Holbo, p. 158.

[124] Chomsky, Noam. Rethinking Camelot. South End Press: Boston, MA, 1993, p. 42-43.

[125] http://flagspot.net/flags/vn-vcong.html#vc (11-14-03). Informational.

[126] http://www.nato.int (11-14-03). Informational.

[127] Bemis, p. 957.; Mann, p. 98-99.

[128] http://nixonfamily.freeservers.com/art10.html (11-25-03). Informational.

[129] http://www.coldwar.org/articles/50s/missile_gap.php3 (11-25-03). Informational

[130] http://nixonfamily.freeservers.com/art10.html (12-4-03).

[131] Bemis, p. 969.

CHAPTER SIX

Kennedy

Just as Eisenhower had inherited a policy of engagement in Vietnam from Truman, so John F. Kennedy (1917-1963)[132] inherited an expanded policy from Eisenhower.

However, this was not a situation, which surprised or confounded President Kennedy. As a senator from Massachusetts, during a time that we now know, he used to prepare himself for a run at the presidency he presented himself consistently as a dedicated Cold Warrior.[133] In his first congressional campaign, he broke with the anti-Cold War faction of the Democratic Party.[134]

As a freshman congressman he said the Truman Administration wasn't being tough enough in the Cold War against International Communism[135] as he became one of the voices asking, "Who Lost China?"[136] While in the House of Representatives, Kennedy supported the work of Senator Joseph McCarthy (1908-1957)[137] with the Senate Sub-Committee on Un-American Activities.[138] In each of his campaigns for re-election the future president worked hard to supply the voters with his anti-Communist credentials. In 1952, during his first campaign for the Senate, he pointed to the fact that while he was in the House he had worked on a labor committee whose investigations had led to the conviction of Communist union officials. In addition, during his entire career in Congress, Kennedy supported every one of America's efforts, both domestic and foreign in waging the Cold War.[139]

During his carefully scripted campaign for President in 1960, Kennedy repeatedly attacked the Eisenhower Administration for America's relative weakness vis-a-vis International Communism. Inventing a non-existent "missile gap"[140] Kennedy, the Cold Warrior promised to increase the funding of defense. And echoing the charges he had once hurled at President Truman during the debates with Nixon, Kennedy charged that it was the Eisenhower Administration which had "Lost Cuba."[141]

A brief look at some of the statements Kennedy made during the election will show that President Kennedy accepted the reality that America was engaged in a world-wide struggle against International Communism. It also makes it clear that he believed that battles in this war would flare-up and when they did, America should respond with forceful action.

> "**We must regain the ability to intervene effectively and swiftly in any limited war anywhere in the world** (emphasis added) -augmenting, modernizing and providing increased mobility and versatility for the conventional forces and weapons of the Army and Marine Corps. As long as those forces lack the necessary airlift and sealift capacity and versatility of firepower, we cannot protect our commitments around the globe-resist non-nuclear aggressions-or be certain of having enough time to decide on the use of our nuclear power."[142]

> "The recognition is not really the crux of our foreign policy. **The real question is what should be done about the harsh facts that China is a powerful and aggressive nation** (emphasis added). The dangerous situation now existing can be remedied only by a strong and successful India, a strong and successful Japan, and some kind of regional group over Southeast Asia which gives these smaller countries the feeling that, in spite of their distaste for a military alliance, they will not be left to be picked off one by one at the whim of the Peiping (sic.) regime."[143]

President Kennedy concurred with his predecessor's domino theory.[144] He also believed that serious questions existed regarding the credibility of America's anticommunist commitments around the world in 1961. Consequently, by 1963 he tripled American aid to South Vietnam and expanded the number of military advisers there from less than seven hundred to more than sixteen thousand.[145] However, the Diem government failed to show significant economic or political progress. Buddhist priests acting as the spiritual leaders of the majority of Vietnamese, staged dramatic protests, including self-immolation, against the dictatorship of the Catholic Diem.[146] Ngo Dinh Nhu,[147] Diem's brother, led a brutal suppression of the Buddhist resistance. Finally, after receiving assurances of noninterference from U.S. officials, South Vietnamese military officers conducted a coup that ended with the murders of Diem and Nhu. Whether these gruesome developments would have led Kennedy to redirect or decrease U.S. involvement in Vietnam is unknown or at least debatable,[148] since Kennedy himself was assassinated three weeks later.

When he finally gained the presidency, Kennedy let the

world know in his Inaugural Address that he would lead the nation as an active Cold Warrior. "Let every nation know, whether it wishes us well or ill, that we will pay any price, bear any burden, meet any hardship, support any friend, oppose any foe, to assure the survival and the success of liberty."[149]

After the election, the outgoing administration briefed Kennedy and several of his new appointees and advisors concerning the situation in Southeast Asia. In this briefing, the outgoing administration expressed its belief that the war in Southeast Asia had wider implications.

In this meeting, President Eisenhower accompanied by members of his senior staff met with president-elect Kennedy and senior members of his transition team. Several subjects were on the agenda but the first subject was the current situation in Laos.

> President Eisenhower opened the discussion on Laos by stating that the United States was determined to preserve the independence of Laos. **It was his opinion that if Laos should fall to the Communists, then it would be just a question of time until South Vietnam, Cambodia, Thailand and Burma would collapse. He felt that the Communists had designs on all of Southeast Asia** (emphasis added), and that it would be a tragedy to permit Laos to fall. ...
>
> President Eisenhower ... **said that the evidence was clear that Communist China and North Vietnam were determined to destroy the independence of Laos. He also added that the Russians were sending in substantial supplies in support of the**

> **Pathet Lao in an effort to overturn the government** (emphasis added).[150]

After making it clear that he thought the battle for Laos was part of the wider conflict of the Cold War the outgoing President warned against any compromise.

> President Eisenhower said it would be fatal for us to permit Communists to insert themselves in the Laotian government. He recalled that our experience had clearly demonstrated that under such circumstances the Communists always ended up in control. He cited China as an illustration.[151]

Then Eisenhower's Secretary of State Christian Herter (1895-1966)[152] expressed the belief that the action to save Laos from falling to the Communists should fit within the framework of existing international agreements designed to forestall outside aggression when he stated,

> if the present government of Laos were to apply to SEATO (Southeast Asia Treaty Organization, information added)[153] for aid under the Pact, Herter was of the positive opinion that the signatories to the SEATO Pact were bound. President Eisenhower agreed with this and in his statement gave the impression that the request for aid had already come from the government of Laos. He corroborated the binding nature of the obligation of the United States under the SEATO Pact. ...[154]

The Secretary continued, highlighting the importance of

this struggle. A struggle he felt was so important that if America's allies would not help, America must bear none-the-less.

> Secretary Herter stated, with President Eisenhower's approval, that we should continue every effort to make a political settlement in Laos. He added, however, that if such efforts were fruitless, then the United States must intervene in concert with our allies. If we were unable to persuade our allies, then we must go it alone.[155]

President Eisenhower now reiterated his belief in the importance of Laos to all of Southeast Asia, again outlining his commitment to the Domino Theory, a theory, which only makes sense within the context of a larger conflict.

> At this point, President Eisenhower said with considerable emotion that **Laos was the key to the entire area of Southeast Asia. He said that if we permitted Laos to fall, then we would have to write off all the area** (emphasis added). He stated that we must not permit a Communist take-over.[156]

That Kennedy accepted and endorsed the views of the outgoing Eisenhower administration as expressed during the presidential transition period is apparent from the following exchange between the newly elected President and the press after his inauguration.

First in his opening statement, the President inherently expressed his adherence to the Domino Theory when he stated, "The security of all Southeast Asia will be endangered if Laos loses its neutral independence."[157] Then he placed it within the context of a wider, global conflict by stating, "Its own safety runs with the safety of us all in real neutrality observed by all."[158]

In answer to a reporter's question, "Mr. President, there appears to be some national unawareness of the importance of a free Laos to the security of the United States and to the individual American. Could you spell out your views on that a little further?"[159] President Kennedy took the opportunity to clarify his belief that the security of one nation would affect the security of its neighbors. In addition, he made it plain that he believed the threat came from Communist aggression when he said, "it's quite obvious that if the Communists were able to move in and dominate this country, it would endanger the security of all, and the peace of all of Southeast Asia."[160]

The President went even further and tied the conflict in Southeast Asia to the wider cause of freedom and specifically to America's own security. "And as a member of the United Nations and as a signatory to the SEATO pact, and as a country which is concerned with the strength of the cause of freedom around the world, that quite obviously affects the security of the United States."[161]

The Kennedy administration was from beginning to end, and from top to bottom committed to the continued American effort in Vietnam. This assertion finds expression in the following statement issued jointly by Vice President Johnson (1908-1973)[162] and the President of South Vietnam, Ngo Dinh Diem during a visit to Vietnam just four months after Kennedy took office.

> "The United States, for its part, is conscious of the determination, energy and sacrifices which the Vietnamese people, under the dedicated leadership of President Ngo Dinh Diem, have brought to the defense

> of freedom in their land.
>
> "The United States is also conscious of its responsibility and duty, in its own self-interest as well as in the interest of other free peoples, to assist a brave country in the defense of its liberties against unprovoked subversion and Communist terror. It has no other motive than the defense of freedom."[163]

As his administration began to take control of the levers of power Kennedy's advisors continued to bombard him with studies, findings and recommendations concerning the situation if Vietnam. These varied sources of advice explained the slowly unraveling confrontation in the terms of the Cold War and their recommendations were uniformly in support of the policy of containment. One well-known report that is often cited as an example of the type of analysis provided to President Kennedy is a report prepared by Secretary of State Dean Rusk (1909-1994)[164] and Secretary of Defense Robert McNamara (b. 1916)[165] dated November 11, 1961.

They first outlined the by now traditional American position that the loss of one nation would inevitably lead to an increased threat if not the ultimate loss of its neighbors. "The loss of South Viet-Nam (sic.) would make pointless any further discussion about the importance of Southeast Asia to the free world; we would have to face the near certainty that the remainder of Southeast Asia and Indonesia would move to a complete accommodation with Communism, if not formal incorporation with the Communist bloc."[166]

The two Cabinet Members went on to tie the fate of Vietnam to the continuance of an international treaty organization designed to provide a Pacific bulwark against Communist aggression, SEATO (Southeast Asia Treaty Organization: information added).[167] They also tied

America's resolve in Vietnam to its continued credibility as an ally in the developing world struggle. "The loss of South Viet-Nam (sic.) to Communism would not only destroy SEATO but would undermine the credibility of American commitments elsewhere."[168]

Then looking at the possibility of domestic destabilization, which they thought would erupt if America "lost" Vietnam they stated, "Further, loss of South Viet-Nam (sic.) would stimulate bitter domestic controversies in the United States and would be seized upon by extreme elements to divide the country and harass the Administration."[169]

The two high-level advisors stated the objective "The United States should commit itself to the clear objective of preventing the fall of South Viet-Nam (sic.) to Communist (sic.),"[170] then moving directly to the practical side of how to avoid the loss of Vietnam, Rusk and McNamara outline how the United States should proceed. "The basic means for accomplishing this objective must be to put the Government of South Viet-Nam (sic.) into a position to win its own war against the Guerrillas. We must insist that that Government itself take the measures necessary for that purpose in exchange for large-scale United States assistance in the military, economic and political fields."[171] Even at this early date, American leaders were expressing the doubts they had concerning the ability of the South Vietnamese to hold their own against the infiltration of men and material from abroad. "At the same time we must recognize that it will probably not be possible for the GVN (Government of Vietnam – information added) to win this war as long as the flow of men and supplies from North Viet-Nam (sic.) continues unchecked and the guerrillas enjoy a safe sanctuary in neighboring territory."[172]

This realization in turn brought a grim assessment that proved to be in the final analysis to have been prophetic "We should be prepared to introduce United States combat forces if that should become necessary for success. Dependent upon the circumstances, it may also be necessary for United States forces to strike at the source of the aggression in North Viet-Nam (sic.)."[173]

Having given their combined analysis of the situation as it then existed the two cabinet members went on to give a detailed recommendation to President Kennedy:

> In the light of the foregoing, the Secretary of State and the Secretary of Defense recommend that:
> 1. We now take the decision to commit ourselves to the objective of preventing the fall of South Viet-Nam (sic.) to Communism and that, in doing so, we recognize that the introduction of United States and other SEATO forces may be necessary to achieve this objective. (However, if it is necessary to commit outside forces to achieve the foregoing objective, our decision to introduce United States forces should not be contingent upon unanimous SEATO agreement thereto.)
> 2. The Department of Defense be prepared with plans for the use of United States forces in South Viet Nam (sic.) under one or more of the following purposes:
>
> > **(a)** Use of a significant number of United States forces to signify United States determination to defend Viet-Nam (sic.) and to boost South Viet-Nam (sic.) morale.
> > **(b)** Use of substantial United States forces to assist in suppressing Viet Cong insurgency short of engaging in detailed counter-guerrilla operations but includ-

ing relevant operations in North Viet-Nam (sic.).

(c) Use of United States forces to deal with the situation if there is organized Communist military intervention.

3. We immediately undertake the following actions in support of the GVN:

. . . **(d)** Provide the GVN with small craft, including such United States uniformed advisers and operating personnel as may be necessary for quick and effective operations in effecting surveillance and control over coastal waters and inland waterways....

(e) Provide such personnel and equipment as may be necessary to prove the military-political intelligence system beginning at the provincial level and extending upward through the Government and the armed forces to the Central Intelligence Organization.

(f) Provide such new terms of reference, reorganization and additional personnel for United States military forces as are required for increased United States participation in the direction and control of GVN military operations and to carry out the other increased responsibilities which accrue to MAAG under these recommendations....

(i) Provide individual administrators and advisers for insertion into the Governmental machinery of South Viet-Nam (sic.) in types and numbers to be agreed upon by the two Governments....[174]

Just as throughout his pre-presidential congressional career President Kennedy continued to believe in and to express his commitment to the validity of the "Domino Theory" regarding the situation in Southeast Asia. His answer to a reporter's question in 1963 aptly expresses his public, though implied, enunciation of this fundamental tenet of American foreign policy:

> **Q:** "Mr. President, the Mansfield committee, sent at your suggestion to the Far East and Europe, has recommended a thorough security reassessment in the Far East and a clamp down, if not a reduction in our aid to that part of the world. Would you have any comment on this, sir?"
>
> **A**: "I don't see how we are going to be able, **unless we are going to pull out of Southeast Asia and turn it over to the Communists** (emphasis added), how we are going to be able to reduce very much our economic programs and military programs in South Viet-Nam (sic.), in Cambodia, in Thailand.
>
> "I think that unless you want to withdraw from the field and decide that it is in the national interest to **permit that area to collapse** (emphasis added), I would think that it would be impossible to substantially change it particularly, as we are in a very intensive struggle in those areas.
>
> "So I think we ought to judge the economic burden it places upon us **as opposed to**

> **having the Communists control all of Southeast Asia with the inevitable effect that this would have on the security of India and, therefore, really begin to run perhaps all the way toward the Middle East** (emphasis added). So I think that while we would all like to lighten the burden, I don't see any real prospect of the burden being lightened for the U.S. in Southeast Asia in the next year if we are going to do the job and meet what I think are very clear national needs."[175]

In addition to the foregoing implied endorsement of the "Domino Theory", the President expressly stated his belief and commitment in the following answer to another reporter's question:

> **Q:** "Mr. President, on Laos again, sever**al years ago we heard a great deal about the 'falling domino' theory in Southeast Asia** (emphasis added).
>
> "**Do you look upon Laos in terms of that country alone, or is your concern the effect that its loss would have in Thailand, Vietnam, and so on** (emphasis added)?
> "Would you discuss that?"
>
> **A: "That is correct** (emphasis added). The population of Laos is 2 million and it is scattered. It is a very rough country. It is important as a sovereign power. The people desire to be independent, and it is also important because it borders the Mekong River and,

> quite obviously, **if Laos fell into Communist hands it would increase the danger along the northern frontiers of Thailand. It would put additional pressure on Cambodia and would put additional pressure on South Vietnam which in itself would put additional pressure on Malaya** (emphasis added).
>
> "So **I do accept the view that there is an interrelationship in these countries** (emphasis added) and that is one of the reasons why we are concerned with maintaining the Geneva Accords as a method of maintaining stability in Southeast Asia. It may be one of the reasons why others do not share that interest."[176]

In the following excerpt from an interview with famed television anchors, Chet Huntley (1911-1975)[177] and David Brinkly (1921-2003),[178] President Kennedy took the opportunity of a nationally broadcast interview to place the war in Southeast Asia within the context of a wider struggle and to expressly reaffirm, his belief in the "Domino Theory." He also stated his continued commitment to sustaining the battle in Vietnam, a battle he viewed as a battle in the continuing Cold War.

> **Mr. Huntley:** "Are we likely to reduce our aid to South Viet-Nam (sic.) now?"
>
> ***THE PRESIDENT*:** "I don't think we think that would be helpful at this time. If you reduce your aid, it is possible you could have some effect upon the government structure

> there. On the other hand, you might have a situation which could bring about a collapse. Strongly in our mind is what happened in the case of China at the end of World War II, where China was lost—a weak government became increasingly unable to control events. We don't want that."
>
> **Mr. Brinkley: "Mr. President, have you had any reason to doubt this so-called 'domino theory,'** (emphasis added) that if South Viet-Nam (sic.) falls, the rest of Southeast Asia will go behind it?"
>
> ***THE PRESIDENT*: "No, I believe it. I believe it** (emphasis added). I think that the struggle is close enough. China is so large, looms so high just beyond the frontiers, that **if South Viet-Nam (sic.) went, it would not only give them an improved geographic position for a guerrilla assault on Malaya** (emphasis added) but would also give the impression that the wave of the future in Southeast Asia was China and the Communists. **So I believe it** (emphasis added)."[179]

Finally, in a speech prepared, but due to his assassination, never delivered. Kennedy clearly meant to reaffirm publicly America's commitment to bearing any burden necessary to stop the advance of Communism. The President sought to make it clear that in his view, Vietnam was a battle in the ongoing Cold War, and a domino in a chain. He also would have stated that he believed if the line of defense collapsed in Southeast Asia the forces of

Communism would have continued their advance and that this would have brought a great cost in American lives.

> But American military might should not and need not stand alone against **the ambitions of international communism** (emphasis added). **Our security and strength, in the last analysis, directly depend on the security and strength of others** (emphasis added)—and that is why our military and economic assistance plays such a key role in enabling those who live on the **periphery of the Communist world** (emphasis added) to maintain their independence of choice. Our assistance to these nations can be painful, risky and costly—as is true in Southeast Asia today. But we dare not weary of the task. For our assistance makes possible the stationing of 3.5 million allied troops **along the Communist frontier** (emphasis added) at one-tenth the cost of maintaining a comparable number of American soldiers. **A successful Communist breakthrough** (emphasis added) in these areas, necessitating direct United States intervention, would cost us several times as much as our entire foreign aid program—and might cost us heavily in American lives as well.
>
> About 70 per cent of our military assistance goes to nine key countries located on or near the borders of the Communist bloc—nine countries confronted directly or indirectly with the threat of Communist aggression—Viet Nam (sic.), Free China, Korea, India, Pakistan, Thailand, Greece,

> Turkey and Iran. No one of these countries possesses on its own the resources to maintain the forces which our own chiefs of staff think needed in the common interest. Reducing our efforts to train, equip and assist their armies can only encourage **Communist penetration** (emphasis added) and require in time the increased overseas deployment of American combat forces. And reducing the help needed to bolster these nations that undertake to help defend freedom can have the same disastrous result."[180]

In addition, from the conclusion of this same speech Kennedy boldly stated that it was America's duty to be ever vigilant in the defense of freedom guarding the walls.

> We in this country, in this generation, are—by destiny rather than choice—the **watchmen on the walls of world freedom** (emphasis added). We ask, therefore, that we may be worthy of our power and responsibility—that we may exercise our strength with wisdom and restraint—and that we may achieve in our time and for all time the ancient vision of "peace on earth, good will toward men." That must always be our goal—and the righteousness of our case must always underlie our strength. For as was written long ago: "Except the Lord keep the city, the watchman waketh but in vain."[181]

As a matter of policy, Kennedy did try to reduce tensions between the United States and the Soviet Union.

However at the same time he made it very clear that he completely supported the Truman Doctrine and its commitment to the containment of International Communism. In the name of objectivity, remember during these years the foreign policy of the liberal democracies lurched and danced to the bombastic rhetoric of the Communist dictators just as the 1930s had listened to the boastful claims of the Fascists. At that time the leadership of International Communism as personified in the bellicose, shoe-pounding, Nikita Khrushchev (1894-1971),[182] declared at every opportunity that the Soviet Union would support so-called "wars of national liberation"[183] waged by Communist insurgents throughout the world. Their actions and rhetoric seemed to imply that the Totalitarian leaders of International Communism not only believed in the Domino Theory but also intended to push down every domino they could.

To Kennedy the Cold Warrior his acceptance of the reality of the Cold War and the validity of the Domino Theory were sufficient reasons to hold the line in Vietnam.[184] To those who perpetuate the myth that President Kennedy sought to lead America to an early disengagement from Vietnam remember that he increased America's troop numbers from 500 to more than 16,000.[185] In addition, he sanctioned the direct involvement of America in the political life of South Vietnam when he approved the coup against President Diem.[186] Hardly the acts of a leader who planned to withdraw American forces and leave South Vietnam to its fate.[187]

---

[132] http://www.cs.umb.edu/jfklibrary (11-14-03). Informational.

[133] Chomsky, p. 45.

[134] http://mcadams.posc.mu.edu/progjfk5.htm (11-14-03).

[135]Mann, p. 28; http://www.bartleby.com/65/ke/KennedyJF.html (11-25-03).

[136] http://mcadams.posc.mu.edu/progjfk5.htm (12-3-03).

[137] http://www.apl.org/history/mccarthy/biography.html (11-17-03). Informational.

[138] http://mcadams.posc.mu.edu/progjfk2.htm (11-14-03).

[139] http://mcadams.posc.mu.edu/progjfk5.htm (11-25-03); Herring, p. 43.

[140] Ibid. Informational.

[141] http://www.jfklibrary.org/60-2nd.htm (11-25-03)

[142] http://www.mtholyoke.edu/acad/intrel/pentagon2/ps2.htm (11-20-03). Senator John F. Kennedy's Statement on Limited War in Congressional Record, June 14, 1960, p. 11631. Source: The Pentagon Papers, Gravel Edition, Volume 2, p. 798.

[143] http://www.mtholyoke.edu/acad/intrel/pentagon2/ps3.htm (11-20-03). Senator John F. Kennedy's Statement on the Dangerous Role of the People's Republic of China, *Washington Daily News*, September 22, 1960. Source: The Pentagon Papers, Gravel Edition, Volume 2, p. 799.

[144] Chomsky, p. 47; http://mcadams.posc.mu.edu/progjfk5.htm (11-14-03).

[145] Ibid.

[146] http://www.angelfire.com/nb/protest/viet.html (11-25-03). Informational.

[147] http://www.vietnam-war.info/figures/ngo_dinh_nhu.php (11-17-03). Informational.

[148] McNamara, Robert S. In Retrospect. Times Books: New York, 1995, pp. 52-61; Chomsky, p. 47.

[149] John F. Kennedy's Inaugural Address, January 20, 1961, http://www.infoplease.com/ipa/A0878607.html / (10-2-03).

[150] For the full text of Memorandum of Conference on January 19, 1961 between President Eisenhower and president-elect Kennedy on the Subject of Laos, see the Appendix.

[151] Ibid.

[152] http://ilovefreedom.com/quotations/Christian_Herter.htm (11-14-03). Informational.

[153] http://www.austlii.edu.au/au/other/dfat/treaties/1955/3.html (11-14-03). Informational.

[154] McNamara, pp. 35-37, passim; For the full text of Memorandum of Conference on January 19, 1961 between President Eisenhower and

president-elect Kennedy on the Subject of Laos, see the Appendix.

[155] Ibid.

[156] Ibid.

[157] http://www.mtholyoke.edu/acad/intrel/pentagon2/ps5.htm (11-20-03). Statement by President Kennedy on the Importance of Laos. New York Times, March 24, 1961. Source: *The Pentagon Papers,* Gravel Edition, Volume 2, pp. 799-800.

[158] Ibid.

[159] Ibid.

[160] Ibid.

[161] Ibid.

[162] http://www.lbjlib.utexas.edu (11-14-03). Informational.

[163] http://www.mtholyoke.edu/acad/intrel/pentagon2/ps10.htm (11-20-03). Joint Communique Issued at Saigon by the Vice President of the United States and the President of Viet-Nam, May 13, 1961. Department of State Bulletin, June 19, 1961, p. 956. Source: The Pentagon Papers, Gravel Edition, Volume 2, p. 803.

[164] http://www.ourgeorgiahistory.com/chronpop/304 (11-14-03).

[165] http://globetrotter.berkeley.edu/McNamara/mcnamarabio.html (11-14-03).

[166] For a more complete text of Excerpts from Rusk-McNamara Report to Kennedy, November 11, 1961 see Appendix.

[167] http://www.austlii.edu.au/au/other/dfat/treaties/1955/3.html (11-18-03). Informational

[168] For a more complete text of Excerpts from Rusk-McNamara Report to Kennedy, November 11, 1961 see Appendix.

[169] Ibid.

[170] Ibid.

[171] Ibid.

[172] Ibid.

[173] Ibid.

[174] For a more complete text of Excerpts from Rusk-McNamara Report to Kennedy, November 11 1961, see the Appendix.

[175] http://www.mtholyoke.edu/acad/intrel/pentagon2/ps29.htm (11-20-03). Excerpts from President Kennedy's News Conference, March 6, 1963. Public Papers of the Presidents, Kennedy, 1963, p. 243. Source:

The Pentagon Papers, Gravel Edition, Volume 2, pp. 816-817.

[176] http://www.mtholyoke.edu/acad/intrel/pentagon2/ps31.htm (11-20-03). President Kennedy's View of the "Domino Theory," News Conference, April 24, 1963. Public Papers of the Presidents, Kennedy, 1963, p. 343. Source: The Pentagon Papers, Gravel Edition, Volume 2, pp. 818-819.

[177] http://www.museum.tv/archives/etv/H/htmlH/huntleychet/huntley-chet.htm (11-14-03). Informational

[178] http://www.museum.tv/archives/etv/B/htmlB/brinkleydav/brinkley-dav.htm (12-17-03). Informational.

[179] http://www.mtholyoke.edu/acad/intrel/pentagon2/ps38.htm (11-20-03). President Kennedy's NBC Interview, September 9, 1963. Department of State Bulletin, September 30, 1963, p. 499. Source: The Pentagon Papers, Gravel Edition, Volume 2, pp. 827-828.

[180] http://www.mtholyoke.edu/acad/intrel/pentagon2/ps43.htm (11-20-03). President Kennedy's Remarks Prepared for Delivery at the Trade Mart in Dallas, November 22, 1963. Public Papers of the Presidents, Kennedy, 1963, p. 890. Source: The Pentagon Papers, Gravel Edition, Volume 2, pp. 830-831.

[181] Ibid.

[182] http://www.geocities.com/CapitolHill/9854/nikita.htm (11-14-03). Informational.

[183] http://www.airpower.maxwell.af.mil/airchronicles/aureview/1980/sep-oct/little.html (11-25-03).

[184] Cooper, pp.409-411; Mann, p. 244.

[185] http://mcadams.posc.mu.edu/progjfk5.htm (12-3-03).

[186] http://www.polytechnic.org/faculty/gfeldmeth/chart.Vietnam.html (11-14-03); Chomsky, p. 73.

[187] http://mcadams.posc.mu.edu/stjohn.htm (12-5-03). Informational.

CHAPTER SEVEN

Johnson

The intensity and tone of the Cold War began to evolve as the 1960's progressed. It was becoming apparent that neither side was the great monolith that the other side had imagined. Accusing their erstwhile patrons of being counter-revolutionaries Communist China in a loudly trumpeted break with the Soviet Union began following its own counsel in foreign relations. This new bipolar situation in the Communist block opened the door for several Communist countries to begin playing one Communist center of power against the other seeking to gain the maximum support from one or both. The fluidity of this situation caused a major split in the ranks of the Communist countries. Some followed China while many others, because of ideology or military domination remained loyal to the Soviet Union. However, despite these cracks in the facade of International Communism the United States continued to recognize that crusading Communism of whatever stripe was merely the current ideological cover for the advancing Totalitarianism of the modern police state.

Economic and social developments caused major shifts in the balance of world power during the 1960's. Massive aid programs provided by America led to the rapid re-industrialization of Japan[188] and West Germany[189] making them again major players on the world stage. Their reemergence as well as the increasing strength of Communist China led to the development of new and more varied relationships among nations.

In the West, France began to criticize the United States eventually withdrawing from the NATO. The French became more and more obstructionist of American leadership couching their attacks in the language of independent leadership for Europe. West Germany followed the French lead while remaining in NATO. They sought a rapprochement based upon negotiated economic and political relationships with the other European countries, including East Germany. All of the countries of Europe began moving towards a stronger union as a counterbalance to the overwhelming power of both the United States and the Soviet Union.

The assassination of President Kennedy had thrust Lyndon Baines Johnson into this maelstrom of great power rivalry and ideological competition that defined the Cold War of the 1960s.

President Lyndon Johnson is the victim of one of the most widely accepted mantras of the Vietnam myth. In essence, this mantra states that President Kennedy had planned to disengage from Vietnam. However, after his death President Johnson, the creature of the Military-Industrial Complex,[190] greatly expanded a local civil war into a massive invasion of the Asian landmass by the resource robbing Americans. This mantra is widely accepted by those who worship at the altar of liberalism and it forms a vital part of the JFK iconology of the left. Over the last forty years this mantra, repeated over and over in books, depicted in movies, pontificated upon on television sets, and in classrooms across America has become "common knowledge" for those who accept rather than inspect the truisms of the establishment.

However, even a cursory inspection of this assertion exposes the whole cloth, which makes it up. In 1963, the last year of his life President Kennedy did more than talk about his desire to hold the line in Vietnam. Indeed his actions spoke even louder than his words, proclaiming that he was not inclined to surrender the field to International Communism in Southeast Asia. Looking at the political developments in South Vietnam during 1963 we see the clearest of indications that Kennedy considered this as an ongoing engagement and not as a matter of declining interest.[191]

When we follow the chain of evidence in the plot to remove South Vietnamese President Ngo Dinh Diem we find that this was not the work of "rogue" CIA agents following the dictates of their Military-Industrial puppet masters. The evolution of this covert action and the orders for its execution lead directly to the highest levels in the Kennedy administration.[192] In addition according to the voluminous evidence now available it becomes clear that Kennedy did not concur in the decision to oust Diem because he was oppressing the religious and civil liberties of his people. Instead, it was because the President saw Diem and his corrupt authoritarian pseudo-democracy as a road-block to victory in this latest battle of the Cold War.

First Kennedy applied mounting pressure to try to force Diem to change, but when that failed he personally authorized the coup of November 1, 1963.[193] Those who promote the pacific intentions of President Kennedy fail to explain why he interfered so dramatically in the internal politics of South Vietnam. If he intended to pull out it would have been easier; to say nothing of more ethical to leave the exiting government in place than to subvert it, build a new one, and then leave?[194]

As the investigation of this liberal mantra progresses,

the evidence mounts that it was not only Kennedy's desire but also his intention to remain in Vietnam until America achieved victory. Kennedy's principle advisors were all held-over by the Johnson administration. And these advisors, who had counseled President Kennedy to stay the course in Vietnam were right there to advise President Johnson to move from a limited advisory role to the full commitment of United States ground forces.

Above all, Lyndon Johnson was a political operative. He cut his political teeth during the up-roar over the charges that the Truman administration had "lost" China.[195] He campaigned with Kennedy in 1960 attacking the Eisenhower administration for having "lost" Cuba." Now, as the President he knew he would face re-election soon after taking office in 1964, he did not intend to bear the onus of having "lost" South Vietnam.[196]

The Kennedy authorized plot to overthrow Diem, brought about an interval of political and military instability that did not end until the election of Nquyen Van Theiu (1923-2001)[197] as president of South Vietnam in 1967. Thus by his direct actions, Kennedy bequeathed President Johnson only two choices, complete disengagement or complete commitment. The decision to overthrow Diem which led to leadership by a cabal of politically unsophisticated military officers left Johnson with no chance to turn the war over to the Vietnamese.[198] Almost immediately, he also faced the rapid deterioration of the military situation, which the Kennedy coup fostered rather than forestalled. Then, advised by the held-over Kennedy-appointed clique that surrounded him Johnson made the fateful decision to expand radically America's commitment to Vietnam from giving support and training to direct military involvement in the next great battle of the Cold War. All the Johnson administration needed now was a plausible excuse.

While campaigning as the "Peace Candidate," Johnson

used (what some call) an alleged[199] North Vietnamese attack on U.S. Navy vessels in August 1964 as the impetus for the sweeping Gulf of Tonkin Resolution.[200] This resolution authorized what Johnson and his Kennedy-appointed advisors interpreted as the unlimited use military forces in Vietnam including the bombing of Communist North Vietnam. Domestically these actions secured a landslide victory for Johnson in the November election. However, they did not convince the Communists that they should stop their campaign to subvert and conquer South Vietnam.

By the summer of 1965, President Johnson still faced a continual decline in the military situation. The constantly shifting military and political environment of post-coup Saigon could not mount nor sustain a credible war effort against the highly motivated insurgents.[201] The proud President did not intend to be the first president of the United States to lose a war. Faced with the very real possibility of defeat and again advised by his Kennedy-appointed staff to press the issue, to fight the Cold War. Consequently, Johnson chose to convert the Vietnam War from a war fought mainly by the proxy soldiers of South Vietnam "advised" by Americans into a vast campaign directly involving large numbers of American ground troops.[202]

In a memo from National Security Advisor McGeorge Bundy (1919-1997)[203] to President Johnson, dated February 7,1965, the President was again advised to escalate the war. Bundy said, "We believe that the best available way of increasing our chance of success in Vietnam is the development and execution of a policy of sustained reprisal against North Vietnam a policy in which air and naval action against the North is justified by and related to the whole Viet Cong campaign of violence and terror in the South."[204]

But while advocating a greatly expanded war Bundy also clearly stated, "that we are not attempting to destroy or conquer North Vietnam."[205] He tied the need for escalation to the affect this would have on the moral of our allies as well as on our enemies. "The Vietnamese increase in hope could well increase the readiness of Vietnamese factions themselves to join together in forming a more effective government... We think it plausible that effective and sustained reprisals, even in a low key, would have a sustained depressing effect upon the morale of Viet Cong cadres in South Vietnam. This is the strong opinion of CIA Saigon. It is based upon reliable reports of the initial Viet Cong reaction to the Gulf of Tonkin episode, and also upon the solid general assessment that the determination of Hanoi and the apparent timidity of the mighty United States are both major items in Viet Cong confidence."[206]

One very interesting point is that Bundy urged this policy even though he was not sure whether it would succeed or not. He went so far as to advise that a failure would be preferable to doing nothing both with our allies and with domestic constituents. "We cannot assert that a policy of sustained reprisal will succeed in changing the course of the contest in Vietnam. … What we can say is that even if it fails, the policy will be worth it. **At a minimum it will damp down the charge that we did not do all that we could have done, and this charge will be important in many countries, including our own** (emphasis showing the domestic political considerations added)."[207] The National Security Advisor was also ready to point out that the successful prosecution of the course of action he advised, massive, sustained engagement would have a dampening effect on possible future advances by America's foes. "Beyond that, a reprisal policy to the extent that it demonstrates **U.S. willingness to employ this new norm in counterinsurgency will set a higher price for the future upon all adventures of guerrilla warfare, and it should therefore somewhat increase our ability to deter such adventures** (emphasis highlighting the wider applications sought from the policies in Vietnam added)."[208] He also emphasized the dangers of failure, "We must recognize, however, that that ability will be gravely weakened if there is failure for any reason in Vietnam...."[209]

The foregoing example is an apt representation of the advice President Johnson received from his circle of Kennedy-appointed military and political officials. President Johnson heeded this advice, advice that defined America's engagement in Vietnam as the next battle of the Cold War. He too saw the war in Vietnam from beginning to end as an episode within the larger strategic context of the Cold War and he consistently expressed this belief as the rationale behind America's involvement.

Repeatedly President Johnson tried to explain to the American people that the war in Vietnam was necessary to safeguard the freedom of others and as ultimately the only way to safeguard our own freedom. He demonstrated this belief when he stated "We fight because we must fight if we are to live in a world **where every country can shape its own destiny. And only in such a world will our own freedom be finally secure** (emphasis added)."[210]

President Johnson also strove to keep his voice above the din of counter-culture reaction by declaring that American military involvement was not aggression it was instead response to outside aggression. To make this fact clear he asked the question, "Why must this Nation hazard its ease, and its interest, and its power for the sake of a people so far away?"[211] So that he could provide the answer, "The first reality is that North VietNam (sic.) has attacked the independent nation of South Viet-Nam (sic.). Its object is total conquest."[212] While acknowledging that this invasion was aided and abetted by a fifth-column of fellow-travelers in the south "Of course, some of the people of South Viet-Nam (sic.) are participating in attack on their own government."[213] He shared the reality that our intelligence revealed "trained men and supplies, orders and arms, flow in a constant stream from north to south."[214]

President Johnson also used public discourse to assert that the war in Vietnam was part of a wider struggle against the forces of International Communism. He stated his belief that the struggle in Southeast Asia was neither completely indigenous nor self-directed when he said, "Over this war and all Asia is another reality: the deepening shadow of Communist China. The rulers in Hanoi are urged on by Peking."[215] He also made known his conviction that America waged this battle against an enemy who was moving internationally, an enemy that had already conquered some nations and attacked others. "This is a regime which has destroyed freedom in Tibet, which has attacked India, and has been condemned by the United Nations for aggression in Korea."[216]

The President publicly stated that we fought as allies of the South Vietnamese because we had promised to do so. "We are there because we have a promise to keep. Since 1954 every American President has offered support to the people of South Viet-Nam (sic.). We have helped to build, and we have helped to defend. Thus, over many years, we have made a national pledge to help South Viet-Nam (sic.) defend its independence."[217]

Johnson's conviction that our struggle in Vietnam had consequences that went far beyond Southeast Asia as illustrated in his statement, "We are also there to strengthen world order."[218] In addition, his belief in the critical nature of our involvement in Vietnam vis-a-vis the wider struggle of the Cold War is evident when he said, "Around the globe, from Berlin to Thailand, are people whose well-being rests, in part, on the belief that they can count on us if they are attacked. To leave Viet-Nam (sic) to its fate would shake the confidence of all these people in the value of an American commitment and in the value of America's word.

The result would be increased unrest and instability, and even wider war."[219]

This was not a one-time expression for President Johnson. He hammered away at the wider implications of the war in Vietnam. "We are also there because there are great stakes in the balance. Let no one think for a moment that retreat from Viet-Nam (sic.) would bring an end to conflict. The battle would be renewed in one country and then another. The central lesson of our time is that the appetite of aggression is never satisfied. To withdraw from one battlefield means only to prepare for the next."[220] To show it would take resolve to stop the floodtide of the advancing forces of Totalitarianism he compared the war in Vietnam to past experiences which made up a part of the Cold War experience. "**We must say in Southeast Asia as we did in Europe** (emphasis added) in the words of the Bible: "Hitherto shalt thou come, but no further."[221]

As to America's goals President Johnson fit in perfectly with the three previous presidents when he stated, "Our objective is the independence of South Viet-Nam, (sic.) and its freedom from attack. We want nothing for ourselves only that the people of South Viet-Nam (sic.) be allowed to guide their own country in their own way."[222]

President Johnson did not however seek a declaration of war from congress. Instead, he followed the course of his mentor President Truman ala-Korea as he chose to fight a limited war with no mobilization of the home front.[223] In response to the pleas of his commanders on the ground, President Johnson sent an ever-increasing number of troops, by 1968 these numbered more than 500,000. A vast navy and airforce supported the ground forces. The supposedly limited air strikes against North Vietnam eventually (by 1967) came to total a greater aggregate tonnage than all of the ordinance dropped during World War II.[224]

The United Sates forces led by Gen. William

Westmoreland (born 1914)[225] following the example of General Ridgway and his Korean "Meat Grinder" adopted a policy of attrition.[226] In addition, as is always the case with this brutal strategy it's design is to inflict such heavy losses on the enemy that their will to fight is broken. Throughout history, such diverse military leaders as Attila, Genghis Khan, and William Tecumseh Sherman have used attrition to gain victory. In the late 1960s, the Johnson administration accepted the military arguments for the application of this policy and the American public began to hear of "body counts"[227] as a euphemism for victory.

Westmoreland's headquarters began claiming that the scales were tipping in America's favor. He asserted that through aggressive search-and-destroy missions American forces destroyed the military assets of the enemy faster than the North could re-supply them. Then in January 1968, came the surprise of the Tet Offensive.[228] Striking seemingly at will throughout South Vietnam, the Vietcong supported by large contingents of North Vietnamese regulars seized many towns and cities. They even managed to penetrate the compound of the United Sates Embassy in Saigon. After weeks of hard fighting the American forces and their South Vietnamese allies ultimately crushed the offensive all but eliminating, the Vietcong as a cohesive fighting force independent of the North Vietnamese.[229] However, the importance of the Tet Offensive lies not in its lasting military affect. Militarily the Tet Offensive was disastrous to the Communist forces.[230] It was in the political arena that it had its greatest impact.[231] Both the breadth and the ferocity of the fighting highlighted the fact that there would be no near end to the war as General Westmoreland had optimistically predicted.[232]

Following the Tet Offensive, the political fallout spread like a pall across the American landscape.[233] Fueled by the rising tide of domestic protest led by a segment of the population, which did not see the Vietnam War as a battle in the Cold War. They instead viewed it as an independent evil somehow existing in a parallel universe devoid of strategic influences. Moreover, though a large segment of the voting public continued to support the war[234] America's political leaders began an agonizingly slow disengagement of United States forces. Another casualty of the Tet Offensive and its resulting political readjustment was President Johnson. A prisoner of the policies he inherited and the architect of a limited war he reacted to the public outcry by first putting ever-tightening restrictions on the bombing of the North. Simultaneously he began to put out peace feelers and sought to begin peace talks with the Totalitarian Communist rulers of North Vietnam. In addition, in what must have been the bitterest decision of his career he withdrew as a candidate for reelection so that he could pursue peace on a full-time basis.[235]

---

[188] http://collections.ic.gc.ca/kingcoal/5/pacificrim/afterwar.html (11-26-03). Informational.

[189] http://www.marshallfoundation.org/about_gcm/marshall_plan.htm (11-26-03). Informational.

[190] http://coursesa.matrix.msu.edu/~hst306/documents/indust.html (11-14-03). Informational.

[191] Chomsky, pp. 105-148, passim; Mann, p.726-727.

[192] http://www.gwu.edu/~nsarchiv/NSAEBB/NSAEBB101 (11-14-03). Informational.

[193] http://www.gwu.edu/~nsarchiv/NSAEBB/NSAEBB101/ (11-25-03).

[194] http://mcadams.posc.mu.edu/progjfk5.htm (12-10-03).

[195] Donovan, p. 43.

[196] Mann, p. 312.

[197] http://www.cikadenet.dk/vietnam/Nguyen_Van_Thieu.htm (11-14-03). Informational.

[198] Berman, Larry. Lyndon Johnson's War. W. W. Norton & Co.: New York, 1989, pp. xi-xiii, 9, 203; Herring, pp. 110-113, passim; Karnow, pp.324-326, passim; McNamara, p. 105.

[199] http://www.fair.org/media-beat/940727.html (11-25-03).

[200] Donovan, pp.54-59; Karnow, pp. 344-345; http://www.luminet.net/~tgort/tonkin.htm (11-14-03). Informational.

[201] Mann, pp. 310-311.

[202] Berman, pp. xi-xiii, 9, 203; Chomsky, pp. 96-97; Donovan, pp. 63, 64, 68-72, 96; Karnow, p. 327; Mann, pp.438-458, passim.

[203] http://www.english.upenn.edu/~afilreis/50s/bundy-obit.html (11-14-03). Informational.

[204] For more complete text of Excerpts from McGeorge Bundy's Memo to President Johnson, February 7 1965, see the Appendix.

[205] Ibid.

[206] Ibid.

[207] Ibid.

[208] Ibid.

[209] Ibid.

[210] For a more complete text of Excerpts from Speech Given by President Johnson at Johns Hopkins University, on April 7 1965, see the Appendix.

[211] Ibid.

[212] Ibid.

[213] Ibid.

[214] Ibid.

[215] Ibid.

[216] Ibid.

[217] Ibid.

[218] Ibid.

[219] Ibid.

[220] Ibid.

[221] Ibid.

[222] Ibid.

[223] Millet, Allan R. & Peter Maslowski. For the Common Defense. The Free Press: New York, 1994, p.580

224 http://www.aftermathpictures.com/aftermat/bombing.html (11-25-03).

225 http://www.vietnampix.com/popww.htm (11-25-03). Informational.

226 Millet, p.580.

227 http://www.11thcavnam.com/education/myth_body_counts_were_falsified.htm (11-26-03). Informational

228 http://hubcap.clemson.edu/~eemoise/viet8.html (11-25-03). Informational.

229 http://www.720mpvietnamproject.org/21-communist%20forces/history-vc/vc-history.html (11-25-03).

230 Millet, p. 88, Herring, p. 191.

231 Ibid, pp. 191-192.

232 Mann, p. 570.

233 Karnow, p546.

234 http://www.seanet.com/~jimxc/Politics/Mistakes/Vietnam_support.html (11-25-03).

235 http://www.pbs.org/ladybird/shattereddreams/shattereddreams_doc_re_elect.html (11-25-03).

CHAPTER EIGHT

Nixon

In 1953, as one of his first of many foreign tours as the official representative of President Eisenhower Vice President Richard M. Nixon (1913-1994)[236] visited Vietnam for the first time. At that time, the United States stood in support of the re-institution of the French colonial regime. This effort would of course end in the complete pullout of the French after their disastrous defeat at Dien Bien Phu. On this first visit, Vice President Nixon became convinced that the French were losing the war. He also left with the impression that their failure to use, train, and equip the indigenous citizens of their colony to fight for themselves against the aggression of International Communist would be their undoing. [237]

After his defeat by Kennedy in the presidential election of 1960, Nixon spent much of his time out of the country, traveling the world. Three times between 1961 and 1968, Richard Nixon met with American commanders, troops, and local leaders in South Vietnam as he sought to understand the situation.[238] In all of his travels, he scrupulously followed what was at the time the accepted American policy of never criticizing United States policy while abroad.

However, when he traveled within the United States, he used his many speaking engagements to raise his serious reservations concerning the policies of the Johnson administration. He was convinced that the United States was making the same mistake as the French respecting the use of indigenous troops against the aggression of International Communism. Further, he saw that the United States policy of offering bombing halts in exchange for progress in negotiations known; "gradualism"[239] was counter-productive. He believed this because it gave the North Vietnamese Communists the impression that the American leaders lacked the necessary determination to prosecute the war.

The 1968 Campaign

Nineteen sixty-eight marked Richard Nixon's second try for the presidency. Vietnam was a constant theme in his campaign.[240] He staked out a policy, which promised he would "end the war and win the peace in Vietnam."[241] One of the most cherished myths of the Left is that Nixon claimed to have a "secret plan" to end the war. However, a careful (or even a cursory) search of his statements proves that he never made such a statement.[242]

The year opened with North Vietnamese regulars mounting a siege of the American base at Khe Sahn[243] in January which some thought would end up as America's Dien Bien Phu. Then in February came the surprise of the TET Offensive.[244] It was apparent to all observers that 1968 would clearly be a presidential election year influenced by Vietnam.

As a sitting President Johnson had not anticipated any challenge for the nomination. He was so confident that he did not even file to get his name on the ballot for the February, 1968 New Hampshire primary. When they counted the votes the president received 49.6% of the vote while Senator Eugene McCarthy (born 1916)[245] after tireless campaigning as a write-in candidate received 41.9% of the vote.[246] However, the next morning the story that the newspapers trumpeted was McCarthy's upset "Victory!" McCarthy had broken with the administration over the war and had come out strongly critical of the president, his advisors, and his policies. By-passing the party machines and the party stalwarts McCarthy, running as an avowed antiwar candidate appealed primarily to younger voters.[247]

Reading the political handwriting on the wall Robert Kennedy (1925-1968)[248] soon announced his candidacy for the Democrat nomination.[249] Then on March 31, in a move that shocked the nation President Johnson, unexpectedly dropped out of the contest.[250] Immediately after the President's withdrawal Vice President Hubert Humphrey (1911-1978),[251] announced that he too would be a candidate for the presidency. Throughout the long primary campaign, as the sitting Vice President Humphrey spoke out in defense of the policies of the Johnson administration. Conversely, Senators Kennedy and McCarthy were both highly critical of Johnson's war policy.

Then on April 4, 1968, the nation faced another great shock whit the assassination of Martin Luther King Jr. Following the death of King riots erupted in cities across the country as civil rights leaders warned ominously of a "Long Hot Summer."[252]

In the battle for the Democratic nomination, both Kennedy and McCarthy faced what appeared an impossible task. The problem that confronted these "outsider" candidates was that party leaders and not primaries chose most delegates to the convention. So Humphrey did not bother to compete in the primaries where Kennedy and McCarthy became ever more bellicose and ever more anti-war. Therefore, instead of slugging it out before the people the Vice President made the rounds and appealed to the workers of the party. Humphrey had worked hard for the party for many years. As the campaign moved from state to state Kennedy and McCarthy drew millions of supporters to what were essentially "beauty contest" primaries[253] while Humphrey steadily gained the votes of actual delegates to the convention. [254]

Locked in a dead heat for second place Kennedy and McCarthy continued to fight it out in the press and in the primaries until they reached the pivotal primary, which occurred in California on June 4. This time, McCarthy's 41.8% wasn't enough to gain him a victory and Kennedy won the primary with 46.3%. That evening, in the ballroom of the Ambassador Hotel in Los Angeles as he walked through the kitchen of the hotel a man stepped out of the crowd and shot Kennedy three times at close range. He died within 24 hours.[255] Hammered by events 1968 reeled from a second assassination as the nation bleeding in a far off war, with a lame-duck president, and the beginnings of a cultural war at home staggered towards the election.

In the Republican Party 1968 didn't produce all the sparks that their opponents did. Instead, it was a year to return to a familiar face and a long accepted leader. Richard Nixon had spent the years since his defeat in 1960 and his abortive retirement in 1962 traveling the world and working for the party. He projected the image of a man who was well prepared for the position of president and commander-in-chief. He had no problem securing the Republican nomination and it seemed like his time had finally arrived. As the year progressed, Nixon in one of the first campaigns based almost entirely in the media emphasized two themes. He spoke of how the administration had lost the will to win as the war bogged down in Vietnam. In addition, he missed no opportunity to comment on the waves of riots and protests sweeping the country. Nixon summed up these two themes in his two main campaign slogans "Peace with

Honor" and "Law and Order."

Regarding his position on Vietnam Nixon sounded vague. Yes, he spoke of new leadership that would end the war with honor. He said that he had a plan but he never revealed what the specifics of that plan would be, thus contributing to the idea of a "secret" plan.[256] He did this because if a candidate for president made specific proposals it might hamper the work of the Johnson Administration in their ongoing negotiations or that it might compromise his own freedom of action once he became president.[257]

Now, late in the election came an unusual episode that if true is a blot upon American politics. Some believe that while he spoke of his desire to end the war Nixon was privately worried that the Johnson Administration would pull what we would now call, an "October Surprise." Through diplomatic channels, Johnson was proposing to halt the massive bombing of North Vietnam in return for the inclusion of the South Vietnamese in the Paris peace talks. In order to counter this some believe that using unofficial contacts Nixon sought to persuade President Thieu of South Vietnam to refuse to enter negotiations. Nixon's supposed message stated that the South Vietnamese should refuse to join the peace talks in 1968 because they would get more support from a President Nixon then they would from a President Humphrey. Whether any contacts from the Nixon campaign ultimately had any influence we can only imagine, we do know that Thieu refused to participate in the peace talks.[258]

In September, Hubert Humphrey broke with the Johnson Administration by proposing that a complete halt to the bombing of North Vietnam without waiting for the quid-pr-quo that Johnson had always demanded would be his program to secure peace.[259] For most of the campaign, Nixon held a commanding lead. However, as is often the case the polls began to narrow as November approached.

Then Johnson announced a unilateral bombing halt on October 31, just days before the election.[260] If he meant this to give an edge to Humphrey in the election, he almost succeeded.

Thus in the last days of the election Humphrey began to gain significantly on Nixon. However, there was another factor in the race George Wallace (1919-1998),[261] a Democrat and his American Freedom Party.[262] Portraying himself as a conservative Wallace drew many Southerners away from what at that time was their traditional loyalty to the Democratic Party. In a reverse of his situation in 1960, this time, with all the votes counted Nixon won in a very close popular vote. 43.42% voted for Nixon, 42.72% for Humphrey with 13.53% going for Wallace.

Consequently on January 20, 1969, Richard Nixon became the fifth President of the United States to face the question, "How do we end American involvement in Vietnam?" He faced a situation that had built up over many years. It rested upon Truman's commitment to "Contain" International Communism and on Eisenhower's decision to build a bulwark against the spread of Communist Totalitarianism throughout Southeast Asia by replacing the French in Indochina. It had grown through President Kennedy's decisions to enlarge the force of advisors from a few hundred to more than 16,000 and to interfere in the internal politics of South Vietnam. It had mushroomed because of President Johnson's massive infusion of military support to forestall the collapse of South Vietnam as he had struggled to pick up the pieces after the coup against Diem.

All of these decisions, over many years meant that Nixon now faced a highly complex and volatile situation. A situation where America not only had over 500,000 soldiers in Vietnam and more than 300 men being held prisoners of war in North Vietnam. At the same time, the American public had divided as never before over the course our foreign policy. In addition on his inauguration day President Nixon faced a situation without parallel in the history of the United States. For the first time, the nation had willingly "changed horses in the middle of the stream." For the first time, America had rejected a presidential administration in the midst of war and they looked hopefully to a new leader to win the battle and secure the peace.

President Nixon entered upon the duties of his office committed to ending the war.[263] However; he was not willing to sacrifice neither, the security and freedom of South Vietnam, nor the perception of our allies that the United States remained a reliable ally in the Cold War. But just as each preceding president had found himself forced to make certain decisions by the actions of his predecessor, Nixon would enter office constrained by Johnson's unilateral bombing halt and by the so-far fruitless negotiations in Paris. Negotiations, which seemed designed to serve only the public relation interests of the Communist North Vietnamese.

The nightly news filled the living rooms of America with graphic pictures of the war and with the news of protests.[264] This became such a dominant theme in the media that many came to believe that everyone was against the war. However, the polls taken throughout this period always showed a large segment of the people backed the government's handling of the war.[265] As his first term progressed, President Nixon followed the course he had spoken of in his campaign, seeking a peace with honor. Although at times the protests were massive and often violent, he refused to allow the demands of this almost overtly anti-American minority to disrupt his policies. Pointing to the polls[266] as he claimed the support of the majority of the American people, he sought to find an end to the war without damaging America's credibility amongst its allies and without allowing the first domino to fall.

To achieve his peace with honor the new President knew he needed to move on two fronts, foreign and domestic. Believing that a major reason for much of the protests, especially those on college campuses was the military draft, he sought to replace it with a lottery system[267] thereby bringing a measure of stability back to the domestic scene. In addition, Nixon also sought to initiate a process he referred to as "Vietnamization."[268] By this he meant that American troops should be progressively replaced by South Vietnamese troops believing that they should bear the brunt of the fighting (and the casualties) in defending their own country. Thus avoiding one of the major mistakes, he had perceived in the French war in Indochina. To maximize his efforts he also provided the South Vietnamese Army with better weapons and expanded training. The peace talks had by this time broken down. In response, the Nixon Administration sought to drive the Communists back to the bargaining table by renewing and expanding the bombing and the mining of North Vietnam's harbors.[269] Diplomatically he attempted to bring pressure to bear upon North Vietnam through their Chinese and Soviet allies.

The Communist North Vietnamese began violating Cambodia in the mid-sixties. As the decade moved to a close, the regular North Vietnamese Army used the dense jungles of the Vietnamese – Cambodian border regions to move supplies from north to south. They also used these areas as a launching pad for attacks against the South Vietnamese government forces.

In March 1969, seeking to disrupt the enemy's re-supply routes and staging areas President Nixon ordered the bombing of those Cambodian areas held and used by the North Vietnamese.[270] It was not long after the commencement of this bombing that the Communists North Vietnamese accepted the American offer to begin secret negotiations.[271] The bombing of Cambodia did much to derail the Communists strategic and tactical war plans.

On May 14, 1969, President Nixon made his first major address about Vietnam over nationwide TV and radio. He began by placing the situation within an historical context and framing the debate.

> We can have honest debate about whether we should have entered the war. We can have honest debate about the past conduct of the war. But the urgent question today is what to do now that we are there, not whether we should have entered on this course, but what is required of us today.
>
> Against that background, let me discuss, first, what we have rejected, and second, what we are prepared to accept.
>
> We have ruled out attempting to impose a purely military solution on the battlefield.
>
> We have also ruled out either a one-sided withdrawal from South Vietnam or the acceptance in Paris of terms that would amount to a disguised defeat.[272]

The President continued by stating his belief that America's credibility and its consequent ability to maintain a deterrent to the advances of International Communism through a system of alliances was inherently tied to its willingness to stand by its agreements and its pledges.[273]

> **Abandoning the South Vietnam people, however, would jeopardize more than lives in South Vietnam. It would threaten our longer-term hopes for peace in the world. A great nation cannot renege on its pledges, A great nation must be**

worthy of trust (emphasis added).

When it comes to maintaining peace, "prestige" is not an empty word. I am not speaking of false pride or bravado - they should have no place in our policies. I speak rather of the respect that one nation has for another's integrity in defending its principles and meeting its obligations.

If we simply abandoned our efforts in South Vietnam, the cause of peace might not survive the damage that would be done to other nations' confidence in our reliability (emphasis added).

Another reason stems from debates within the communist world between those who argue for a policy of confrontation with the United States and those who argue against it. **If Hanoi were to succeed in taking over South Vietnam by force- even after the power of the United States had been engaged - it would greatly strengthen those leaders who scorn negotiation, who advocate aggression, who minimize the risks of confrontation. It would bring peace now, but it would enormously increase the danger of a bigger war later** (emphasis added).

If we are to move successfully from an era of confrontation to an era of negotiation, then we have to demonstrate - at the point at which confrontation is being tested - that confrontation with the United States is costly and unrewarding.

Almost without exception, the leaders of non-communist Asia have told me that

> **they would consider a one-sided American withdrawal from South Vietnam to be a threat to the security of their own nations** (emphasis added).[274]

His peace proposal went beyond anything previously offered by the United States.

> In this spirit, let me be explicit about several points:
>
> We seek not bases in South Vietnam.
>
> We insist on no military ties.
>
> We are willing to agree to neutrality if that is what the South Vietnam people freely choose.
>
> We believe there should be an opportunity for full participation in the political life of South Vietnam by all political elements that are prepared to do so without the use of force or intimidation.
>
> We are prepared to accept any government in South Vietnam that results from the free choice of the South Vietnam people themselves.
>
> We have no intention of imposing any form of govt upon the people of South Vietnam, nor will we be a party to such coercion.
>
> We have no objection to reunification, if that turns out to be what the people of South Vietnam and the people of North Vietnamese want; we ask only that the decision reflect the free choice of the people concerned.[275]

The President then clearly and explicitly stated that

America had only limited goals in the prosecution of war in Indochina.

> In pursuing our **limited objective** (emphasis added), we insist on no rigid diplomatic formula. Peace could be achieved by a formal negotiated settlement. Peace could be achieved by an informal understanding, provided that the understanding is clear and that there were adequate assurance that it would be observed. Peace on paper is not as important as peace in fact.[276]

Nixon also clearly and specifically addressed the matter of the ongoing negotiations to end the war. He made it clear that the United States sought neither the conquest nor the total defeat of North Vietnam but instead the right of determination for the people of Indochina.

> This brings us, then, to the matter of negotiations.
>
> We must recognize that peace in South Vietnam cannot be achieved overnight. A war which has raged for so many years will require detailed negotiations and cannot be settled at a single stroke.
>
> What kind of settlement will permit the South Vietnam people to determine freely their own political future? Such a settlement will require the withdrawal of all non-South Vietnam forces from South Vietnam and procedures for political choice that give each significant group in South Vietnam a real opportunity to participate in the political life of the nation.[277]

To accomplish this the President did not require any change of government in the North or even its renunciation of its goal of reunification. Instead, all he gave as an American goal was the withdrawal of foreign forces.

> To implement these principles, I reaffirm now our willingness to withdraw our forces on a specified timetable. **We ask only that North Vietnamese withdraw its forces** (emphasis added) from South Vietnam, Cambodia, and Laos into North Vietnam, also in accordance with a timetable.
>
> We include Cambodia and Laos to ensure that these countries would not be used as bases for a renewed war. The Cambodian border is only 35 miles from Saigon; the Laotian border is only 25 miles from Hue.
>
> Our offer provides for a simultaneous start on withdrawal by both sides; agreement on a mutually acceptable timetable; and for the withdrawal to be accomplished quickly.[278]

Regarding North Vietnamese forces, he declared his willingness to accept the fiction that they had no forces in the South as long as they withdrew those forces and promised not to re-introduce them.

If North Vietnamese wants to insist that it has no forces in South Vietnam, we will no longer debate the point - provided that its forces cease to be there and that we have reliable assurances that they will not return.[279]

Near the end of his statement, the President clarified one last time the bottom line of American goals in South Vietnam.

> This, then, is the outline of the settlement

> that we seek to negotiate in Paris. Its basic terms are very simple: **mutual withdrawal of non-South Vietnam forces from South Vietnam and free choice for the people of South Vietnam** (emphasis added).
>
> To make very concrete what I have said, I propose the following measures, which seem to me consistent with the principles of all parties.[280]

However Nixon was careful to express America's continuing support for the lasting independence of South Vietnam and its full participation in any negotiations affecting it future.

These proposals are made on the basis of **full consultation with President Thieu** (emphasis added).

> As soon as agreement can be reached, all non-South Vietnam forces would begin withdrawals from South Vietnam.
>
> Over a period of twelve months, by agreed-upon stages, the major portions of all United States Allied and other non-South Vietnam forces would be withdrawn. At the end of this 12-month period, the remaining US, Allied, and other non-South Vietnam forces would move into designated base area and would not engage in combat operations.
>
> The remaining United States and Allied forces would move to complete their withdrawals as the remaining North Vietnamese forces were withdrawn and returned to North Vietnam.
>
> An international supervisory body, acceptable to both sides, would be created

for the purpose agreed upon between the two sides.

This international body would begin operating in accordance with an agreed timetable and would participate in arranging supervised cease-fires.

As soon as possible after the international body was functioning, elections would be held under agreed procedures and under the supervision of the international body.

Arrangements would be made for the earliest possible release of prisoners of war on both sides.

All parties would agree to observe the GA of '54 regarding Vietnam and Cambodia, and the Laos accords of '62.

I believe this proposal for peace is realistic and takes account of the legitimate interests of all concerned. **It is consistent with President Thieu's six points** (emphasis added). It can accommodate the various programs put forth by the other side. **We and the govt of South Vietnam** (emphasis added) are prepared to discuss its details with the other side. Secretary Rogers is now in Saigon and will be **discussing with President Thieu** (emphasis added) how, together, we may put forward these proposed measures most usefully in Paris. He will, as well, be consulting with our other Asian allies on these measures while on his Asian trip. However, I would stress that these proposals are not offered on a take-it-or-leave-it basis. We are quite willing to consider other approaches consistent with

> our principles.
>
> We are willing to talk about anybody's program - Hanoi's four points, the NLF's ten points - provided it can be made consistent with the few basic principles I have set forth here. Despite our disagreement with several of its points, we welcome the fact that the NLF has put forward its first comprehensive program. We are continuing to study it carefully. However, we cannot ignore the fact that immediately after the offer, the scale of enemy attacks stepped up and American casualties increased.
>
> Let me make one point very clear. If the enemy wants peace with the United States, that is not the way to get it.
>
> I have set forth a peace program tonight which is generous in its terms. I have indicated our willingness to consider other proposals. No greater mistake could be made than to confuse flexibility with weakness or being reasonable with lack of resolution. I must make clear, in all candor, that if the needless suffering continues, this will affect other decisions. Nobody has anything to gain by delay.[281]

President Nixon ended his statement by expressing the resolve of the American government. A resolve not to succumb to the campaign of pressure exerted by the forces of International Communism, both on the field of battle or in the leftist offense waged on the campuses and in the media of America. A campaign designed to undermine the will of the people to bear the burden in the defense of liberty.

> Reports from Hanoi indicate that **the enemy has given up hope for a military victory in South Vietnam but is counting on a collapse of American will in the United States** (emphasis added). They could make no greater error in judgment.
>
> Let me be quite blunt. Our fighting men are not going to be worn down; our negotiators are not going to be talked down; our allies are not going to be let down.
>
> In my campaign for the Presidency, I pledged to end this war in a way that would increase our chances to win true and lasting peace in South Vietnam, in the Pacific, and in the world. I am determined to keep that pledge. If I fail to do so, I expect the American people to hold me accountable for that failure.[282]

Then in July 1969, while on the American Pacific Island of Guam, President Nixon outlined his vision for America's involvement in a post-Vietnam Asia. In a statement, which has since been called the Nixon Doctrine he stated that in the future the United States would continue to stand by its allies in the fight against International Communism. It would continue to fulfill its historic role as the storehouse of democracy. However, in the future it would be American policy to expect the nations of the area to supply the troops.

THE NIXON DOCTRINE

> Three principles as guidelines for future American policy toward Asia:
>
> - First, the United States will keep all of its treaty commitments.

- Second, we shall provide a shield if a nuclear power threatens the freedom of a nation allied with us or of a nation whose survival we consider vital to our security.
- Third, in cases involving other types of aggression, we shall furnish military and economic assistance when requested in accordance with our treaty commitments. But we shall look to the nation directly threatened to assume the primary responsibility of providing the manpower for its defense.[283]

Being a student of history and having been involved in high diplomatic circles throughout the period of the First Indochina War the President believed that one of the reasons the French met defeat lay in the fact that they had overlooked the desire of the people to fight in their own defense. The colonial prejudices of the French had kept them from using the manpower resources of those Vietnamese who supported them fully.[284]

In response to this belief, the President announced a policy he referred to as "Vietnamization" in 1969 this policy, realizing that the government of South Vietnam faced a highly trained and well-supplied enemy in the regular North Vietnamese Army. The Communist invaders, trained and supplied by the forces of International Communism posed a formidable obstacle to peace. To counter this Nixon proposed that America provide training and equipment for a South Vietnamese Army capable of meeting the threat.

Just as Johnson had tied, bombing to the level of Communist activity so too President Nixon connected the withdrawal of American troops to the progress made in his effort of Vietnamization.[285] The many critics of Nixon's policies in Vietnam often fail to mention that during his first term as president he reduced our troop level in Vietnam by approximately 90%.[286] In the heat of battle the courage and determination and resourcefulness of the American trained Army of South Vietnam proved time and again that these people were willing and able to defend their own freedom.

November 3, 1969 marked the date when President Nixon delivered what many believe was his most powerful and effective speech. In this, his famous "Silent Majority" speech President Nixon called upon the Americans who supported the government of the United States in its battle against International Communism to rally behind him as he pursued peace with honor in Vietnam. In this very moving and effective speech, the President sought to educate the public concerning the history of American involvement. He also eloquently stated the both cases for America's limited objectives and for the continuation of the Cold War effort to contain Totalitarian International Communism.

> I believe that one of the reasons for the deep division about Vietnam is that many Americans have lost confidence in what their Government has told them about our policy. The American people cannot and should not be asked to support a policy which involves the overriding issues of war and peace unless they know the truth about that policy.
>
> Tonight, therefore, I would like to answer some of the questions that I know are on the minds of many of you listening to me. How and why did America get involved in Vietnam in the first place? How has this administration changed the policy of the previous administration? What has really happened in the negotiations in Paris and on

the battlefront in Vietnam? What choices do we have if we are to end the war? What are the prospects for peace? Now, let me begin by describing the situation I found when I was inaugurated on January 20:

The war had been going on for four years. One thousand Americans had been killed in action. The training program for the South Vietnamese was behind schedule; 540,000 Americans were in Vietnam with no plans to reduce the number. No progress had been made at the negotiations in Paris and the United States had not put forth a comprehensive peace proposal. The war was causing deep division at home and criticism from many of our friends as well as our enemies abroad.

In view of these circumstances there were some who urged that I end the war at once by ordering the immediate withdrawal of all American forces. From a political standpoint this would have been a popular and easy course to follow. After all, we became involved in the war while my predecessor was in office. I could blame the defeat which would be the result of my action on him and come out as the peacemaker. Some put it to me quite bluntly: This was the only way to avoid allowing Johnson's war to become Nixon's war.

But I had a greater obligation than to think only of the years of my administration and of the next election. **I had to think of the effect of my decision on the next generation and on the future of peace and**

freedom in America and in the world (emphasis added).

Let us all understand that the question before us is not whether some Americans are for peace and some Americans are against peace. The question at issue is not whether Johnson's war becomes Nixon's war. **The great question is: How can we win America's peace?** (emphasis added)

Well, let us turn now to the fundamental issue. **Why and how did the United States become involved in Vietnam in the first place? Fifteen years ago North Vietnam, with the logistical support of communist China and the Soviet Union, launched a campaign to impose a communist government on South Vietnam by instigating and supporting a revolution** (emphasis added).

In response to the request of the Government of South Vietnam, President Eisenhower sent economic aid and military equipment to assist the people of South Vietnam in their efforts to prevent a communist takeover. Seven years ago, President Kennedy sent 16,000 military personnel to Vietnam as combat advisers. Four years ago, President Johnson sent American combat forces to South Vietnam.

Now, many believe that President Johnson's decision to send American combat forces to South Vietnam was wrong. And many others — I among them — have been strongly critical of the way the war has been conducted.

But the question facing us today is:

Now that we are in the war, what is the best way to end it? (emphasis added)

In January I could only conclude that the precipitate withdrawal of American forces from Vietnam would be a disaster not only for South Vietnam but for the United States and for the cause of peace.

For the South Vietnamese, our precipitate withdrawal would inevitably allow the Communists to repeat the massacres which followed their takeover in the North 15 years before; They then murdered more than 50,000 people and hundreds of thousands more died in slave labor camps.

We saw a prelude of what would happen in South Vietnam when the Communists entered the city of Hue last year. During their brief rule there, there was a bloody reign of terror in which 3,000 civilians were clubbed, shot to death, and buried in mass graves.

With the sudden collapse of our support, these atrocities of Hue would become the nightmare of the entire nation — and particularly for the million and a half Catholic refugees who fled to South Vietnam when the Communists took over in the North.

For the United States, this first defeat in our nation's history would result in a collapse of confidence in American leadership, **not only in Asia but throughout the world** (emphasis added).

Three American presidents have recognized the great stakes involved in Vietnam and understood what had to be done.

In 1963, President Kennedy, with his characteristic eloquence and clarity, said:

> ... we want to see a stable government there, carrying on a struggle to maintain its national independence. We believe strongly in that. We are not going to withdraw from that effort. **In my opinion, for us to withdraw from that effort would mean a collapse not only of South Vietnam, but Southeast Asia** (emphasis added). So we are going to stay there.

> President Eisenhower and President Johnson expressed the same conclusion during their terms of office.
>
> For the future of peace, precipitate withdrawal would thus be a disaster of immense magnitude. A nation cannot remain great if it betrays its allies and lets down its friends. Our defeat and humiliation in South Vietnam without question would promote recklessness in the councils of **those great powers who have not yet abandoned their goals of world conquest** (emphasis added). This would spark violence wherever our commitments help maintain the peace — in the Middle East, in Berlin, eventually even in the Western Hemisphere. Ultimately, this would cost more lives. It would not bring peace; it would bring more war.[287]

He also reiterated his proposals for peace.

> We have offered the complete withdrawal of all outside forces within one year.
>
> We have proposed a cease-fire under international supervision.
>
> We have offered free elections under international supervision with the Communists participating in the organization and conduct of the elections as an organized political force. And the Saigon Government has pledged to accept the result of the elections.
>
> We have not put forth our proposals on a take-it-or-leave-it basis. We have indicated that we are willing to discuss the proposals that have been put forth by the other side. We have declared that **anything is negotiable except the right of the people of South Vietnam to determine their own future** (emphasis added). At the Paris peace conference, Ambassador Lodge has demonstrated our flexibility and good faith in 40 public meetings.[288]

He enlightened the American public regarding the intransigence of the Communists.

> Hanoi has refused even to discuss our proposals. They demand our unconditional acceptance of their terms, which are that we withdraw all American forces immediately and unconditionally and that we overthrow the Government of South Vietnam as we leave.[289]

The President further illustrated the intransigence by speaking of the non-progress of his ongoing efforts to obtain a negotiated peace settlement.

> But the effect of all the public, private and secret negotiations which have been undertaken since the bombing halt a year ago and since this administration came into office on January 20 can be summed up in one sentence: No progress whatever has been made except agreement on the shape of the bargaining table.

Well now, who is at fault?

> It has become clear that the obstacle in negotiating an end to the war is not the President of the United States. It is not the South Vietnamese Government.
>
> The obstacle is the other side's absolute refusal to show the least willingness to join us in seeking a just peace. And it will not do so while it is convinced that all it has to do is to wait for our next concession, and our next concession after that one, until it gets everything it wants.
>
> There can now be no longer any question that progress in negotiation depends only on Hanoi's deciding to negotiate, to negotiate seriously.
>
> I realize that this report on our efforts on the diplomatic front is discouraging to the American people, but the American people are entitled to know the truth — the bad news as well as the good news — where the lives of our young men are involved.[290]

In referring to the Nixon Doctrine and its implications for the future of American involvement in the defense of the free world against the forces of Totalitarian International Communism the President said:

> We Americans are a do-it-yourself people. We are an impatient people. Instead of teaching someone else to do a job, we like to do it ourselves. And this trait has been carried over into our foreign policy. In Korea and again in Vietnam, the United States furnished most of the money, most of the arms, and most of the men to **help the people of those countries defend their freedom against Communist aggression** (emphasis added).
>
> Before any American troops were committed to Vietnam, a leader of another Asian country expressed this opinion to me when I was traveling in Asia as a private citizen. He said: "When you are trying to assist another nation defend its freedom, U.S. policy should be to help them fight the war but not to fight the war for them."
>
> After I announced this policy, I found that the leaders of the Philippines, Thailand, Vietnam, South Korea, and other nations which might be **threatened by Communist aggression** (emphasis added) welcomed this new direction in American foreign policy.[291]

In consequence of the Nixon Doctrine, the administration began the long process of extricating itself from the massive intervention initiated by the Johnson administration and the Vietnamization of the war.

> The defense of freedom is everybody's business — not just America's business. And it is particularly the responsibility of the people whose freedom is threatened. In the previous administration, we Americanized the war in Vietnam. In this administration, we are Vietnamizing the search for peace.
>
> The policy of the previous administration not only resulted in our assuming the primary responsibility for fighting the war, but even more significantly did not adequately stress the goal of strengthening the South Vietnamese so that they could defend themselves when we left.
>
> The Vietnamization plan was launched following Secretary Laird's visit to Vietnam in March. Under the plan, I ordered first a substantial increase in the training and equipment of South Vietnamese forces.
>
> In July, on my visit to Vietnam, I changed General Abrams' orders so that they were consistent with the objectives of our new policies. Under the new orders, the primary mission of our troops is to enable the South Vietnamese forces to assume the full responsibility for the security of South Vietnam.[292]

President Nixon then continued speaking of the early results of his changes in policy application regarding the prosecution of the war.

> Two other significant developments have occurred since this administration took office.

> **Enemy infiltration** (emphasis added), infiltration which is essential if they are to launch a major attack, over the last three months is less than 20 percent of what it was over the same period last year. Most important — **United States casualties have declined** during the last two months to the lowest point in three years.[293]

The President tied the idea of peace in Vietnam to the goal of peace in the world, thus emphasizing its placement within the larger context of the Cold War.

> It is a plan which will end the war and serve the cause of peace — **not just in Vietnam but in the Pacific and in the world** (emphasis added).[294]

He also remarked what a unilateral withdrawal would mean, again placing it within the broader context.

> In speaking of the consequences of a precipitate withdrawal, I mentioned that our allies would lose confidence in America.[295]

In a prescient statement, concerning what would later appear as the hesitation, fear and calamitous timidity of the Carter Administration.

> Far more dangerous, we would lose confidence in ourselves. Oh, the immediate reaction would be a sense of relief that our men were coming home. But as we saw the consequences of what we had done, inevitable remorse and divisive recrimination would

> scar our spirit as a people.[296]

Addressing the leadership of America in the Cold War and in the struggle of the free nations of the world against the advancing forces of International Communism President Nixon continued:

> I know it may not be fashionable to speak of patriotism or national destiny these days. But I feel it is appropriate to do so on this occasion.
>
> Two hundred years ago this nation was weak and poor. But even then, America was the hope of millions in the world. Today we have become the strongest and richest nation in the world. And the wheel of destiny has turned so that **any hope the world has for the survival of peace and freedom will be determined by whether the American people have the moral stamina and the courage to meet the challenge of free world leadership** (emphasis added).
>
> Let historians not record that when America was the most powerful nation in the world we passed on the other side of the road and **allowed the last hopes for peace and freedom of millions of people to be suffocated by the forces of totalitarianism** (emphasis added).[297]

This speech brought forth a tremendous response. The White House mailrooms flooded with tens of thousands of letters and telegrams supporting the President in his quest for peace with honor.[298] Throughout his presidency, until the Watergate scandal destroyed his political career

President Nixon enjoyed the solid support of the Silent Majority.[299]

The unflagging support which, this silent majority offered in the face of the continued aggression of International Communism stands juxtaposed to the tactics of the vocal minority. In his speech the President acknowledged that, "Honest and patriotic Americans have reached different conclusions as to how peace should be achieved." However, it was not these Americans who led the almost rabid peace-at-any-cost organizations that organized so many of the demonstrations. Often, the goal seemed to be not just protest but instead provocation. Finding many allies among the up-and-coming generation of left-wing professors on the nation's college campuses, they loudly proclaimed their dedication of free speech while doing their best to make theirs the only voice heard.

On November 15 1970, as part of a nationwide campaign of demonstrations, one of the largest gatherings in the history of Washington occurred with "Moratorium Day" as more than 500,000 protesters loudly protested the war in the glare of overwhelming press coverage.[300] Nixon still encouraged by the reaction to his "silent majority" speech responded by affirming his intention to guide the policies of the United States according to his vision for combating aggression and not by the demonstrations of a vocal minority.

During this time there were thousands of incidents from bombings to break-ins that showed this vocal minority was committed to violence in their attempt to force their will upon the nation. Today we would call this domestic terrorism. Then we called it a "Peace Movement."[301]

In great part due to the determination and steadfastness of President Nixon, this nationwide terrorist program did not have its desired effect. The great silent majority continued to support the government in its attempt to find a peace with honor, a peace that would stop the dominos from falling.

In the closing days of 1969, disturbing information concerning and action by American soldiers in a small village named My Lai[302] surfaced. In this action which, occurred during the Communist Tet offensive in 1968 American soldiers were charged with killing 175 unarmed civilians. After an extensive investigation, Lieutenant William Calley, Jr.[303] faced a court-martial for his role in what the Defense Department termed the murder of non-combatants. After his conviction in 1970, Lieutenant Calley went to prison.[304]

The leaders of the anti-war movement attempted to use this as proof that America was prosecuting an "illegal" war by "illegal" means. It is interesting to note the blatant double standard they applied when it came to war crimes. While the Calley case dominated the national news, both print and broadcast, countless incidents of Communist atrocities never even made the news, such as the thousands massacred in Hue[305] during the unsuccessful Tet Offensive.[306]

Moreover, in sharp contrast to the Communists who rewarded the perpetrators of atrocities with promotions, medals and parades[307] the Americans tried and convicted those involved. [308]

Knowing that the Communists operating from sanctuaries in Cambodia continued to have an advantage in that they could give their hard-pressed troops rest and re-supply with impunity. Militarily this made no sense. Therefore on April 30 1970, President Nixon ordered and subsequently told the nation that the American forces in Vietnam and their South Vietnamese allies had initiated an operation aimed at denying the enemy his sanctuary in Cambodia.[309] Furthermore, the President stated that this incursion was in answer to the call of the Cambodian government for help in freeing itself of the North Vietnamese forces occupying its border areas.

> North Vietnam in the last two weeks has stripped away all pretense of respecting the sovereignty or the neutrality of Cambodia. Thousands of their soldiers are invading the country from the sanctuary from the sanctuaries; they are encircling the Capital of Phnom Penh. Coming from these sanctuaries, as you see here, they have moved into Cambodia and are encircling the Capital. **Cambodia, as a result of this, has sent out a call to the United States, to a number of other nations, for assistance** (emphasis added). Because if this enemy effort succeeds, Cambodia would become a vast enemy staging area and a springboard for attacks on South Vietnam along 600 miles of frontier, a refuge where enemy troops could return from combat without fear of retaliation. **North Vietnamese men and supplies could then be poured into that country** (emphasis added), jeopardizing not only the lives of our own men but the people of South Vietnam as well.[310]

The President unequivocally defined the limited nature and scope of the incursion. He stated that the United States did not intend to invade Cambodia. This was instead only an incursion mounted for a specific purpose and that America guaranteed its withdrawal. Nixon continued that the attacks by the joint American-South Vietnamese force would only affect areas occupied and controlled by the North Vietnamese.

> **This is not an invasion of Cambodia** (emphasis added). The areas in which these

> attacks will be launched are completely occupied and controlled by North Vietnamese forces. **Our purpose is not to occupy the areas** (emphasis added). Once enemy forces are driven out of these sanctuaries and once their military supplies are destroyed, we will withdraw.[311]

The President went on to clarify his reasons for ordering the incursion.

> Now, let me give you the reasons for my decision. A majority of the American people, a majority of you listening to me, are for the withdrawal of our forces from Vietnam. The action I have taken tonight is indispensable for the continuing success of the continuing success of that withdrawal program. A majority of the American people want to end this war rather than to have it drag on interminably. The action: have taken tonight will serve that purpose.
>
> A majority of the American people want to keep the casualties of our brave men in Vietnam at an absolute minimum. The action I take tonight is essential if we are to accomplish that goal. **We take this action not for the purpose of expanding the war into Cambodia, but for the purpose of ending the war in Vietnam and winning the just peace we all desire** (emphasis added). We have made and we will continue to make every possible effort to end this war through negotiation at the conference table rather than through more fighting on the battlefield.[312]

The statement spoke of the direct link between the war in Vietnam and its wider implications. These implications both domestically and internationally which again showed the understanding of the Nixon administration that Vietnam existed as one battle in a much wider war. It also clearly recognized the enemy as "the forces of totalitarianism and anarchy."

> My fellow Americans, **we live in an age of anarchy, both abroad and at home. We see mindless attacks on all the great institutions which have been created by free civilizations in the last 500 years. Even here in the United States, great universities are being systematically destroyed. Small nations all over the world find themselves under attack from within and from without** (emphasis added).
>
> If, when the chips are down, the world's most powerful nation, the United States of America, acts like a pitiful, helpless giant, **the forces of totalitarianism and anarchy will threaten free nations and free institutions throughout the world** (emphasis added). It is not our power but our will and character that is being tested tonight. The question all Americans must ask and answer tonight is this: Does the richest and strongest nation in the history of the world have the character to meet a direct challenge by a group which rejects every effort to win a just peace, ignores our warning, tramples on solemn agreements, violates the neutrality of an unarmed people, and uses our prisoners as hostages?[313]

This incursion ended in June 1970, just as the President had promised. Highly successful, many believe that it forestalled the Communists' plan for a massive Spring offensive by capturing or destroying massive stocks of weapons and food. But the reaction of the vocal minority, which was determined to protest and undermine the war effort, came swift and sure as demonstrations exploded on many college campuses. Governors across the nation responded by calling out the National Guard. Thousands were arrested and at Kent State in Ohio, in answer to a shower of rocks and other debris one guard unit fired into a crowd killing four students.[314]

So far, the negotiations that President Johnson had initiated with the Communists of North Vietnam had proved fruitless. President Nixon met this challenge by opening "secret" negotiations.

The President chose his National Security Advisor, Dr. Henry Kissinger (born 1923)[315] for this delicate work. The idea of opening this secret channel sought to stop the Communists from gaining an advantage in the spin put on such talks by the mainly sympathetic American media. This work of Dr. Kissinger eventually led to the agreement, which brought the longest war in American history to an end.

President Nixon knew that unless he convinced the Communists the United States would do whatever necessary to bring the war to an honorable conclusion they would never see negotiations other than the opportunity to gain their objectives by another means. It became apparent that the Communists doubted this assumption several times throughout the long process of ending the war. To cite one example in 1972, while the President prepared for a major summit with his Russian counterpart, Leonid Brezhnev (1906-1982)[316] and as peace talks, both public and private languished the Communists launched a series of major offensives. Possibly, the North Vietnamese Communists thought that Nixon would passively continue to withdraw troops and refrain from bombing in fear of jeopardizing a successful summit. If this was their calculation, they were soon surprised when the President instead ordered massive bombing of the northern capital of Hanoi and of their one major port facility at Haiphong.

The leaders of the Anti-War Movement attacked this forceful response and countered with massive demonstrations and widespread unrest but Nixon stood his ground. In addition, in answer to this willingness to pursue peace with honor and this courage in the face of attack the Communists returned to the negotiations.

Feeling the bight but still doubting the resolve of American power, the Communists of North Vietnam and their backers in the Kremlin and China repeatedly stalled the negotiations as they pushed harder on the battlefield.

Each time President Nixon met the challenge with appropriate action. Moreover, although the protesters tried their hardest to convince the nation that theirs represented the overwhelming majority opinion they could never convince anyone but themselves and the media. At least they could not at the time though thirty years of shaping the presentation of history has now indoctrinated generations of succeeding Americans.

In 1972 President Nixon stood for re-election. In this round he faced George McGovern (B. 1922)[317] the outspoken leader of the far-left fringe of the Democrat Party. While President Nixon easily won the election it was during this time of social upheaval and turmoil that some of his followers initiated the incident that would swell to become the "Watergate Scandal"[318] which would eventually destroy his presidency.

The peace-at-any-cost movement shouted and yelled that America should admit its guilt and unilaterally withdraw from Vietnam. Coincidentally this was the same position the Communists offered in negotiations. Despite the great pressure, President Nixon led the nation unwaveringly toward his goal of peace with honor meeting each new attack with an appropriate response until the signing of the final peace agreement on January 27, 1973.[319]

The Communists held more than 300 American service men as prisoners of war when President Nixon entered office. During his terms in office this number nearly doubled. In addition, in contravention to the Geneva Conventions (which North Vietnam had signed) the Communists not only treated these brave souls in a very harsh and degrading way they also used them to further their propaganda war.

The Nixon administration tried many times to gain the release of the POWs. They offered to exchange prisoners at a rate of 10 to 1, they offered humanitarian supplies, but nothing could over-ride the desire of the Communists to use these brave men as bargaining chips in their game of international conquest.[320]

When the Paris Peace Accord was signed it made provision for the immediate release of all of the American POWs.[321]

Finally, after so many years of American involvement in the Vietnam War ended with honor. However, this hard won peace would continue to exist, only if all the parties honorably fulfilled the commitments they had made.

---

236 http://www.whitehouse.gov/history/presidents/rn37.html (12-17-03). Informational.

237 Nixon, Richard M. The Memoirs of Richard Nixon. Grosset & Dunlap: New York, 1978, pp.122-126, passim.

238 Ibid., pp.256-58, 271, 282-283.

239 http://etext.lib.virginia.edu/journals/EH/EH41/Friedman41.html (11-15-03). Informational.

240 Nixon, pp. 289, 298, 300, 318.

[241] For the full text of President Nixon's Silent Majority Speech, see the Appendix.

[242] http://www.nixonlibrary.org/Research_Center/Vietnam/Nixon_Role.shtml (11-26-03); Nixon, p. 298.

[243] Herring, pp 188-189; Millett, p. 588; http://www.war-stories.com/khesanh-02.htm (11-15-03). Informational.

[244] http://www.pbs.org/wgbh/amex/vietnam/107ts.html (12-5-03). Informational.

[245] http://people.mnhs.org/authors/biog_detail.cfm?PersonID=McCa281 (11-15-03). Informational.

[246] http://www.politicallibrary.org/TallState/1968dem.html (11-25-03).

[247] Mann, pp. 589-594, passim.

[248] http://www.arlingtoncemetery.net/rfk.htm (11-15-03). Informational.

[249] Karnow, p. 559.

[250] Ibid., p. 579; Donovan, pp.170-171, passim.

[251] http://www.spartacus.schoolnet.co.uk/USAhumphreyH.htm (11-15-03). Informational.

[252] http://www.yorkdispatch.com/Stories/0,1413,138~27257~1206255,00.html (11-25-03). Informational.

[253] http://www.usatoday.com/news/opinion/e1106.htm (11-26-03). Informational.

[254] Mann, pp. 605-606, 608-614, 616-619, passim.

[255] http://www.geocities.com/verisimus101/rfk/assasination.htm (11-25-03). Informational.

[256] Nixon, p. 298.

[257] Ibid.

[258] Though there has been much written about this "supposed" incident there is no actual evidence that it occurred.

[259] Ibid., p.318.

[260] Ibid, p. 328; Herring, pp. 216-217; Mann, pp.623-624.

[261] http://www.cnn.com/US/9809/14/wallace.obit/ (11-25-03). Informational.

[262] Known today as the American Independent Party. http://en2.wikipedia.org/wiki/American_Independent_Party (12-5-03). Informat-

ional

[263] Nixon, p. 298.

[264] Ibid., p. 350.

[265] http://www.seanet.com/~jimxc/Politics/Mistakes/Vietnam_support.html (11-25-03).

[266] http://www.vwip.org/mb/public.htm (12-5-03); http://www.coursework bank.co.uk/coursework/american_public_opinion_during_vietnam_584/ (12-5-03). Informational

[267] http://www.landscaper.net/draft.htm (12-5-03). Informational.

[268] Herring, pp 198-199, passim; Mann, p.642-644, passim; Nixon, p. 392; http://history.acusd.edu/gen/20th/RN/page002.html (11-15-03). Informational.

[269] Nixon, pp. 605-608, passim.

[270] Ibid., pp. 381-382, passim.

[271] Ibid., p. 394; Karnow, pp. 623-624; Herring, pp225, 227, 228, 245; Mann, pp. 693-694.

[272] For the full text of President Nixon's Report On Vietnam May 14 1969, see the Appendix.

[273] Herring, p.223.

[274] For the full text of President Nixon's Report On Vietnam May 14 1969, see the Appendix.

[275] Ibid.

[276] Ibid.

[277] Ibid.

[278] Ibid.

[279] Ibid.

[280] Ibid.

[281] Ibid.

[282] Ibid. ; Nixon, p384, 391-392, passim.

[283] http://en.wikipedia.org/wiki/Nixon_Doctrine (11-19-03); Nixon, pp. 394, 397.

[284] http://www.nixonlibrary.org/Research_Center/Vietnam/Nixon_Role.shtml (12-2-03); Nixon, pp.122-126, passim.

[285] Karnow, p. 593.

[286] Herring, pp. 226, 233, 240-241, 243, passim; Karnow, pp.593, 594-

595, 598, 608, 627, 636, passim; Mann, pp. 637-638, 650, 678-679, passim.

287 Nixon, pp. 401-414, passim; For the full text of President Nixon's 'Silent Majority' Speech, see the Appendix.

288 Ibid.

289 Ibid.

290 Ibid.

291 Ibid.

292 Ibid.

293 Ibid.

294 Ibid.

295 Ibid.

296 Ibid.

297 Ibid.

298 Nixon, p. 410.

299 "General public support remained well above 50 percent throughout the war years."

Kissinger, Henry. Ending the Vietnam War: A History of America's Involvement in and Extrication from the Vietnam War. Simon & Schuster, (Forward) as excerpted on http://www.washingtonpost.com/wp-srv/style/longterm/books/chap1/endingthevietnamwar.htm (10-13-03)

300 Herring, p. 230; Mann, pp.637, 640-642, passim; Nixon, pp.399, 400, 401-402, 403, 404, 405, 412-413, passim; Wells, Tom. The War Within. Henry Holt & Co.: New York, 1994, pp. 441-444.

301 http://dsausa.org/about/history.html (11-25-03).

302 Karnow, pp.24, 468, 530, 601; Herring, pp. 215, 242; Mann, pp. 648-649; Nixon, pp. 499-500; http://www.pbs.org/wgbh/amex/vietnam/trenches/mylai.html (11-15-03). Informational.

303 http://www.law.umkc.edu/faculty/projects/ftrials/mylai/myl_bcalleyhtml.htm (11-15-03). Informational.

304 Ibid. Calley was pardoned in 1974 and eventually pardoned by President Nixon. Informational.

305 http://www.vcdh.virginia.edu/HIUS316/mbase/docs/hue.html (11-15-03). Informational.

306 http://www.pbs.org/wgbh/amex/vietnam/107ts.html (11-15-03).

[307] http://www.vhcma.org/fact.html (12-17-03).

[308] http://www.nixonlibrary.org/Research_Center/Vietnam/Nixon_Role.shtml (12-2-03).

[309] Ibid.; http://www.geocities.com/nixonkissingerpeacemaker/part2/part2ch5.html (11-15-03). Informational.

[310] http://chnm.gmu.edu/hardhats/cambodia.html (12-2-03); Herring, pp. 154, 211, 234-237, passim; Karnow, pp. 605-610, passim; Mann, pp. 655-661, passim; Millett, pp. 591-592; Nixon, pp. 445-459, 467-468, passim; For the full text of President Nixon's statement on the Cambodian invasion, see the Appendix.

[311] Ibid.

[312] Ibid.

[313] Ibid.

[314] http://members.aol.com/nrbooks/chronol.htm (11-25-03); Herring, p. 237; Karnow, p. 611; Mann, pp. 661, 671; Nixon, pp. 456-457; Wells, pp. 424; 438.

[315] http://www.nobel.se/peace/laureates/1973/kissinger-bio.html (11-15-03). Informational.

[316] http://www.cnn.com/SPECIALS/cold.war/kbank/profiles/brezhnev (11-15-03). Informational.

[317] http://www.mcgovernlibrary.com/george.htm (12-17-03). Informational.

[318] http://watergate.info/ (12-17-03).

[319] For the full text of the Paris Peace Accord, see the Appendix.

[320] Nixon, pp. 348, 584-585, 595, 691-692, 694-695, 707, 734, 812.

[321] Ibid, pp. 859-869, passim.

CHAPTER NINE

War Goals and Aims

TRUMAN

The goals and aims, the strategy of the United States in the Indochina Wars remained constant from beginning to end: the containment of Communism.[322] However, the tactics evolved over time, from support for the French, to support for the Diem regime, through massive direct involvement to Vietnamization.

Looking back over the span of decades it is easy to lose sight of the contemporaneous perceptions which led the leaders of the United States to commit this country to a war half-way around the world. As we view these perceptions separated as we are by the safety and security of time, in the search for understanding we must strive to appreciate the context in which they existed.

Originally, the United States perceived the attempt by Communist North Vietnam to subjugate an independent South Vietnam as the next battle to stop the spread of the openly aggressive Totalitarian forces of International Communism. These leaders could not help but recall the (then fresh) experience of the forces of democracy folding before the belligerence of a previous incarnation of crusading Totalitarianism in Munich in 1938.[323] They had just fought a long and arduous war as the terrible consequence, which this failure of resolve had dictated. Therefore, it is not surprising that the leaders of the United States were determined to stand firm against the advancing forces of Totalitarianism in its International Communism incarnation. We must remember that at the time the leaders of International Communism loudly and repeatedly announced their aim of world domination just as the Fascist leaders had done before them.

Reacting to this perception, the United States led by President Truman initially supported the French in their effort to reestablish control over its former colonies in Indochina as a means of "containing" the spread of Communism. This American policy led to a steady escalation of U.S. involvement.

EISENHOWER

Having inherited a policy of supporting the French in Indochina from his predecessor President Eisenhower avoided direct military intervention while steadily increasing the level of aid until the disastrous defeat of the French at Dien Bien Phu in 1954. The Geneva Agreements, which ended French involvement and to which the United States was not a party provided for a North-South partition of Vietnam until elections could be held. The United States immediately began to support the creation of an independent democratic regime in South Vietnam as a counterbalance to the already existing Totalitarian Communist regime of Ho Chi Minh in the North.

Although the United States paid approximately 80% of French costs, Eisenhower refused to send troops to support the French. However, after they surrendered he did choose to support the newly re-organized South Vietnamese government as the best available means to hold the line against the advancing forces of International Communism. President Eisenhower fervently believed that the American people could only understand the on-going conflict in Vietnam and America's involvement in it within the context of the Cold War. He clearly states his purpose for America's continuing aid to the government in South Vietnam in the following letter:

Eisenhower's Letter of Support to Ngo Dinh Diem, October 23, 1954.

> Dear Mr. President: I have been following with great interest the course of developments in Viet-Nam, (sic.) particularly since the conclusion of the conference at Geneva. The implications of the agreement concerning Viet-Nam (sic.) have caused grave concern regarding the future of a country temporarily divided by an artificial military grouping, weakened by a long and exhausting war and **faced with enemies without and by their subversive collaborations within** (emphasis added). Your recent requests for aid to assist in the formidable project of the movement of several hundred thousand loyal Vietnamese citizens away from areas which are passing under a de facto rule and political ideology which they abhor, are being fulfilled. I am glad that the United States is able to assist in this humanitarian effort. We have been exploring ways and means to permit our aid to Viet-Nam (sic.) to be more effective and to make a greater contribution to the welfare and stability of the government

of Viet-Nam (sic.). I am, accordingly, instructing the American Ambassador to Viet-Nam (sic.) to examine with you in your capacity as Chief of Government, how an intelligent program of American aid given directly to your government can serve to assist Viet-Nam (sic.) in its present hour of trial, provided that your Government is prepared to give assurances as to the standards of performance it would be able to maintain in the event such aid were supplied. **The purpose of this offer is to assist the Government of Viet-Nam (sic.) in developing and maintaining a strong, viable state, capable of resisting attempted subversion or aggression through military means** (emphasis added). The Government of the United States expects that this aid will be met by performance on the part of the Government of Viet-Nam (sic.) in undertaking needed reforms. It hopes that such aid, combined with your own continuing efforts, will contribute effectively toward **an independent Viet-Nam** (sic.) (emphasis added) endowed with a strong government. Such a government would, I hope, be so responsive to the nationalist aspirations of its people, so enlightened in purpose and effective in performance, that it will be respected both at home and abroad and discourage any who might wish to impose a foreign ideology on your free people.

Sincerely,

Dwight D. Eisenhower[324]

Eisenhower became the first American president to enunciate the Domino Theory. This theory expressed the belief that if the forces of International Communism succeeded in conquering all of Vietnam, they would soon conquer all of Southeast Asia.

The Domino Theory

By 1954, it became obvious that the French effort to defeat the Communist forces entrenched in North Vietnam had failed. In March, the French faced the loss of an entire army at Dien Bien Phu. The France appealed to the United States to intervene through massive and sustained military involvement. However, Eisenhower decided this would not serve American interests and therefore he did not send any aid to the beleaguered French army which subsequently surrendered in early May. Although he did not come to France's aid, Eisenhower saw that the French defeat if not somehow countered could ultimately result in the triumph of International Communism throughout Indochina.

The following excerpts from a Presidential Press Conference held on April 7, 1954 shows both the public interest and perceptions through the questions asked but the President's thoughts in his answers.

> **Question by Robert Richards, Copley Press: Mr. President, would you mind commenting on the strategic importance of Indochina for the free world** (emphasis added)? I think there has been, across the country, some lack of understanding on just what it means to us.
>
> **The President.** You have, of course, both the specific and the general when you talk about such things. First of all, you have the

specific value of a locality in its production of materials that the world needs.

Then you have the possibility that many human beings pass under a dictatorship that is inimical to the free world.

Finally, you have broader considerations that might follow what you would call the "falling domino" principle. You have a row of dominoes set up, you knock over the first one, and what will happen to the last one is the certainty that it will go over very quickly. So you could have a beginning of a disintegration that would have the most profound influences (emphasis added).

Now, with respect to the first one, two of the items from this particular area that the world uses are tin and tungsten. They are very important. There are others, of course, the rubber plantations and so on.

Then with respect to more people passing under this domination, Asia, after all, has already lost some 450 million of its peoples to the Communist dictatorship, and we simply can't afford greater losses.

But **when we come to the possible sequence of events, the loss of Indochina, of Burma, of Thailand, of the Peninsula, and Indonesia following** (emphasis added), now you begin to talk about areas that no only multiply the disadvantages that you would suffer through the loss of materials, sources of materials, but now you are talking about millions and millions of people.

Finally, the geographical position achieved thereby does many things. **It turns**

> **the so-called island defensive chain of Japan, Formosa, of the Philippines and to the southward; it moves in to threaten Australia and New Zealand** (emphasis added).
>
> It takes away, in its economic aspects, that region that Japan must have as a trading area or Japan, in turn, will have only one place in the world to go that is, toward the Communist areas in order to live.
>
> So, **the possible consequences of the loss are just incalculable to the free world** (emphasis added).[325]

KENNEDY

Just as Eisenhower had inherited a policy of engagement in Vietnam from Truman, so John F. Kennedy inherited an expanded policy from Eisenhower.

This was not a situation, which surprised or confounded President Kennedy. As a senator from Massachusetts, during a time that we now know, he prepped for a run at the presidency he presented himself consistently as a dedicated Cold Warrior. As early as his first congressional campaign, he had declared his independence from the anti-Cold War faction of the Democratic Party.

The Kennedy administration was from beginning to end, and from top to bottom committed to the continued American effort in Vietnam. This assertion is evidenced by the following statement issued jointly by Vice President Johnson and the President of South Vietnam; Ngo Dinh Diem during a visit to Vietnam just four months after JFK took office.

> "The United States, for its part, is conscious

> of the determination, energy and sacrifices which the Vietnamese people, under the dedicated leadership of President Ngo Dinh Diem, have brought to the defense of freedom in their land.[326]

Vice President Johnson went on to point out that he, as a representative of the American government acknowledged and supported the idea that the conflict in Vietnam was part of a wider struggle when he said, “”The United States is also conscious of its responsibility and duty, **in its own self-interest as well as in the interest of other free peoples, to assist a brave country in the defense of its liberties against unprovoked subversion and Communist terror** (emphasis added). It has no other motive than the defense of freedom.”[327]

As his administration began to take control of the levers of power Kennedy's advisors continued to bombard him with studies, findings and recommendations concerning the situation if Vietnam. These varied sources of advice consistently explained the slowly unraveling confrontation in the terms of the Cold War and their recommendations were uniformly in support of the policy of containment.

Excerpts from Rusk-McNamara Report to Kennedy, November 11, 1961.

1. United States National Interests in South Viet-Nam.

> The deteriorating situation in South Viet-Nam (sic.) requires attention to the nature and scope of United States national interests in that country. **The loss of South Viet-Nam (sic.) to Communism would involve the transfer of a nation of 20 million people from the free world to**

> **the Communism bloc. The loss of South Viet-Nam would make pointless any further discussion about the importance of Southeast Asia to the free world; we would have to face the near certainty that the remainder of Southeast Asia and Indonesia would move to a complete accommodation with Communism, if not formal incorporation with the Communist bloc** (emphasis added).[328]

Throughout his tenure, President Kennedy continued to believe in and to express his commitment to the validity of the Domino Theory regarding the situation in Southeast Asia. His answers to a reporter's question in 1963 expresses his public, though implied, enunciation of this fundamental belief of American foreign policy:

> **Q:** "Mr. President, the Mansfield committee, sent at your suggestion to the Far East and Europe, has recommended a thorough security reassessment in the Far East and a clamp down, if not a reduction in our aid to that part of the world. Would you have any comment on this, sir?"
>
> **A**: "I don't see how we are going to be able, **unless we are going to pull out of Southeast Asia and turn it over to the Communists** (emphasis added), how we are going to be able to reduce very much our economic programs and military programs in South Viet-Nam (sic.), in Cambodia, in Thailand.

> "I think that unless you want to withdraw from the field and decide that it is in the national interest to permit that area to collapse, I would think that it would be impossible to substantially change it particularly, as we are in a very intensive struggle in those areas.
>
> "So I think we ought to judge the economic burden it places upon us **as opposed to having the Communists control all of Southeast Asia with the inevitable effect that this would have on the security of India and, therefore, really begin to run perhaps all the way toward the Middle East** (emphasis added). So I think that while we would all like to lighten the burden, I don't see any real prospect of the burden being lightened for the U.S. in Southeast Asia in the next year if we are going to do the job and meet what I think are very clear national needs."[329]

In addition to the foregoing implied endorsement of the Domino Theory, the President expressly stated his belief and commitment in the following answer to another reporter's question, which again also shows the contemporaneous interest and perceptions of the reporter:

> **Q:** "Mr. President, on Laos again, several years ago we heard a great deal about the 'falling domino' theory in Southeast Asia.
>
> "Do you look upon Laos in terms of that country alone, **or is your concern the effect**

> **that its loss would have in Thailand, Vietnam, and so on?** (emphasis added). "Would you discuss that?"
>
> **A:** "That is correct. The population of Laos is 2 million and it is scattered. It is a very rough country. It is important as a sovereign power. The people desire to be independent, and it is also important because it borders the Mekong River and, quite obviously, **if Laos fell into Communist hands it would increase the danger along the northern frontiers of Thailand. It would put additional pressure on Cambodia and would put additional pressure on South Vietnam which in itself would put additional pressure on Malaya** (emphasis added).
>
> "So **I do accept the view that there is an interrelationship in these countries** (emphasis added) and that is one of the reasons why we are concerned with maintaining the Geneva Accords as a method of maintaining stability in Southeast Asia. It may be one of the reasons why others do not share that interest."[330]

To Kennedy the Cold Warrior his acceptance of the reality of the Cold War and the validity of the Domino Theory were sufficient reasons to hold the line in Indochina. To those who perpetuate the myth that Kennedy was leading America to an early disengagement from Vietnam. President Kennedy increased America's troops in Vietnam from several hundred to more than 16,000 and his involvement in the coup which removed President Diem created a power vacuum which ultimately required the massive engagement initiated by his successor.[331]

JOHNSON

As stated earlier, President Lyndon Johnson is the victim of one of the most widely accepted mantras of the Vietnam myth. In essence, this mantra states that President Kennedy had planned to disengage from Vietnam but after his untimely (and to some still mysterious) death, Johnson the tool of the military-industrial complex expanded the America's previous limited involvement into a full-blown war.

However, even a cursory inspection of this assertion exposes the whole cloth, which makes it up. In 1963, the last year of his life President Kennedy, the committed Cold Warrior did more than talk about his desire to hold the line in Vietnam. Indeed his actions spoke even louder than his words, proclaiming that he was not inclined to surrender the field to International Communism in Southeast Asia. Looking at the political developments in South Vietnam during 1963 we see the clearest of indications that Kennedy saw this as an ongoing engagement and not as a matter of declining interest.

Those who promote the pacific intentions of President Kennedy fail to explain why he interfered so dramatically in the internal politics of South Vietnam. If he intended to pull out it would have been easier; to say nothing of more ethical to leave the exiting government in place than to subvert it, impose a new one, and then leave?

The evidence shows that it was Kennedy's intention to remain in Vietnam until America achieved victory. After Kennedy's assassination all of his principle advisors were held-over by the Johnson administration. Moreover, these advisors, who had counseled President Kennedy to stay the course in Vietnam, advised President Johnson to move from a limited advisory role to the full commitment of United States ground forces.

Thus by his direct actions in the Diem coup, and indirectly through his remaining staff, Kennedy bequeathed President Johnson only two choices, complete disengagement or complete commitment. Almost immediately, Johnson faced the rapid deterioration of the military situation, which the Kennedy coup fostered rather than forestalled. Then, advised by the Kennedy-appointed clique that surrounded him Johnson made the fateful decision to expand radically America's commitment to Vietnam from giving support and training to direct military involvement in what they all saw as the next great battle of the Cold War.

Excerpts from Speech Given by President Johnson at Johns Hopkins University, April 7, 1965.

> We are also there because there are great stakes in the balance. **Let no one think for a moment that retreat from Viet-Nam** (sic.) **would bring an end to conflict. The battle would be renewed in one country and then another. The central lesson of our time is that the appetite of aggression is never satisfied. To withdraw from one battlefield means only to prepare for the next** (emphasis added). We must say in Southeast Asia as we did in Europe in the words of the Bible: "Hitherto shalt thou come, but no further."...
>
> **Our objective is the independence of South Viet-Nam** (sic.) (emphasis added) and its freedom from attack. We want nothing for ourselves only that the people of

> South Viet-Nam (sic.) be allowed to guide their own country in their own way. We will do everything necessary to reach that objective. And we will do only what is absolutely necessary.[332]

NIXON

Richard Nixon became the fifth President of the United States to face the question, "How do we end American involvement in Vietnam?" He faced a situation that had built up over many years. It rested upon Truman's commitment to "Contain" International Communism. On Eisenhower's decision to stop the dominos from falling by build a bulwark against the spread of International Communism throughout Southeast Asia by replacing the French in Indochina. It had grown through President Kennedy's decisions to enlarge the force of advisors from a few hundred to more than 16,000 and to interfere in the internal politics of South Vietnam. It had mushroomed because of President Johnson's massive infusion of military support to forestall the collapse of South Vietnam as he had struggled to pick up the pieces after Kennedy's coup against Diem.

All of these decisions, over many years meant that Nixon now faced a highly complex and volatile situation. A situation where America had over 500,000 soldiers in Vietnam and more than 300 men being held as prisoners of war in North Vietnam. At the same time, the American public had divided as never before over the course our foreign policy. In addition, on his inauguration day President Nixon faced a situation without parallel in the history of the United States. For the first time, the nation had willingly "changed horses in the middle of the stream." For the first time, America had rejected a presidential administration in the midst of war and they looked hopefully to a new leader to win the battle and secure the peace.

President Nixon entered upon the duties of his office committed to ending the war. However, he was willing to sacrifice neither the security nor freedom of South Vietnam, nor the perception of our allies that the United States remained a reliable ally in the wider Cold War. But just as each preceding president had found himself forced to make certain decisions by the actions of his predecessor, Nixon would enter office constrained by Johnson's unilateral bombing halt and by the so-far fruitless negotiations in Paris. Negotiations, which seemed designed only to serve the public relation interests of the Communist North Vietnamese.

Under the rubric "Peace with Honor" the Nixon administration advanced three goals: (1) withdrawal of U.S. Forces, (2) turning the war back over to the Vietnamese through "Vietnamization" (3) the return of American prisoners of war.[333] This change of tactics, just as similar readjustments did not effect the overall strategy of stopping the advance of International Communism.

As becomes apparent from this study of America's involvement in the War in Vietnam the United States initially entered the conflict under the belief that it constituted the "NEXT" battle in the already decades old Cold War. The American political and military leaders following in the footsteps of other American leaders sought to fight a limited war such as we had fought against Spain in the 1890s[334] and against North Korea in the 1950s.

Therefore, while winning every major engagement in the South and almost entirely eliminating the indigenous Viet Cong they limited their aggressive action to bombing the sanctuaries and staging areas of the Communists forces in North Vietnam, Cambodia, and Laos. Moreover, though they sent several brief but limited incursions into Cambodia and Laos, they never invaded North Vietnam, the source and direct conduit for this latest thrust of the advancing tide of

International Communism.

Many have disparaged this strategy as forcing our soldiers to fight with "one hand tied behind their back." However, as we look back from a future made secure by the sacrifices of the very leaders and soldiers so many are so quick to defame we should view this strategy of limited war within its proper context.[335] One battle in the much larger conflict between the forces of freedom and the aggressive forces of International Communism, the last and greatest attempt by twentieth century Totalitarianism to conquer the world, the Cold War.

This larger field of attention is readily apparent in many statements made from successive American Presidents.

President Truman almost immediately after the Allied victory over the Fascist Totalitarians faced with the intransigence and belligerence of Totalitarian International Communism. In this standoff, he enunciated **the Truman Doctrine**. This doctrine would be the lynchpin for U.S. diplomacy and military action for the next forty plus years as the Cold War ebbed and flowed around the globe. Truman opened the storehouse of democracy to hold the line against the gathering darkness, declaring, **"It must be the policy of the United States to support free peoples who are resisting attempted subjugation by armed minorities or by outside pressures"**[336]

President Eisenhower faced an implacable enemy, which had already swallowed a sizable portion of the globe. An enemy with the largest armed forces ever gathered. An enemy which loudly proclaimed its intention to "Bury" the United States and the rest of the Free World under an iron blanket of totalitarian slavery. Seeing the strategic significance of Vietnam, having enunciated the "Domino Theory" which asserted that if Vietnam fell all of Southeast Asia would then be in jeopardy and if Southeast Asia fell, "Finally, the geographical position achieved thereby does many things. **It turns the so-called island defensive chain of Japan, Formosa, of the Philippines and to the southward; it moves in to threaten Australia and New Zealand** (emphasis added)."[337]

President Kennedy assumed the presidency in the wake of his charges of a "Missile Gap" and of a deteriorating situation vis-a-vis the forces of the crusading International Communist Totalitarians. He campaigned as the most effective person to lead the nation in the Cold War. His Inaugural Address served notice that he would lead America into battle. "Let every nation know, whether it wishes us well or ill, that we will pay any price, bear any burden, meet any hardship, support any friend, oppose any foe, to assure the survival and the success of liberty."[338]

From the beginning of his presidency, President Kennedy framed the war in Vietnam within the context of the wider struggle. "The United States is also conscious of its responsibility and duty, in its own self-interest as well as in the interest of other free peoples, to assist a brave country in the defense of its liberties against unprovoked subversion and Communist terror. It has no other motive than the defense of freedom."[339]

"The best and the brightest" as his hand-picked Eastern Establishment think-tank of advisors was known consistently advised by that in Vietnam America faced the forces of International Communism and that this battle had wider implications. His Secretary of State, Dean Rusk and his Secretary of Defense, Robert MacNamara typified this advice when the said:

> The deteriorating situation in South Viet-Nam (sic.) requires attention to the nature and scope of United States national interests in that country. The loss of South Viet-Nam (sic.) to Communism would

> involve the transfer of a nation of 20 million people from the free world to the Communism bloc. **The loss of South Viet-Nam** (sic.) **would make pointless any further discussion about the importance of Southeast Asia to the free world; we would have to face the near certainty that the remainder of Southeast Asia and Indonesia would move to a complete accommodation with Communism, if not formal incorporation with the Communist bloc** (emphasis added). The United States, as a member of SEATO, has commitments with respect to South Viet-Nam (sic.) under the Protocol to the SEATO Treaty. Additionally, in a formal statement at the conclusion session of the 1954 Geneva Conference, the United States representative stated that the United States "would view any renewal of the aggression . . . with grave concern and seriously threatening international peace and security."
>
> **The loss of South Viet-Nam (sic.) to Communism would not only destroy SEATO but would undermine the credibility of American commitments elsewhere** (emphasis added).[340]

Finally, using biblical imagery Kennedy starkly illustrated his belief that America stood on guard against the forces of and encroaching evil,

> We in this country, in this generation, are—by destiny rather than choice—**the watchmen on the walls of world freedom**

> (emphasis added). We ask, therefore, that we may be worthy of our power and responsibility—that we may exercise our strength with wisdom and restrain—and that we may achieve in our time and for all time the ancient vision of "peace on earth, good will toward men." That must always be our goal—and the righteousness of our case must always underlie our strength. For as was written long ago: "Except the Lord keep the city, the watchman waketh but in vain."[341]

President Johnson in many ways stepped into a role written by and for his predecessor. However, by temperament, philosophy, and inclination he supported the role to which he sacrificed his own political career and reputation. Moreover, there can be no doubt that he too saw the conflict in Vietnam as a battle within the larger context of the Cold War.

> Viet Nam (sic.) is far away from this quiet campus. We have no territory there, nor do we seek any. ...
>
> Why must this Nation hazard its ease, and its interest, and its power for the sake of a people so far away?
>
> We fight because we must fight if we are to live in a world where every country can shape its own destiny. And only in such a world will our own freedom be finally secure....
>
> The first reality is that North VietNam (sic.) has attacked the independent nation of South Viet-Nam (sic.). Its object is total conquest.
>
> Of course, some of the people of South

Viet-Nam (sic.) are participating in attack on their own government. But trained men and supplies, orders and arms, flow in a constant stream from north to south....

Over this war and all Asia is another reality: the deepening shadow of Communist China (emphasis added). The rulers in Hanoi are urged on by Peking. This is a regime which has destroyed freedom in Tibet, which has attacked India, and has been condemned by the United Nations for aggression in Korea.

Why are these realities our concern? Why are we in South Vietnam?

We are there because we have a promise to keep. Since 1954 every American President has offered support to the people of South Viet-Nam (sic.). We have helped to build, and we have helped to defend. Thus, over many years, we have made a national pledge to help South Viet-Nam (sic.) defend its independence. And I intend to keep that promise...

We are also there to strengthen world order. **Around the globe, from Berlin to Thailand, are people whose well-being rests, in part, on the belief that they can count on us if they are attacked** (Emphasis added). To leave Viet-Nam (sic) to its fate would shake the confidence of all these people in the value of an American commitment and in the value of America's word. The result would be increased unrest and instability, and even wider war.

We are also there because there are great

> stakes in the balance. **Let no one think for a moment that retreat from Viet-Nam** (sic.) **would bring an end to conflict. The battle would be renewed in one country and then another. The central lesson of our time is that the appetite of aggression is never satisfied. To withdraw from one battlefield means only to prepare for the next** (emphasis added). We must say in Southeast Asia as we did in Europe in the words of the Bible: "Hitherto shalt thou come, but no further."... [342]

President Nixon campaigned on a platform promising an end to the war in Vietnam. However, from beginning to end he consistently enunciated goals in terms of the standard rhetoric of the Cold War.

> **Abandoning the South Vietnam people, however, would jeopardize more than lives in South Vietnam. It would threaten our longer term hopes for peace in the world**(emphasis added). A great nation cannot renege on its pledges, A great nation must be worthy of trust.
>
> When it comes to maintaining peace, "prestige" is not an empty word. I am not speaking of false pride or bravado - they should have no place in our policies. I speak rather of the respect that one nation has for another's integrity in defending its principles and meeting its obligations.
>
> **If we simply abandoned our efforts in South Vietnam, the cause of peace might not survive the damage that would be**

> **done to other nations' confidence in our reliability** (emphasis added).
>
> Another reason stems from debates within the communist world between those who argue for a policy of confrontation with the United States and those who argue against it. **If Hanoi were to succeed in taking over South Vietnam by force- even after the power of the United States had been engaged - it would greatly strengthen those leaders who scorn negotiation, who advocate aggression, who minimize the risks of confrontation. It would bring peace now, but it would enormously increase the danger of a bigger war later** (emphasis added).
>
> In my campaign for the Presidency, **I pledged to end this war in a way that would increase our chances to win true and lasting peace in South Vietnam, in the Pacific, and in the world** (emphasis added). I am determined to keep that pledge.[343]

Therefore, it becomes apparent that the leadership of the United States consistently considered Vietnam as one more battle in a much larger war. As stated many times by our presidents just as in Korea, the goal in Vietnam was **NEVER** to conquer North Vietnam. Instead, America sought to bring about a stable, independent South Vietnam able to hold the line against the aggressive intentions of its Communist northern counterpart.

TRUMAN

To most Americans after World War II International

Communism appeared to be the opposite of everything they thought worthwhile. The Totalitarian aggressors who led International Communism, just as the Fascist Totalitarians before them disdained democracy, disregarded human dignity, pursued a policy of aggression that declared its intention to conquer the world. Furthermore, they built up a highly integrated block of states with command economies that did not enter into peaceful trade with the rest of the world but sought instead to build a new world based upon their ideology.

Seeing International Communism as a political plague, which could spread from nation to nation the leaders of the United States espoused their belief in the Domino Theory. This theory held that as one nation fell to the onslaught of International Communism its neighbors would come under increased pressure.

In 1949, when someone "lost" China to the Communists the political leaders in America began to fear that Indochina could well be next. This belief, that the advancing tide of Communism would seek to swallow one country after another prompted Truman to give aid to the French as they struggled to reinstate the colonial control they had lost during World War II.[344]

EISENHOWER

President Eisenhower reacted to the loss by the French in Indochina by stepping into the gap. The following excerpt from his letter of support to President Diem of South Vietnam expressed his belief that this was necessary to forestall a collapse of the democratic opposition in Vietnam.

> We have been exploring ways and means to permit our aid to Viet-Nam (sic.) to be more effective and to make a greater contribution

to the welfare and stability of the government of Viet-Nam (sic.). I am, accordingly, instructing the American Ambassador to Viet-Nam (sic.) to examine with you in your capacity as Chief of Government, how an intelligent program of American aid given directly to your government can serve to assist Viet-Nam (sic.) in its present hour of trial, provided that your Government is prepared to give assurances as to the standards of performance it would be able to maintain in the event such aid were supplied. **The purpose of this offer is to assist the Government of Viet-Nam** (sic.) **in developing and maintaining a strong, viable state, capable of resisting attempted subversion or aggression through military means** (emphasis added). The Government of the United States expects that this aid will be met by performance on the part of the Government of Viet-Nam (sic.) in undertaking needed reforms. It hopes that **such aid, combined with your own continuing efforts, will contribute effectively toward an independent Viet-Nam (sic.) endowed with a strong government. Such a government would, I hope, be so responsive to the nationalist aspirations of its people,** (emphasis added) so enlightened in purpose and effective in performance, that it will be respected both at home and abroad and discourage any who might wish to impose a foreign ideology on your free people. [345]

KENNEDY

In referring to the motives of the United States in helping Vietnam maintain its independence stated, "It has no other motive than the defense of freedom."[346] Seeking to follow this motive and achieve the goal of a safe and stable South Vietnam President Kennedy increased the American presence and intervened directly in the domestic political situation through his complicity in the over throw of President Diem.

JOHNSON

Adding his voice to the growing line of American presidents who were required by circumstance to speak-out on Vietnam, President Johnson enunciated the objectives of the United States when he said:

> Viet Nam (sic.) is far away ... We have no territory there, nor do we seek any. **Our objective is the independence of South Viet-Nam,** (sic.) **and its freedom from attack** (emphasis added). We want nothing for ourselves only that the people of South Viet-Nam (sic.) be allowed to guide their own country in their own way. We will do everything necessary to reach that objective. [347]

NIXON

President Nixon reiterated his view of American objectives clearly and often:

> **Our objective is the independence of**

South Viet-Nam (sic.), **and its freedom from attack** (emphasis added). We want nothing for ourselves only that the people of South Viet-Nam (sic.) be allowed to guide their own country in their own way. We will do everything necessary to reach that objective. And we will do only what is absolutely necessary.

Almost without exception, the leaders of non-communist Asia have told me that they would consider a one-sided American withdrawal from South Vietnam to be a threat to the security of their own nations (emphasis added).

In this spirit, let me be explicit about several points:

We seek not bases in South Vietnam. We insist on no military ties. (emphasis added). We are willing to agree to neutrality if that is what the South Vietnamese people freely choose. We believe there should be an opportunity for full participation in the political life of South Vietnam by all political elements that are prepared to do so without the use of force or intimidation. We are prepared to accept any government in South Vietnam that results from **the free choice** (emphasis added) of the South Vietnamese people themselves.

We have no intention of imposing any form of govt upon the people of South Vietnam, nor will we be a party to such coercion. We have no objection to reunification, if that turns out to be what the people of South Vietnam and the people of North

> Vietnam want; **we ask only that the decision reflect the free choice of the people concerned** (emphasis added).
>
> In pursuing our **limited objective** (emphasis added), we insist on no rigid diplomatic formula. Peace could be achieved by a formal negotiated settlement. Peace could be achieved by an informal understanding, provided that the understanding is clear and that there were adequate assurance that it would be observed. Peace on paper is not as important as peace in fact.
>
> In my campaign for the Presidency, I pledged to end this war in a way that would increase our chances to win true and lasting peace in South Vietnam, in the Pacific, and in the world. I am determined to keep that pledge. If I fail to do so, I expect the American people to hold me accountable for that failure.[348]

It is only within a framework, which references these oft stated and clearly defined limited goals and objectives that any objective discussion regarding the outcome of the Vietnam War should take place. How can we possibly determine whether we won or lost if we do not clearly discern what we sought to achieve?

---

[322] Donovan. pp. 20-23.

[323] http://web.jjay.cuny.edu/~jobrien/reference/ob66.html (11-26-03). Informational,

[324] t http://www.fordham.edu/halsall/mod/1954-eisenhower-vietnam1.html (11-20-03). Modern History Sourcebook: President Eisenhower: Letter to Ngo Dinh Diem, October 23, 1954

Department of State Bulletin November 15 1954, pp.735-736.

[325] Presidential Press Conference April 7, 1954 http://www.uiowa.edu/~c030162/Common/Handouts/POTUS/IKE.html (11-20-03).

[326] http://www.mtholyoke.edu/acad/intrel/pentagon2/ps10.htm (11-20-03). Joint Communiqué Issued at Saigon by the Vice President of the United States and the President of Viet-Nam, May 13 1961, Department of State Bulletin, June 19 1961, p. 956. Source: The Pentagon Papers, Gravel Edition, Volume 2, p. 803

[327] Ibid.

[328]Sheehan, Neil & E. W. Kenworthy. The Pentagon Papers, Crown Publishing Group, 1971, pp. 150-153.

[329] http://www.mtholyoke.edu/acad/intrel/pentagon2/ps29.htm (11-20-03). Excerpts from President Kennedy's News Conference, March 6, 1963. Public Papers of the Presidents, Kennedy, 1963, p. 243. Source: The Pentagon Papers, Gravel Edition, Volume 2, pp. 816-817

[330] http://www.mtholyoke.edu/acad/intrel/pentagon2/ps31.htm (11-20-03). President Kennedy's View of the "Domino Theory," News Conference, April 24, 1963. Public Papers of the Presidents, Kennedy, 1963, p. 343. Source: *The Pentagon Papers,* Gravel Edition, Volume 2, pp. 818-819.

[331] http://mcadams.posc.mu.edu/progjfk5.htm (12-3-03).

[332] http://vietnam.vassar.edu/doc12.html (11-20-03). Excerpts from Speech Given by President Johnson at Johns Hopkins University, April 7,1965. Public Papers of the Presidents of the United States: Lyndon B. Johnson, 1965, pp. 394-397.

[333] http://www.vietnam.ttu.edu/vietnamcenter/events/2002_Symposium/2002Papers_files/tilford.htm (11-26-03).

[334] http://www.wccusd.k12.ca.us/elcerrito/history/span-amerwar.htm (12-5-03). Informational.

[335] http://www.vwip.org/mb/limited.htm (12-5-03). Informational.

[336] For the full text of the Truman Doctrine see the Appendix.

[337] Presidential Press Conference April 7, 1954. http://www.uiowa.edu/~c030162/Common/Handouts/POTUS/IKE.html (11-20-03).

[338] John F. Kennedy's Inaugural Address, January 20 1961, http://www.infoplease.com/ipa/A0878607.html / (10-2-03).

[339] Joint Communique Issued at Saigon by the Vice President of the United States and the President of Viet-Nam, May 13 1961, Department of State *Bulletin*, June 19 1961, p. 956:

[340] Sheehan and others (eds.), *Pentagon Papers*, pp. 150-153.

[341] http://www.mtholyoke.edu/acad/intrel/pentagon2/ps43.htm (11-20-03). President Kennedy's Remarks Prepared for Delivery at the Trade Mart in Dallas, November 22, 1963. Public Papers of the Presidents, Kennedy, 1963, p. 890. Source: *The Pentagon Papers,* Gravel Edition, Volume 2, pp. 830-831.

[342] Public Papers of the Presidents of the United States: Lyndon B. Johnson, 1965, pp. 394-397.

[343] http://www.usconstitution.com/PresidentNixon'sReportOnVietnam.htm (11-19-03).

[344] http://www.english.uiuc.edu/maps/vietnam/causes.htm (11-18-03). Informational

[345] http://www.fordham.edu/halsall/mod/1954-eisenhower-vietnam1.html (11-20-03). Modern History Sourcebook: President Eisenhower: Letter to Ngo Dinh Diem, October 23, 1954

Department of State Bulletin. November 15, 1954, pp.735-736.

[346] Joint Communique Issued at Saigon by the Vice President of the United States and the President of Viet-Nam, May 13, 1961, Department of State *Bulletin*, June 19, 1961, p. 956:

[347] Public Papers of the Presidents of the United States: Lyndon B. Johnson, 1965, pp. 394-397.

[348] http://www.usconstitution.com/PresidentNixon'sReportOnVietnam.htm (11-19-03).

THE DELIBERATE DELUSION

CHAPTER TEN

Defeat From The Jaws Of Victory

The Legend of Defeat

One old saying states that, "To the victors go the spoils." Another truism seldom adequately appreciated by non-Historians is "Winners write History." The case of Vietnam in the popular consciousness is a case in point. While this book by its nature and purpose presents and defends the premise that America won the Vietnam War, who won the peace is another matter. Ultimately the winners of the peace shape the perceptions of the future.

It is easy to understand why the Communists of Vietnam continue to foster the perception of their great humanitarian victory as they torture and oppress their own people.[349] They obviously have an interest in portraying themselves as visionary leaders instead of thugs. It is equally easy to understand why the current leaders of our own society join them in this exercise.

It is hard for the swiftly maturing survivors of the anti-war movement to look at their long held beliefs, or to analyze their previous behavior and its consequences with anything short of smug approval. Many have invested their entire lives in maintaining the belief that what they did as idealistic young people mattered and that it exerted a positive influence upon the unfolding of history. For their continued self-esteem, to say nothing of their continued possession of public approval it is vitally important that all sources agree, they were right and those who supported the Vietnam War were wrong. It is vitally important that all sources agree that they saw through the fog of government propaganda and liberated America from a brutal and selfish war fought for economic aggrandizement.

Any deviation from this line of thinking opens the possibility that perhaps the anti-war supporters were not right. Perhaps instead of liberating anyone, they were actually the unwitting accomplices of Totalitarian Communist aggressors who used their naiveté to help enslave millions.[350] If the theory presented in this book is ever reasonably considered, even as a possibility, these counter-culture devotees might be forced to see themselves as the proud supporters of freedom fighters like Ho Chi Minh and Pol Pot (1925-1998)[351] who killed hundreds of thousands perhaps millions in hellish labor camps, forced relocations, and inhuman re-education programs.

A major concern for the aging members of the peace movement remains the protection of their cherished self-image as visionaries. Visionaries who led American society to its current high state of enlightenment, as exemplified by the morality and example of the Clinton Administration. To accomplish this they must at all costs maintain the fiction that the Vietnam War was an isolated event. It must be divorced from its context as one battle in the global conflict, which was the Cold War.

To prove they were right in fomenting, abetting, and participating in actions calculated to undermine the domestic support for American troops deployed in a foreign war they strive always to show that the Vietnam War was unnecessary. They exploit every opportunity to impugn the motives of America's wartime leaders. They consistently assert that American aggression initiated the conflict. They extol the bravery of the protestors in standing up to what they portray as an authoritarian American government and of the Communist aggressors while at the same time casting ridicule on the truly exemplary conduct of the American military.

Moreover, to maintain the seamless perfection of this historical construct everyone must agree that the Vietnam War was a major defeat doomed from the beginning. Anyone who challenges these rigid standards of groupthink faces the fury of the young idealists who have become the entrenched establishment. This self-appointed elite will ignore, ridicule, or in any way possible marginalize anyone who offers a contrary opinion, no matter how well researched, no matter how well presented. During the three decades since our valiant troops came home, that triumvirate of liberal opinion formation and decimation, academia, the media elite and Hollywood have sought to control the debate concerning the war in Vietnam. Until the iron grip of the liberal elite loosens no open or honest debate which questions the approved history of the Vietnam War will occur in a major media forum.

The masterfully created common-knowledge runs like a flowing stream from college campus to front page from major publishing houses to local movie screens. Like a pinwheel turning in the manufactured breeze of a fan America has endured thirty years of an oft-repeated but still illogical legend. This is the legend of idealistic youths valiantly stopping an American government intent on exploiting the vast economic resources of Vietnam. The courage and dedication of the stay-at-home warriors in burning draft-cards and refusing to fight lends color to the legend. In this legend, the reality of actions, which helped the North Vietnamese impose the blessings of Totalitarian Communism on the unwilling citizens of South Vietnam, Cambodia, and Laos, becomes the gift of liberation, the blessing of unity and the peace of the graveyard.

Based on thirty years of biased commentary, beginning in the rice paddies and continued in the lecture hall, a generation of journalists, politicians and historians built careers selling America the legend. Today walls of books, articles, and movies provide citation as evidence that the legend is true. Entire political careers find their foundation in the truth of the legend. To challenge this legend is to court the ridicule of the establishment. However, if opinions contradicting the common knowledge never receive a fair presentation and therefore, never enter the debate, never rise to the level of objective consideration how do we honestly maintain the belief that we live in a free society?

The Deliberate Delusion

The list of deliberate misrepresentations and falsehoods presented for public consumption is long and extensive. They have received so much exposure that they have become common knowledge.

The annexation of South Vietnam by North Vietnam was NOT "Conquest." It was instead the natural result of the Vietnamese people's desire for unity. The light of inspection focuses on the brutality and atrocities of the American occupiers at My Lai while ignoring decades of systematic assassination and torture on the part of the Communists both before and after their conquest in the south. The bombing of North Vietnam becomes the proof of American war crimes while incidents such as the mass slaughter of unarmed people in the city of Hue during the Tet Offensive are glossed over.

The legend portrays the various leaders of South

Vietnam as dupes of the American puppet-masters while Ho Chi Minh is the Father of his Nation and General Giap is the Napoleon of Indochina. The legend ignores the fact that the list of allied victories covers every major engagement including the Tet offensive. It ignores the fact of the highly disproportionate casualty figures (50,000 Americans, 240,000 South Vietnamese verses nearly 1.5 million North Vietnamese and Viet Cong). Instead, the legend holds up the Communists as resourceful freedom fighters who constantly made fools of the drugged up, over confidant, over supplied, and under motivated Americans.

In addition to poor leadership, the legend assumes an aggressive American army of occupation consisting almost completely of poor draftees with an unfairly high proportion of minorities. Actually, a majority of those who served and of those who died volunteered. Moreover, though African-Americans accounted for more than 13% of the draft-age population they made up approximately 12.5% of the American Army in Vietnam.[352]

The antiwar movement in America receives a different treatment as the legend winds its way through the pinnacles of power, the hallowed halls of academia, the gate of the media, and long-reach of Hollywood. Controlling the debate and shaping the public image in such a way that few would ever realize many of the prominent anti-war leaders had a dedication not to peace but to seeing a social(ist) revolution in America. They seized upon the war as an opportunity to mobilize masses of people who would never have followed them if they knew what their true motives were. They merely used the war as a vehicle to gain prominence and to push their agenda much as Lenin used the First World War. The legend speaks of them as brave souls willing to risk police brutality to stop the aggression of a series of American administrations bent on imposing democracy on the world.

The legend unabashedly tells us that the Tet Offensive

spelled the doom of American dreams of military conquest. It ignores the fact that although the Communists achieved some stunning initial victories the allies eventually defeated them, furthermore, after Tet the indigenous Viet Cong for all practical purposes ceased to exist as a cohesive fighting force. The communist invaders had counted on a massive uprising of the South Vietnamese population to join them in throwing the American's and their puppets into the sea. However, this positive popular response never materialized and so the Communists killed as many civilians as they could.[353]

Then from 1969 onward President Nixon successfully implemented his program of Vietnamization. This program dramatically cut American involvement and casualties with the burden of the war carried by the increasingly efficient South Vietnamese Army.

In addition, while it is true that the anti-war movement succeeded in radicalizing a large portion of the American population, especially among the draft-age young a sizable (silent) majority of the people remained loyal supporters of the war policy of the government. Even with Watergate and the constant media barrage of distortions public opinion polls continued to give evidence of massive support for holding the line against the aggression of International Communism. This carried over into majority support for such controversial aspects of the war as the continued bombing of North Vietnam, and the mining North Vietnamese harbors.

Almost forgotten is the fact that the negotiators of the 1973 Paris Peace Accords won the Nobel Peace Prize.[354] Lost in a flood of pictures showing terrified people clinging to the under-carriages of helicopters as Communist tanks rolled into Saigon it is seldom mentioned that the Paris Peace Accords promised an end to infiltration and free elections. The evacuation pictures have so engulfed the imagination of the perpetrators and victims of the legend that most people now think this is how the American Army left Vietnam.

Few remember that the American Army had withdrawn two years before the final evacuation after forcing the Communists to abandon the idea of winning in the field. However, instead of coming home as one huge victorious army as the Americans did after World War I and World War II, the brave but forgotten victorious veterans of Vietnam came home piecemeal to face the legend alone.

Soon after the signing of the Paris Peace Accords political events in the United States spiraled out of control.

Due to the ever-mushrooming Watergate scandal, President Nixon resigned. The so-called Watergate Congress that came in 1974 had a disproportionate number of anti-war Democrats. Many of them had participated in the anti-war movement and were now moving from the picket lines to the avenues of power. Almost immediately, the new congress began cutting support to South Vietnam. The very support America had repeatedly promised to the government of South Vietnam, military supplies, spare parts and other logistical equipment necessary to operate a modern army.

The first effect of this betrayal was the collapse of South Vietnamese moral. In addition, while the new leaders of American foreign policy began to under-cut and under-fund the South Vietnamese the forces of International Communism in the Soviet Union, China continued to pour material support into North Vietnam.

Seeing the fruition of the long effort to undermine America's will to win the Communist leaders of North Vietnam ordered General Giap to begin to planning for the final assault. We cannot over emphasize the importance of these actions by the United States Congress when trying to understand the collapse of South Vietnam. Waiting in the wings like successful lobbyists the Communists launched their final assault. The South Vietnamese under-supplied and with sagging moral watched their initial withdrawal turn into a rout. It is this military collapse, built upon broken-promises, which provided the pictures of forlorn people clinging for freedom and life to helicopters. Pictures subsequently used by those same anti-war leaders to prove the failure of the American War effort in Vietnam.

Then in contravention to the wisdom of the anti-war rhetoric the dominos began to fall. To the self-congratulating victors of the American Vietnam War debate with Nixon humiliated and the military hobbled all was now right with the world. But to the suffering millions of Cambodia's killing fields and the desperate boat people who soon clogged the shipping lanes of the Pacific life in the worker's paradise turned out to be death. In America as the young lions of peace settled into the paths of power more than a million South Vietnamese who had trusted in America's promises of support were rounded up and shipped off for re-education. The victorious Communists worked or tortured tens of thousands to death while many more spent decades behind barbed wire as the blessings of "peace" swallowed generations. Generations of people descended from those who fought for freedom, who believed in American promises have lived as second class citizens, denied equal treatment in their own country by the Communists who had come to "liberate" them.

Perhaps, not all of the dominos fell. Thailand, Malaya, Singapore and Indonesia escaped the collapse. However, to the millions in Cambodia and Laos the collapse of democratic resistance in South Vietnam began a chain reaction that affects them to this day.

After long decades of the all-pervading legend, have we finally reached enough distance to provide an objective look at this generation defining experience?

Today the Vietnam generation sits in their living rooms and dens as their grandchildren play on the floor. Perhaps the time has finally come when they will be able to look through the haze of years and discern the outlines of a past that is not exactly, as the post-war establishment represents it.

Whole lifetimes, entire personalities find their meaning in the sure knowledge that America fought an illegal, immoral, and losing war in Vietnam. People keep their old bumper stickers and pictures from the anti-war movement on prominent display while the veterans keep their medals in dresser drawers. How would the past look to us now if we began to look at the self-indulgence of the "summer of love"[355] for what it really was, an orgy of sex, drugs, and rock-n-roll? What if we suddenly saw the flower power of the anti-war crowd something a bit more sordid than the "Golden Age" so many retro-hippies think it must have been? What if we started admitting that the young men and women who swam against the tide of peer pressure and fought a successful campaign against an implacable foe had been right all along?

---

349 http://www.newsargus.com/newsport/edit/0512000.html (11-26-03).

350 Ibid.

351 http://www.time.com/time/asia/asia/magazine/1999/990823/pol_pot1.html (11-15-03). Informational.

352 http://www.ku.edu/carrie/archives/milhst-l/19990701.mil/msg00139.html (11-18-03).

353 http://hubcap.clemson.edu/~eemoise/viet8.html (11-18-03).

354 http://www.nobel.se/peace/laureates/1973/ (12-17-03).

355 http://www.sftoday.com/enn2/sumdex.htm (12-5-03); http://www.hippy.com/php/index.php (12-5-03). Informational.

CHAPTER 11

Victory On The Battle Field, The Paris Peace Accords, And The Loss Of Vietnam

No agreement is worth more than the honor of those who negotiate and sign it and no agreement is stronger than the integrity of those who implement it.

As presented in the preceding chapter the goals of America were neither to conquer North Vietnam nor to impose freedom upon its masses. America's goals instead consisted of stopping the infiltration (invasion) of the South by the forces of Communist North Vietnam and securing an independent South Vietnam an equal voice in the future of Vietnam thus achieving a "Peace with Honor."[356]

To the advancing tide of International Communism, negotiation existed only as just one more step to achieve their goals of domination. However as can be seen in Korea and Vietnam they never began negotiations until they saw that their military option was stalled and they never agreed to a cease fire until they were beaten on the field. Moreover, as can also be seen through the examples of Korea and Vietnam, they never honored the obligations they agreed to unless the military resolve of the free nations of the world stood resolute and determined.

In Korea America has borne the burden these many years to ensure that the Communists of North Korea did not renew their invasion of the South. Even a cursory review of the history of the Totalitarian state of North Korea for the last fifty years shows that if America had followed a course of action similar to the one followed in Vietnam a similar fate would have befallen South Korea. If America had withdrawn all its forces in 1952, and then voted in 1954, not to re-supply South Korea is there any doubt that the forces of International Communism would have again raised the red flag Seoul? Is there any doubt that if we followed this course of action today the slave armies of North Korea would cross the demilitarized zone within a short time? Only the continued commitment of America preserves the peace in Korea. Conversely, the lack of commitment brought about the collapse of democratic resistance in South Vietnam.

Using Korea as the model, the leaders of America sought to end the war and preserve the peace. Perhaps naively, they trusted in the success of Vietnamization to allow the United States to withdraw all of its forces instead of leaving them as a trip-wire as had been done in Korea. This may have been a miss-calculation but it was not the signal of abject desertion of our allies. America promised the South Vietnamese a continuous re-supply to maintain equality with the Communist forces.

If the United States believed the South Vietnamese were capable of dealing militarily with the Communist troops which the agreement allowed to remain in the South it is then fair to ask the question, "Why did the Paris Accords fail?"

And answer a secondary question, "At what level did each side maintain their forces in the field?" This reveals the answer to the primary question. It is also in the answer to this secondary question, which reveals that the failure of the

United States Congress to live up to the promises made by successive administrations was the cause for the loss of Vietnam.

During the critical period from 1973 when the Paris Peace Accords were signed to 1975 when South Vietnam fell, Communist military aid to North Vietnam increased four-fold. During the same period, the American Congress slashed military aid to South Vietnam from more than $2.5 billion in 1973 to a mere $700 million in 1975.[357] This massive reduction in American military aid to South Vietnam, in contravention of our promise to maintain their forces combined with continued infiltration of troops and supplies by North Vietnam into the South, also in direct contravention to the agreement signed by the leaders of North Vietnam, created a major disequilibrium of forces by 1975.

This study turns now to the sad history which flowed as a result of the failure of the government of the United States, led by Congress to live up to its promises to the people of South Vietnam.

On June 19, 1973, the Congress of the United States, led by Senator J. William Fulbright, passed the Case-Church Amendment. This amendment forbade American military involvement in Southeast Asia, as of August 15, 1973. The amendment passed with a veto-proof vote of 278 to 124 in the House and 64-26 in the Senate making it impervious to a presidential veto.[358] This Amendment, which directly contravened American promises, opened the way for the Communists of North Vietnam to launch another invasion of the South, with no fear of American intervention.

This unilateral action by the Congress of the United States induced President Nixon to write to the Democrat Speaker of the House, Speaker Carl Albert and the Democrat Majority Leader of the United States Senate Mike Mansfield. He gave vent to his serious concerns regarding the serious consequences, which he felt, might be their result:

> The abandonment of a friend will have a profound impact in other countries, such as Thailand, which have relied on the constancy and determination of the United States, and I want the Congress to be fully aware of the consequences of its action. ... I can only hope that the North Vietnamese will not draw the erroneous conclusion from this Congressional action that they are free to launch a military offensive in other areas of Indochina. North Vietnam would be making a very dangerous error if it mistook the cessation of bombing in Cambodia for an invitation to fresh aggression or further violations of the Paris agreements. The American people would respond to such aggression with appropriate action.[359]

President Nixon later confessed in his memoirs, that Congress having removed any possibility of a military response had left him with only had words with which to threaten North Vietnam.[360] Subsequent events proved that, the North Vietnamese also were well aware of this fact. The Nixon Administration knew of North Vietnam's intentions. In addition, they fully intended to honor the agreements made to the government and people of South Vietnam. But the ever accelerating dissolution of the President's ability to shape events caused by the Watergate scandal gave the Democrat-controlled Congress the power to abandon the promises and desert the ally we had supported for so long.

Henry Kissinger, the essential American figure involved with the negotiations to end the war shared his views of what the Nixon administration hoped would be the result of ending the war on America. He also revealed why he thought those hopes were dashed.

> There will be debate about why South Vietnam succumbed forever, and there are so many people on every side of that debate with vested interests in their position, that it seems almost impossible to achieve a reconciliation. So I can only give you my view. Our view was that the ending of the war might bring about a measure of national reconciliation in the United States, in the sense that those who wanted an end to the war had achieved their objectives, and those who wanted honor in the sense of not condemning people who had relied on us to live under communist rule, they had achieved their objective. So we thought it would be possible to achieve levels of assistance to South Vietnam which, together with the military equipment we were leaving behind, would enable them to resist all but a total military invasion; and that if an all-out assault was started in South Vietnam, we would reintroduce American air and sea power. That was our basic view. I believe it is an open question whether it could have succeeded, because we cut off aid almost immediately. In the first year of peace, we gave $2 billion, which is what we thought was the appropriate level. The second year that was cut to a billion; the third year it was cut to 700 million, while fuel prices were rising. So that the South Vietnamese army was not only required to fight alone, but it

> had to cut their ammunition expenditures by 70%, air power by 80%. And the final collapse occurred at a moment when the Congress was debating a total cut-off of aid and was discussing some terminal grant. How long Vietnam could have lasted, I don't know. **In 1975, it was killed by American domestic politics** (emphasis added). Whether it would have lasted much longer, is a question that will be debated forever.[361]

Dr. Kissinger spoke his mind concerning the effect of renunciation by Congress of the administration's policy in Vietnam, the effect of this renunciation on the negotiations, and the final impact of the complete withdrawal of American troops when he said,

> It was a tragic situation in Vietnam. We had withdrawn, over a period of four years, 520 of the 550,000 troops we found there, at a rate of about 150,000 a year; and we were down to 30,000 troops, and we had to retreat without a debacle, which was not easy, and we were now down to the last 30,000 troops plus (Fluff?) air and naval forces. I have great sympathy for Thieu, and at the same time I have great sympathy for our problem. We faced 65 congressional resolutions in the year 1972 alone, that were urging unilateral withdrawal from Vietnam. We would need a congressional supplementary appropriation in January of the following year for the excessive expenditure that we had... excessive in terms of the yearly budget... we had incurred in resisting the North Vietnamese

> offensive. So we felt, when the North Vietnamese accepted, and exceeded actually in accepting, what Nixon had proposed publicly nine months earlier, that we had no choice except to proceed. On the other hand, Thieu was faced with a situation no American ally has ever been asked to undertake, namely the total withdrawal of American forces. **We haven't done that in Korea, we haven't done that in Europe, we've never done it anywhere** (emphasis added). So we probably did not take into sufficient consideration... but frankly, if we had, I don't know whether we could have come to a different conclusion: the shock to the South Vietnamese political system of the sudden total withdrawal of American forces.[362]

And to make it perfectly clear that he felt that it was a dissolution of presidential power that precipitated the collapse of America's resolve to fulfill its commitments to South Vietnam Dr. Kissinger stated,

> **The effect of Watergate was that the President lost his executive ability to defend the agreement** (emphasis added), and that a weird situation developed, in which it was held that the United States had no right to enforce an agreement for which 50,000 Americans had died. **Within three months of Watergate becoming a public issue, and in more or less the same week as the public hearing started, the Congress passed a resolution prohibiting American military action in, over or near Indochina,**

> **which removed any threat** (emphasis added) of American... and eventually passed a whole series of acts which prohibited the transfer of equipment from one of the Indochinese countries to another, and a whole series of restrictions on the use of American advisers. And above all, it cut American aid so substantially that only by the strictest rationing could the South Vietnamese continue at all. So **I think Watergate made it impossible to implement the agreement** (emphasis added). And the question then is: how long could it have been maintained? It's the debatable question. I believe for quite a bit. [363]

After using the intervening four months to increase their infiltration of men and material into South Vietnam, in October of 1974 the leaders of North Vietnam decided to launch an all-out invasion of South Vietnam in 1975.

On December 13 1974, North Vietnam overtly violated the Paris Peace Accords by attacking Phuoc Long Province[364] in South Vietnam this first step is done to test President Ford's resolve. Bowing to the force of the new congressional realities, President Ford responds with diplomatic protests but no military force.

By January of 1975, the North Vietnamese Army supplied and advised by the forces of International Communism ranked as the fifth largest in the world.[365] The plans for their all-out invasion of the South called for more than 20 divisions of the regular North Vietnamese Army to lead the irregular forces of the surviving Viet Cong.[366]

The fact that America was not living up to its obligations is clearly shown when in January of 1975 Secretary of Defense James Schlesinger while testifying before

Congress, stated that the United States was not living up to its earlier promise to South Vietnam's President Thieu of "severe retaliatory action" in the event North Vietnam violated the Paris peace treaty.[367]

At a press conference also in January of 1975, President Ford indicated that the United States would not intervene to stop this new invasion of South Vietnam.[368]

In February of 1975 the leader of the North Vietnamese Army, General Van Tien Dung (1917-2002)[369] enters South Vietnam to take direct command in preparation for the final offensive. This final offensive begins on March 10, 1975 when 25,000 soldiers of the regular North Vietnamese Army attack Ban Me Thuot[370] in the Central Highlands. Although the Communists had anticipated a long siege Ban Me Thuot falls on March 11 when more than half of the 4000 South Vietnamese soldiers defending it surrender or desert.

Seeing his forces crumbling due to the lack of adequate supplies and acknowledging the low moral this lack caused in the armed forces South Vietnamese President Thieu faces a tough decision. Knowing that no help will be forthcoming, he decides on March 13, 1975 that he has no other option than to abandon the Highlands region and the two northern-most provinces of South Vietnam to the invading Communists. This decision brings about the collapse of national resolve. Seeing their country dissolve around them those who wanted to escape the coming Communist takeover soon jammed the roads blocking any effective withdrawal of the masses of troops ordered to fall back. This turns what should have been an orderly advance to the rear to well-prepared defensive positions into a rout known as "the convoy of tears."[371]

Seeing their long-time opponent nearing total collapse the leaders of North Vietnam decided to abandon the two-year plan they have devised for the total subjugation of the South. Instead, they seek to achieve total victory by May of

1975. Now in swift order the cities of South Vietnam surrender to the invaders, Quang Tri City falls on March 19, 1975, Tam Ky on March 24, 1975.

After a short siege, Hue falls on March 25, 1975. This brings about the disintegration of the South Vietnamese Army as they break and join hundreds of thousands of refugees fleeing south. The rout continues as Chu Lai is disserted on March 26, 1975. On March 28 1975, the North Vietnamese Army begins a massive bombardment of Da Nang. On March 30 1975, the mighty fortress-city of Da Nang falls with the surrender of more than 100,000 South Vietnamese soldiers.

This begins, on March 31, 1975 what the Communists called the "Ho Chi Minh Campaign," the final assault on Saigon. The resistance of the South Vietnamese Army finally stiffened on April 9, 1975 at Xuan Loc less than 40 miles from Saigon as they attempted to hold off more than 40,000 advancing soldiers of the North Vietnamese Army.

It was at this juncture that America once again intervened diplomatically. Not in the promised "sever retaliatory action"[372] against the Communists who had broken their agreements but instead against our erstwhile ally when on April 20, 1975 the American Ambassador Graham Martin met with President Thieu and pressured him to resign.

On April 21, 1975, President Thieu resigned. During his speech to the people of South Vietnam, he read the letter he had received from then President Nixon in 1972. The latter that had pledged "severe retaliatory action" if South Vietnam was ever again invaded. Through many tears, Thieu soundly condemned the Paris Peace Accords, and the ally, which had abandoned them "The United States has not respected its promises. It is inhumane. It is untrustworthy. It is irresponsible."[373] After the speech, President Thieu left the country for exile.[374]

After more than two weeks and a heroic stand Xuan

Loc[375] falls on April 22.

The North Vietnamese Army now swollen to more than 100,000 strong began its final advance on Saigon. On April 23, in a speech President Ford tells the world that the renewed conflict in Vietnam is "a war that is finished as far as America is concerned."[376]

By April 27, the Communists surround Saigon, trapping more than 30,000 South Vietnamese soldiers inside the city. In complete disregard for the civilian population, the North Vietnamese invaders mercilessly shell the city. As the government continues to breakdown widespread, rioting and looting convulse the city.

Immediately appealing for a cease-fire General Duong Van "Big" Minh (1916-2001)[377] becomes the new President of South Vietnam on April 28. Sensing that complete victory is within their grasp, the leaders of North Vietnam ignore this appeal. On April 29, shells begin falling at Tan Son Nhut Air Base.[378] Again; American soldiers die in Vietnam as the Communists shoot several guards stationed at the gate of the sprawling base.

Led by Communist sympathizers, South Vietnamese civilians begin to loot the now unprotected air base. Congress having sown the wind President Ford now reaps the whirlwind as he orders "Operation Frequent Wind,"[379] to begin the evacuation of 7000 Americans and South Vietnamese from Saigon. At the base frantic civilians, begin swarming the helicopters. The evacuation now shifts to the American embassy, walled and guarded by Marines. Thousands of South Vietnamese civilians, fearing the coming bloodbath storm the walls in their attempt to get into the compound. This is the chaotic scene, which produced the vivid pictures of terror-stricken people clinging to helicopters. These are the pictures that have been used ever since as evidence that the American military were driven out of Vietnam, although the withdrawal of American Ground

Forces (excluding embassy and base guards) had been peacefully completed two years earlier.

Off the coast of Vietnam, three American aircraft carriers stood by to accommodate the exodus of refugees. In the confusion, many South Vietnamese pilots attempting to flee the collapse of their country also landed on the carriers. The rush of incoming flights caused a glut on the decks of the carriers, a glut which, the flight crews could not handle. Consequently, many of the helicopters were pushed overboard to make room for more arrivals. The videos of this discarded ordinance falling into the sea has joined the scenes of desperate people hanging to the bottoms of helicopters as part of oft repeated image of America's "defeat" at the hands of the Communists in Vietnam.

On April 30, 1975 at 8:35 a.m., the last Americans, ten Marines from the embassy, depart Saigon, ending after more than thirty years the American military presence in Vietnam. As President Minh broadcasts a message of unconditional surrender invaders raise the red and blue Viet Cong flag over the presidential palace and the War in Vietnam is finally over.

The end had come. American soldiers had fought bravely and successfully for decades, finally forcing the Communist invaders to sign the Paris Peace Accords that fulfilled the American war goals, limited as they were. This was an agreement negotiated in good faith by the leaders of the Nixon Administration. However, it also came to be an agreement undermined by the actions of a run-away Congress. A Congress led by the peace-at-any-cost wing of the Democrat Party, the long-time opponents of Richard Nixon, and the large number of members elected during the turmoil of the Watergate scandal. This Watergate class of congressmen had campaigned on their opposition to the President, their opposition to the war, and their commitment to end the American presence in Vietnam no matter what the cost.

Ultimately the leaders of South Vietnam, both military and political must bear the responsibility for the loss of the war. It was after all "their" war. However, the government of the United States must also accept some major responsibility. The abject refusal of the Democrat-dominated American Congress to live up to the promises made by five successive American administrations to the government and people of South Vietnam during the two years, which intervened between the signing of the Paris Peace Accords and the fall of Saigon are a sad testimony to the bravery and sacrifice made by so many for so long.

---

[356] For the full text of the Paris Peace Accords, see the Appendix.

[357] http://www.ehistory.com/vietnam/essays/theend/0007.cfm (10-13-03)

[358] http://www.bbc.co.uk/dna/h2g2/A715060 (11-15-03).

[359] http://www.nixonfoundation.org/Research_Center/1973_pdf_files/1973_0229.pdf (11-15-03).

[360] Nixon, Richard. The Memoirs of Richard Nixon. Grosset & Dunlap: New York, NY. 1978, p. 888.

[361] http://www.gwu.edu/~nsarchiv/coldwar/interviews/episode-16/kissinger3.html (11-15-03).

[362] Ibid.

[363] Ibid.

[364] http://www.flyarmy.org/panel/battle/75010100.HTM (11-15-03). Informational.

[365] http://www.ichiban1.org/html/history/1975_present_postwar/nvn_invasion_1975.htm (11-15-03).

[366] Ibid.

[367] Ibid.

[368] http://www.grunt.com/hownorthvietnamwonthewar.htm (12-5-03). Informational.

[369] http://www.britannica.com/eb/article?eu=414860 (11-15-03).

Informational.

[370] http://www.dposs.com/k9/buonmethout.htm (11-15-03). Informational.

[371] http://news.bbc.co.uk/2/low/asia-pacific/716609.stm (11-26-03).

[372] http://www.ichiban1.org/html/history/1975_present_postwar/nvn_invasion_1975.htm (11-18-03).

[373] Ibid.

[374] http://news.bbc.co.uk/onthisday/hi/dates/stories/april/21/newsid_2935000/2935347.stm (12-5-03).

[375] http://www.generalhieu.com/xuanloc-m.htm (11-15-03). Informational.

[376] http://hnn.us/articles/1574.html (11-15-03).

[377] http://www.encyclopedia.com/html/M/Minh-D1uo.asp (11-15-03). Informational.

[378] http://www.dposs.com/k9/tansonhut.htm (11-15-03). Informational.

[379] http://www.fas.org/man/dod-101/ops/frequent_wind.htm (11-15-03). Informational.

CHAPTER TWELVE

Conclusion

In the History of the United States no other war except the Civil War has divided the nation during its prosecution and branded its perceptions afterwards as much as Vietnam. Questions of national ethics, national goals, the limits of power, and need for consensus rose to the fore as a new polarization between the two major parties replaced the hitherto bipartisan prosecution of the Cold War. The loud protests, the swirling caldron of riots, and the cultural dislocation also resembled no other experience in our national saga than the Civil War. In their reaction to both the trauma and the outcome of the War Between the States, Northern politicians spent a generation "waving the bloody shirt" while Jim Crow erected a cruel wall of apartheid, which lasted longer than a generation. So too the legacy of Vietnam has altered the platform, policies, and conduct of American politicians ever since.

Looking back over the long history of American wars it is notable that the only war, which might be termed "Questionable" to a sizable percentage of the population of the United States, is Vietnam.

It is true that a sizable minority did oppose the

Revolution. This vocal and committed minority took up arms in defense of their beliefs. However, those who remained after the war and who became the founding citizens of the Republic not only supported this primary war but also had been willing to hazard their lives and sacred honor to see it through.

Before the War of 1812 trade policies meant to harm the enemy, which instead punished the livelihood of American merchants, did indeed bring controversy and protest. However, the encroachments of the British on the high seas and along the Canadian border finally provoked America to declare war. Once the fighting began the vast majority of the population put their shoulder to the wheel as merchants and planters, mechanics and frontiersmen joined together to uphold the national honor.

The Mexican War sparked debate and dissent at the time and has been questioned many times since but while it was underway even vocal opponents joined the fray to support the American cause.

The great national divisions of the Civil War are obvious in its nature, but within the two separate camps, North and South the clear majority of citizens pulled together for victory.

Many Historians judge the Spanish American War to be a war manufactured by journalists and used by politicians solely to establish an American Empire. While this may have sparked debate between scholars of succeeding generations contemporaneously the American public whole heatedly embraced and vigorously prosecuted the war to a successful conclusion.

In a similar fashion, pundits of following generations have questioned the necessity of entering the First World War. Some have sighted the relative similarity between the antagonist's political and social systems as proof that American intervention was not as much to "Make the World

Safe for Democracy" as it was to protect the interests of America's Anglophile elite. However, there was no discernable protest or traceable anti-war movement when our government sent the doughboys "Over There."

For the purposes of this thumbnail sketch of American wars suffice it to say World War II united this country as never before as millions of men rushed to the recruiting stations vowing to "Remember Pearl Harbor!"

Although there was national criticism of **HOW** the United States government prosecuted the Korean War, there was never any question about **WHY** we had to fight. The national will to stop the spread of Totalitarian International Communism faced the initial impact and withstood the grinding reality of this first "limited" war of the twentieth century.

The various other "interventions" "police actions" and "incursions" which marked the hot phases of the Cold War from the Congo to the Cuban Missile crises all enjoyed the overwhelming support of the American people. Perhaps the fact that the majority of the electorate as well as the majority of those called upon to serve had experienced the worldwide crusade against Totalitarianism we know as World War II explains this support. Perhaps in this understanding and commitment to defend freedom against the second great wave of twentieth century Totalitarianism in the Cold War the "Greatest Generation" again proved how deserving they are of this honorific title.

Then the tide of American History crashed against the shoals of Vietnam. The Boomer Generation, fresh from a "Summer of Love"[380] and bristling as a result of a self-perceived techno-social generation gap refused to take their place alongside the proceeding generations who trusted their government, opposed its enemies, and "rallied round the flag." Every generation strives to find its voice. America has experienced a "Lost" generation, a "Swing" generation, and a "Beat" generation. Coincidence decided that Vietnam would collide with the "Hippie" generation. A sizable minority of this generation rejected the political leaders who sought to send them off to war. They and embraced a cadre of anti-leaders who sent them off to protest, burn draft cards, and riot. As the anti-war movement grew it gained supporters in the academic community, the social elite and in the media. Using their socially provided platforms they succeeded in convincing themselves that if they were not the majority they were the only ones who understood the war and who judged it correctly. So it was only in Vietnam that in the midst of war the American public tore itself apart in debate concerning the validity of the war itself.

Leading the Allies to victory in World War II brought America to the fore as the preeminent, almost hegemonic world power, the undisputed leader of the free world. However, at the end of this global battle instead of enjoying the fruits of a hard-won peace the Democracies of the West found themselves locked in a life-or-death struggle with the forces of International Communism. As the post-war years unfolded, and the Totalitarians systematically "liberated" Poland, Czechoslovakia, Hungary, Rumania, Bulgaria, Yugoslavia, Albania, China, North Korea the freedom loving people of the west watched in growing alarm as history seemed to be repeating itself.

Then when North Korea supported and urged on by the Soviets and the Chinese invaded South Korea the West found the resolve to resist. This resistance paid off and after years of war, the world returned to the same stalemate that had initially prompted the clash. Through the 1950s, the battle raged in Indochina as the French sought to re-impose their old empire and the Communists sought to expand their new empire. The United States as the western super-power, the storehouse of democracy supported the French. After the Geneva Conventions divided the former colony into its component parts, the U. S. supported the South Vietnamese, the Cambodians and the Laotians in their quest for freedom. Blowing hot and cold through the emerging nations of Africa to the steaming jungles of Latin America the Cold War raged around the world. Then Cuba fell to the Communists and America rededicated itself to stopping the advance of Communism.

Since the fall of Communism it may seem easy to pontificate on how the West made the mistake of seeing a monolithic International Communism when in fact the block split in many ways. Now it appears easy to see how unthinking overreactions and oversimplifications led to faulty assumptions. However, during the heat of battle none of the combatants ever enjoys the luxury of the 20/20 vision provided by the safety of years and the security of victory.

The misconceptions of both sides led to situations that proved deadly and dangerous. The West saw a monolithic threat banging its shoe on a table screaming, "We will bury you!" The Soviets saw an enemy that encircled them, that declared their system to be an aberration in human history and that began almost immediately to re-arm the Germans. The Chinese looked through age-old eyes of xenophobic self-interest and sought to replace the hegemony of the West in Asia with what they considered the natural order of things, a Chinese Hegemony.

Acting upon their individual beliefs and perceptions both sides made their calculations and pushed their agendas.

How does this understanding of various Cold War perspectives relate to the war in Vietnam? How did they lead to America's involvement in this the longest and most controversial of wars?

Some scholars advance the theory of an ever-deepening quagmire. Soviet and Chinese support for any revolution anywhere collided with American determination to maintain the status quo. America began by supporting the French. Then she stepped in when the French left and supported the

South Vietnamese until it became apparent that these clients could not successfully prosecute the war. Then the fear of dominos falling led to direct intervention until by the late 1960s America had embraced the tar-baby of a land war in Asia within the broader context of the Cold War.

The Kennedy administration, fresh from is "victory" in the Cuban missile crisis[381] believed if they remained resolute the Communists would eventually swerve out of the way as they escalated their way into an international game of "chicken" in Southeast Asia. In the yet unperceived twilight of Kennedy's life and government an ill-conceived coup deposed Diem and left South Vietnam in the clutches of a politically and militarily inept junta of generals.

The power of circumstance ushered in Lyndon Johnson as the unsophisticated successor to the glamour of "Camelot."[382] In many ways, he operated as a hostage to the enlightened advice of the elitist advisors bequeathed to him by President Kennedy. As the frequently shifting collage of generals and colonels who claimed the right to lead South Vietnam for fun and profit began to teeter towards defeat Johnson had little choice besides surrender or direct engagement. Abruptly a proxy war fought through client states in an obscure corner of the world became a maze of quick sand and mirrors for the United States. Without realizing the tremendous costs that would arise America, after a decade of growing involvement found itself fully engaged facing a resolute foe with a captive a population of millions that it had no compunction about sacrificing, a wily, battle-hardened army led by staunch Stalinist ideologues and supported by both poles of the Communist world.

President Johnson promised the nation "guns and butter."[383] Ever the master of American politics Johnson ran a re-election campaign, which portrayed him as the peace candidate. Following the example of his mentor President Truman, Johnson sought to fight a war without allowing it to interfere with his domestic agenda. In other words, he sought to fight a war without mobilizing the home front.

Then came the Tonkin Gulf Incident. Once the battle was joined Johnson, a veteran of World War II and a resolute Cold Warrior in his own right deferred to the advice of his cabinet and his commanders on the ground.

His elitist advisors smoothly assured Johnson that it was necessary to prove America's resolve to defend South Vietnam. They presented this as the only option, as the only way to show the Communists of North Vietnam that their campaign to conquer the South was doomed to failure. They urged the President to institute a plan consisting of bombing of the North in direct relation to their actions in the South and to a small but substantial American military presence on the ground in the South. They believed that this bombing in retaliation and a small number of American troops would convince the Communists that if they persisted in their infiltration and terrorism they would have to face the full weight of the United States.

At this point a major miscalculation occurred, a miscalculation that escalated into an all-out war. The Best and the Brightest never imagined that after the bloodbath of Korea the Communists would again risk a major military confrontation. Applying the lesson they had erroneously learned from the Cuban Missile Crises Johnson's advisors continued to assume that the Communists would swerve off the road to war as the America juggernaut showed its willingness to become an international train wreck.

This misguided strategy imposed flawed tactics from the beginning. It hamstrung our military to a reflexive campaign of reaction aimed at convincing a determined enemy to surrender their objectives instead of a proactive campaign aimed at victory. This tentative, graduated, seemingly haphazard engagement brought a response on the domestic front. When in 1965 the United States began its first massive bombing campaign, Rolling Thunder[384] antiwar protests first appeared in the cities and on campuses across the country.

President Johnson, ever the political operative, sought to diffuse the mounting wave of protest by announcing a huge government program designed to spur the economic development of Southeast Asia. Johnson meant the plan to show the protestors the dedication of the American government to peaceful development. To accomplish this, the plan included North Vietnam as a potential recipient of American Foreign Aid, "IF" they would stop their infiltration of the South. Johnson and his advisors felt they had scored a masterstroke as the protests began to taper-off. Then the Communists of North Vietnam stunned the American administration when they rejected the offer of aid and renewed their call for the re-unification of Vietnam by any means necessary. As the Viet Cong and their North Vietnamese allies stepped up the campaign of terror in South Vietnam, the United States faced with a direct challenge. Backed into a corner by his own actions, Johnson, following the advice of his cabinet committed more than 100,000 American troops to Vietnam within the next few months.

In fits and starts the Johnson administration moved one way and then another. First, they would expand bombing the North in retaliation for fresh terrorist action in the South. Then they would abruptly stop the bombing so they could lobby Congress for more money, or try to take the edge off domestic protests. It soon became apparent to all that there was no over-all strategy, no cohesive plan to win the war.

Then in 1966 General William Westmoreland emerged as the man with the plan, attrition. The same strategy he had learned while fighting in Korea. The same strategy General Ridgway had used to successfully force the North Koreans and Chinese to the bargaining table. The securing of territory became secondary to the "body count." The number of enemy casualties rose but the Communists skillfully used the coldly calculating brutality of the American strategy to their own benefit as nightly television pictures showed American brutality and shaped American opinion. In addition, as Americans counted body bags and called it pacification the Communists sought to win the hearts and minds of the people. Consequently, every time the Americans and the South Vietnamese allies would stage an incursion into the countryside the Communists would gain new allies and supporters as soon as the Americans would withdraw.

By 1967, Secretary of Defense Robert McNamara told the President that the policy of attrition would never bring the Communists to the bargaining table. However, Johnson still believed that if America unilaterally abandoned the battle it would be a disaster to the wider prosecution of the ongoing Cold War. In 1968 the surprise of the Tet Offensive brought waves of massive protest. Legions of news people began to switch from support for the government to support for the protestors. Moreover, Johnson saw his political life destroyed by McCarthy's "victory" in New Hampshire. This evoked a shocking announcement from the White House. The President decided not to run for re-election so that he could work full-time for peace. In the field, General Abrams replaced Westmoreland as America again looked for a strategy that would bring victory.

After his victory in the 1968 presidential election, Nixon inherited a war he had pledged to end. However, Nixon saw the world in terms of the vast geopolitical struggle between freedom and Totalitarian Communism, which had dominated his political life. Based upon his experience and his assumptions it never entered his mind to withdraw unilaterally from the conflict. He believed that this would unnerve America's allies and embolden America's enemies. His speeches expressed the view that American resolution faced the test in Vietnam. Repeatedly he alluded to the belief that if

America's resolve collapsed in the face of naked aggression the system of alliances, which provided some measure of stability in the bi-polar world of the Cold War would teeter and possibly topple. His private papers and tapes make it abundantly clear that he wanted to end the war. However, he was not ready to abandon the South Vietnamese. He was not willing to sacrifice the honor of America.[385]

Under President Nixon and his trusted advisor Henry Kissinger in some ways America's goal in Vietnam changed substantially from fighting Communist aggression to the demonstration of American resolve, the proof of America's reliability as an ally. In this, the two American leaders had their eyes on a much larger goal. They wanted to exploit the rift between the Soviet Communists and the Chinese Communists. They wanted to change fundamentally the thrust of the Cold War from a strictly bipolar contest wherein the United States carried the burden of countering every move by the Communists into one where they could play the China card. They wanted to change the rules and thereby change the game. To do this they felt they must show the Chinese that America could and would stop the Soviet drive for world domination, thereby opening the door for Sino-America rapprochement.

In the growing climate of revolt erupting from the Watergate scandal, a wounded and weakened presidency limped along trying to stay the course. However, the Democrat-controlled Congress, circling the political blood in the water, packed with anti-war, anti-establishment freshmen displayed no hesitation in following the well-entrenched leaders who had built careers out of opposing the war in Vietnam. On June 19 1973, the Congress of the United States passed the Case-Church Amendment.

This amendment specifically forbade any further involvement by the American military in Southeast Asia. It became effective on August 15, 1973. The amendment passed by 278-124 votes in the House of Representatives and by 64-26 votes in the Senate. Thus giving it enough support to over-ride a presidential veto. This amendment sent the signal to North Vietnam that it would soon be possible to launch a new invasion of the South in direct violation of their sworn agreement. They only needed to wait until American resolve fell short of even giving the South Vietnamese adequate supplies to defend themselves. The Communists now knew they could advance with virtual impunity. America had proudly announced that they would abandon their longtime ally to the aggressors having removed even the threat of direct American intervention.

Finally bleeding from a thousand, political cuts President Nixon resigned the presidency on August 9, 1974 as result of Watergate. Sworn in as the 38th U.S. President, Gerald R. Ford becomes the sixth American leader forced to cope with Vietnam. However, the presidency under the appointed Ford was far different than it had been under popularly elected leaders such as Kennedy, Johnson and Nixon. Ford limped along trying to stay the course. However, his administration was irrevocably hampered by the Congressional ban on intervention. Then in September of 1974 the now Imperial Congress took the next step in handing South Vietnam to the Totalitarian Communists of the North when they voted to appropriate only $700 million for South Vietnam. This constituted a direct refusal of Congress to continue the level of re-supply, which the American government had promised South Vietnam during the negotiations leading up to, the Paris Peace Accords. From this time on the Army of South Vietnam begins to lose its ability to respond to Communist aggression. This action by the American government and its results leads inexorably to a radical decline in South Vietnam's military preparedness, morale, and the national will to survive.

As previously described above, the emboldened

Communists soon launched a full-scale invasion. Encouraged by the abject surrender of the American Congress the Communists advanced as the forces of South Vietnam crumbled. Under supplied, with no hope of further material or even moral support many units simply dissolved into the population. Until finally On April 30, 1975, as the fog of morning and the fog of war rose from the bleeding carcass of Vietnam several North Vietnamese tanks crunched through the deserted streets of a once proud Saigon. Meeting no resistance they barley slowed as they thundered through the gates and into the compound of South Vietnam's presidential palace. Moments later soldiers representing the Totalitarian Communist regime of North Vietnam raise the Communist flag over what had once been the seat of a free South Vietnam and for good or ill the Vietnam War was over.

Finally, The Dominos Fell [386]

In March of 1975, the Pathet Lao[387] supported by strong North Vietnamese forces launched an all-out attack throughout the country. The Pathet Lao singled out the Hmong, longtime allies of the American and staunch defenders of the government of a free Laos as enemies who received no mercy.[388] Later the Pathet Lao would brag of destroying their tribal enemies who valiantly opposed their road to power for more than fifteen years. Under supplied and abandoned by their American allies the forces of a free Laos surrendered on August 23 and the Pathet Lao entered Vientiane and set up revolutionary committees to run the country. So the conquest of Laos by the forces of Totalitarian Communism, which had begun in the 1950s, which had been opposed by every American administration since Truman was completed.

On January 1, 1975, The Khmer Rouge[389] in Cambodia opened a nation-wide offensive targeted on capturing the Cambodian capital. The forces of a free Cambodia crumbled due to the lack of supplies and the hopelessness of their situation and the victorious Communist Khmer Rouge units entered Phnom Penh on April 17, 1975

The intervening years since the collapse of South Vietnam, there have been millions of people murdered as a result of the imposition of Totalitarian Communism on the countries of Indochina. These murders have flowed as the inevitable result of the failure of the American Congress to live up to the promises made in good faith to our allies. The prophetic voices of American leaders and the correctness of our attempt to stop the advance of Totalitarianism is shown in the brutal re-education camps of Vietnam, the "seminars" of the Pathet Lao, the exile of the Hmong,[390] and the killing fields of Cambodia. The absolute horror imposed upon these brave people by the nightmare of Totalitarian Communism stands as monument to the actions of our Congress.[391]

In the end, the American forces and their allies had won every major battle it fought against the North Vietnamese and the Viet Cong. They inflicted vastly disproportionate casualties on their Communist enemies. The allies forced the Totalitarians to the negotiation table and eventually forced them to sign the Paris Peace Accords. These Accords met America's war goals of a stop to Communist Infiltration and the recognition of South Vietnam, a "Peace with Honor."

However, ultimately the forces of freedom lost the peace because the Congress of the United States no longer supported the belief that Vietnam constituted a pivotal battle in the larger context of the Cold War. It had become for them instead a local matter, which no longer affected the vital interests of the United States

It is not the valiant men and women who fought so long, so hard, and so victoriously, who should bear the burden of this defeat. **They won their war.** They defeated a determined and resourceful enemy on the battlefield. They sacrificed their innocence, their youth, their health, and in all too many cases their lives to give the people of Indochina a chance at freedom.

No, the responsibility for snatching defeat from the jaws of victory lies directly with two groups. First at the feet of the leaders of the peace-at-any-cost faction of the Anti-war movement who worked so hard and so successfully to undermine America's resolve. Secondly, at the feet of the Congress of the United States who broke every promise five successive administrations had made. Leaders who exploited the turmoil of a selfish generation, the expediency of a presidential scandal, and the resulting temporary weakness of the executive branch to erase the victory won by America's valiant army.

Having recapped the progression of the war we must now turn to the central question of this work, "Who won the Vietnam War?"

To know who won we must know what the goals were. The author must admit since the conquest of South Vietnam marked the goal of North Vietnam, from its viewpoint it did "Win" the war, however, as previously established the goal of the United States was never to conquer North Vietnam. It was instead to stop the invasion of South Vietnam by its aggressive Communist neighbor and to win for the people of South Vietnam the right to determine their own future free of military intimidation. The following excerpts from a speech by President Johnson aptly express these goals:

Excerpts from Speech Given by President Johnson at Johns Hopkins University, April 7,1965.

We are also there because there are great

> *stakes in the balance.* **Let no one think for a moment that retreat from Viet-Nam** (sic.) **would bring an end to conflict. The battle would be renewed in one country and then another. The central lesson of our time is that the appetite of aggression is never satisfied. To withdraw from one battlefield means only to prepare for the next** (emphasis added). We must say in Southeast Asia as we did in Europe in the words of the Bible: "Hitherto shalt thou come, but no further."...
>
> **Our objective is the independence of South Viet-Nam** (sic.)**, and its freedom from attack** (emphasis added). We want nothing for ourselves only that the people of South Viet-Nam (sic.) be allowed to guide their own country in their own way. We will do everything necessary to reach that objective. And we will do only what is absolutely necessary.[392]

The Paris Peace Accords accomplished these goals. The following excerpts from an address by President Nixon also make it abundantly clear that in the understanding of the American government the clearly defined objectives and goals for which America had fought found their fulfillment in these Accords. He began by saying, "we today have concluded an agreement to end the war and bring **peace with honor** (emphasis added) in Vietnam and in Southeast Asia."[393] He continued,

> Throughout the years of negotiations, we have insisted on peace with honor. In my addresses to the Nation from this room of

January 25 and May 8, [1972] **I set forth the goals that we considered essential for peace with honor.** (emphasis added)...

In the settlement that has now been agreed to, **all the conditions that I laid down then have been met** (emphasis added). ...

The people of South Vietnam have been guaranteed the right to determine their own future, without outside interference. (emphasis added)...

This settlement meets the goals (emphasis added) and has the full support of President Thieu and the Government of the Republic of Vietnam, as well as that of our other allies who are affected.

The United States will continue to recognize the Government of the Republic of Vietnam as the sole legitimate government of South Vietnam.

We shall continue to aid South Vietnam within the terms of the agreement and we shall support efforts by the people of South Vietnam to settle their problems peacefully among themselves.

We must recognize that ending the war is only the first step toward building the peace. All parties must now see to it that this is a peace that lasts, and also a peace that heals, and a peace that not only ends the war in Southeast Asia, but contributes to the prospects of peace in the whole world.

This will mean that the terms of the agreement must be scrupulously adhered to. We shall do everything the agreement

> requires of us and we shall expect the other parties to do everything it requires of them. We shall also expect other interested nations to help insure that the agreement is carried out and peace is maintained.[394]

That the President expected this to be a lasting agreement that ensured the continuance of South Vietnam as a free and independent nation is affirmed by his statement,

> First, to the people and Government of South Vietnam: By your courage, by your sacrifice, you have won the precious right to determine your own future and you have developed the strength to defend that right. **We look forward to working with you in the future, friends in peace as we have been allies in war** (emphasis added).[395]

To the Communist leaders of North Vietnam he said,

> To the leaders of North Vietnam: As we have ended the war through negotiations, let us now build a peace of reconciliation. For our part; we are prepared to make a major effort to help achieve that goal. But just as reciprocity was needed to end the war, so, too, will it be needed to build and strengthen the peace.[396]

To the leaders of International Communism he said,

> To the other major powers that have been involved even indirectly: Now is the time for mutual restraint so that the peace we have

> achieved can last.[397]

To the American people he directly claimed to have fulfilled the goals of a peace with honor when he said,

> **The important thing was not to talk about peace, but to get peace and to get the right kind of peace. This we have done** (emphasis added).
>
> **Now that we have achieved an honorable agreement** (emphasis added), let us be proud that America did not settle for a peace that would have betrayed our allies, that would have abandoned our prisoners of war, or that would have ended the war for us but would have continued the war for the 50 million people of Indochina. Let us be proud of the 2 1/2 million young Americans who served in Vietnam, who served with honor and distinction in one of the most selfless enterprises in the history of nations. And let us be proud of those who sacrificed, who gave their lives so that the people of South Vietnam might live in freedom and so that the world might live in peace.[398]

To the wives and families of the prisoners of war and MIAs he said,

> In particular, I would like to say a word to some of the bravest people I have ever met-the wives, the children, the families of our prisoners of war and the missing in action. When others called on us to settle on any terms, you had the courage to stand for **the**

> **right kind of peace** (emphasis added) so that those who died and those who suffered would not have died and suffered in vain, and so that, where this generation knew war, the next generation would know peace. Nothing means more to me at this moment than the fact that your long vigil is coming to an end.[399]

Highlighting the fact that he believed this would be a peace that would serve the nation well, a lasting peace he said,

> And I know he would join me in asking for those who died and for those who live, **let us consecrate this moment by resolving together to make the peace we have achieved a peace that will last** (emphasis added).[400]

In the final analysis, it takes people of honor to maintain a "Peace with Honor." The duplicity of the Congress of the United States combined with the treachery of the North Vietnamese Communists repudiated the promises, ignored the guarantees, and besmirched the honor of these hard won accords.

It is upon the faulty foundations of delusion that the Left has successfully sought to make the vision of ignominious defeat into America's shroud of shame.

First, this delusion builds upon the absolute necessity of forcing the Vietnam War out of its proper Cold War context. Once this was accomplished it was no longer a battle in a larger war it became instead a singular event, which it never was. Secondly, keep people ignorant of the fact that American forces withdrew in 1973, not in retreat or defeat but in accordance with a negotiated agreement, which left South Vietnam free and intact. Thirdly, the media and academia ignore the reality that for **two years** North Vietnam appeared to abide by the Accords and South Vietnam continued to exist **AFTER** American forces left thus fulfilling the stated American goals. Finally, the gatekeepers of American society take every opportunity to show the pitiful pictures of people hanging to the undercarriages of helicopters fleeing from the victoriously advancing Communists to build the impression of an American defeat and rout. In addition, it must never be admitted that these are scenes of the evacuation of our embassy staff and Vietnamese supporters **NOT** of our army.[401]

Furthermore, I am well aware that the perceptions presented and the explicit teachings promoted in the media and in academia have successfully shaped the beliefs of generations of Americans. If this were not the case, there would be no need for this book. Repeatedly in words and pictures the drumbeat goes on, "America lost the Vietnam War."

Today many Americans have accepted the established interpretation of events and believe them to be "**THE**" truth, based solidly upon "**THE**" facts. To question this is to question what has become, "Common Knowledge." Today many American leaders, such as politicians, journalists, and historians have built lives and careers on interpreting those events.

For these leaders to continue in their self-declared superiority of "correctness" there is an absolute necessity for the general acceptance by American society of this "dishonorable defeat." To them, this present work represents the basest form of historical heresy, "revisionism." The broad-brush of guilt by association may well appear. This may surface in an attempt to explain away this work by lumping it in with Historians from the past that sought to "revise" history. Referring to it as "an attempt to promote the 'stabin-the-back theory' to explain away the loss of Vietnam" will be the hallmark of this attempt. The author understands that in presenting an alternative to the "accepted" anti-imperial history of America's defining defeat he opens the door to polemics. Polemics aimed at disproving the conclusions drawn by denying the validity of the facts, which form the basis for those conclusions. Polemics aimed at the destruction of the author's credibility as an Historian.

In this work I am directly advancing the premise that **America won the Vietnam War** juxtaposed to the accepted belief that in this mighty battle of the Cold War the United States met with a devastating military defeat. I do not propose some grand conspiracy of the mind (either covert or overt) either in the design, the presentation, or the perpetuation of this delusion of defeat. Instead, I propose a particularly personal conspiracy of the emotions. Those who opposed the war, so many of whom are now the arbiters of the academic establishment, of the government and of the media invested their youth and built their careers on the idea that "they were right!" As I recall the vehemence, the utter passion with which aging protestors and draft card burners who are now professors, politicians and capitalists react when confronted with the statement **"America won the Vietnam War"** this emotional investment becomes clear. The very idea that instead of heroic warriors for peace they may have been dupes for a murderous regime of Stalinist Communists bent upon imposing a Totalitarian nightmare of death and slavery on millions through conquest would shatter their self-image.

Is there any doubt in anyone's mind that if the Congress of the United States had withdrawn of all troops from South Korea in 1954, voted that no matter what happened America would not re-engage, and then voted to cut off even the resupply of material to the South Korean army that today we would see the cruel reality of a Democratic People's

Republic of Korea stretching from China to Pusan? Is there any doubt that if Congress took these actions today, South Korea would be in imminent danger from the Totalitarian Communists of North Korea tomorrow?

Looking back upon the Vietnam War, we must realize that even we who lived through it now look back through more than thirty years of reflection and opinion. I realize that common knowledge often consists of whatever we may learn before we are mature. I also realize that many have come to maturity believing the leftist mantra of America's defeat. A mantra used for many years in the effort to create a malaise ridden American giant hobbled by doubt, a paper tiger unable to bear the responsibilities of a great power. However, it is my hope that after looking at the case free from the society-wide spin of the leftist information filters the reader will reject the oft-repeated myth, the delusion of defeat and realize that:

AMERICA WON

THE VIETNAM WAR!

---

380 http://www.sftoday.com/enn2/sumdex.htm (11-15-03). Informational.

381 http://www.cuba-junky.com/cuba/missile-crisis.html (11-15-03).

382 http://more.abcnews.go.com/sections/us/camelot/ (11-18-03). Informational.

383 http://johnshadegg.house.gov/index.cfm?fuseaction=News.DisplayArticle&Article_id=15 (12-5-03).

384 http://www.multied.com/vietnam/RollingThunder.html (11-26-03).

385 Kissinger, Henry. Ending the Vietnam War: A History of America's Involvement in and Extrication from the Vietnam War , (Forward) as excerpted on http://www.washingtonpost.com/wp-srv/style/longterm/books/chap1/endingthevietnamwar.htm

(10-13-03).

[386] http://www.nixoncenter.org/publications/articles/4_28_00Vietnam.htm (11-17-03) Informational.

[387] http://www.bartleby.com/65/pa/PathetLa.html (11-15-03). Informational.

[388] http://www.hmongnet.org/hmong-au/refugee.htm (11-26-03).

[389] http://www.encyclopedia.com/html/k/khmerr1ou.asp (11-15-03). Informational.

[390] http://www.hmongnet.org (11-15-03). Informational.

[391] Sorley, Lewis. A Better War. Harcourt Brace & Co. :New York, 1999, p.383.

[392] Public Papers of the Presidents of the United States: Lyndon B. Johnson, 1965, pp. 394-397.

[393] For the full text of President Nixon's "Peace With Honor": Radio-television broadcast, dealing with the initialing of the Vietnam Agreement January 23 1973, see Appendix.

[394] Ibid.

[395] Ibid.

[396] Ibid.

[397] Ibid.

[398] Ibid.

[399] Ibid.

[400]Ibid.

[401] Herrington, pp. 175-187, passim.

Appendix

Index of Documents

August 1, 1941

7. Winston Churchill's "Iron Curtain" Speech March 5, 1946

8. Truman Doctrine March 12, 1947

9. Indochina - Additional United States Aid for France and Indochina: Joint Franco-American Communiqué, September 30, 1953

10. The Final Declaration of the Geneva Conference: On Restoring Peace in Indochina, July 21, 1954

11. The American Response to the Geneva Declarations, July 21, 1954

12. Presidential Press Conference April 7, 1954

13. Eisenhower's Letter of Support to Ngo Dinh Diem, October 23, 1954.

14. Memorandum of Conference on January 19, 1961 between President Eisenhower and President-elect Kennedy on the Subject of Laos December 29, 1960/ Prepared by Clark Clifford

15. Kennedy Presidential News Conference March 24, 1961

16. Excerpts from Rusk-McNamara Report to Kennedy, November 11, 1961

17. President Kennedy's News Conference, March 6, 1963

18. President Kennedy's NBC Interview, September 9, 1963

19. Excerpts from McGeorge Bundy's Memo to President Johnson, February 7, 1965

20. Excerpts from Speech Given by President Johnson at Johns Hopkins University, April 7,1965

21. President Nixon's Report On Vietnam May 14, 1969

22. Nixon's 'Silent Majority' Speech November 3, 1969

23. **President Nixon: Cambodian Invasion** May, 1970

24. Paris Peace Accords

25. President Nixon's "Peace With Honor": Radio-television broadcast, 23 January 1973

Yosuke Matsuoka Japan's Foreign Minister's Address At Opening Of Thai-French Indo-China Border Dispute, Mediation Conference

Tokyo, February 7, 1941

YOUR ROYAL HIGHNESS, EXCELLENCIES, AND GENTLEMEN:

I wish first of all to welcome you most heartily, and express my most sincere appreciation of the trouble you have taken in coming such a long way to attend this conference.

It is my firm belief that the establishment of **a sphere of common prosperity throughout Greater East Asia** (emphasis added) is not only Japan's policy, but indeed a historical necessity in the event of world history. And those countries which exist in that sphere can contribute to the peace of Asia as well as to that of the world by their procuring each its own place and enjoying common prosperity amongst them. For that purpose I need hardly say that it is of vital importance that there should be security and stability in this part of East Asia. Therefore, when there arose a dispute concerning the boundary between Thailand and French Indo-China last year, I sincerely wished that the dispute would be amicably settled. Unfortunately, however, hostilities began between the two countries. The Japanese Government considered that it would be undesirable in the interests of the whole East Asia if this state of affairs were allowed to last long, and therefore **we have decided to mediate** (emphasis added) between the two countries.

Now that we have entered upon the task of mediation, it will readily be appreciated that the Japanese Government are prepared to endeavor to bring about the settlement of the dispute with determination and responsibility.

It was most fortunate that the Conference for the Cessation of Hostilities held at Saigon so speedily came to satisfactory end. I wish from the bottom of my heart that both the French and Thai Delegates would show at this Tokyo Conference for the Dispute such a perfect understanding and earnest spirit of cooperation as were manifested by them at the Saigon Conference for the Cessation of Hostilities, so that the dispute may be speedily settled and friendly relations restored between the two countries, thus making an invaluable contribution towards the peace and stability of Greater East Asia[402].

Mediation Terms Of The Thai-French Indo-China Border Dispute

March 11, 1941

1. France cedes to Thailand the district of Paklay, which is mentioned in Article II of the Convention between France and Siam of February 13, 1904, and the region lying to the north of the boundary line between the Province of Battambang and Pursat and the region lying on the right bank of the Mekong River bounded on south by the line running northward along the Longitude from the point touching Grand Lac and the southernmost end of the boundary line between the Provinces of Siem Reap and Battambang to the crossing point of that Longitude and the line of the 15th degree G of the Latitude and then eastward along that line of the Latitude of the Mekong River. However, a small area lying opposite to Stung Treng is reserved

to French Indo-China.

2. All of the above-mentioned ceded territories are to be made demilitarized zones, and French nationals and the people of French Indo-China are to enjoy an absolutely equal treatment with nationals of Thailand through these areas with respect to entry, domicile and occupations and their pursuit.

3. The Government of Thailand will respect the mausolea of the Luang Prabang Royal House situated in the triangular zone lying opposite to Luang Prabang, and afford facilities for its preservation and worship, etc.

4. The Mekong frontier will be fixed in accordance with the principle of the deep-water channel, but the two islands, namely Khong and Khone, will, under the sovereignty of Thailand, be jointly administered by France and Thailand, and the existing French establishments on the islands shall belong to France.

In signing the above-mentioned terms of mediation, letters were exchanged between France and Japan and between Japan and Thailand which have clarified to the effect **that Japan guarantees** (emphasis added) the definitive nature of the settlement of the dispute by the aforementioned terms of mediation and that agreements will subsequently be made with respect to the maintenance of peace in Greater East Asia and the establishment and promotion of the specially closer relations between Japan and Thailand and between Japan and French Indo-China[403].

Exchange Of Letters Between The French Ambassador, Charles Arsène-Henry And Yosuke Matsuoka, Japanese Foreign Minister

To Charles Arsène-Henry, French Ambassador to Japan

Tokyo, March 11, 1941
YOUR EXCELLENCY,

I have the honor to state that the Japanese Government, in view of the greatest importance which they attach to the maintenance of peace in Greater East Asia, have been watching with concern the development of the dispute to which French Indo-China, whose special relations with Japan have grown still closer as a result of the agreement of the 30th August, 1940, is a party against Thailand.

The Japanese Government, from the standpoint of the maintenance of peace in Greater East Asia and recalling the peaceful and friendly spirit which prompted the conclusion of the aforementioned agreement between Japan and France, have offered their mediation to the Governments of France and Thailand with a view to bringing to an end the dispute between French Indo-China and

Thailand. They, therefore, propose to the Government of France their plan of mediation which is presented on separate sheet with confidence that it will be unconditionally accepted by the latter Government. The **Japanese Government are prepared**, (emphasis added) upon its acceptance by the French Government, **to guarantee to the Government of France** (emphasis added) that the settlement of the said dispute through the mediation plan submitted by them will be definitive and irrevocable.

The Japanese Government, on the other hand, entertain no doubt that the Government of France, on their part, will endeavor for the maintenance of peace in Greater East Asia and especially for the establishment of good neighborly and amicable relations between Japan and French Indo-China, as well as for the promotion of closer economic relations between Japan and French Indo-China, and that **they will declare to the Japanese Government that they will not enter into any agreement or understanding with a third Power or Powers regarding French Indo-China envisaging economic or military cooperation aimed either directly or indirectly against Japan** (emphasis added).

It is understood that the aforementioned guarantee by the Japanese Government and the declaration of the French Government shall by formal documents be confirmed simultaneously with the conclusion of a treaty for the settlement of the dispute between France and Thailand.

I avail myself of this opportunity to renew to Your Excellency the assurance of my highest consideration.

YOSUKE MATSUOKA

To Yosuke Matsuoka, Japanese Foreign Minister
Tokyo, March 11,

MONSIEUR LE MINISTRE,

By the letter under today's date, Your Excellency was good enough to inform me as follows: (See text of the foregoing letter)

I have the honor to acknowledge the receipt of the above letter and to inform Your Excellency that the Government of France are disposed, under the present situation, to accede to the instance of the Japanese Government, although they are not obliged to renounce the benefits of their treaties freely negotiated and concluded with the Government of Thailand, either from the standpoint of the local situation or from that of the fortunes of arms. The Government of France, being constantly solicitous of the maintenance of peace in Greater East Asia, have never taken initiative of such a nature as of disturbing that peace, but testify to their fidelity to the basic spirit which inspired the agreement of August 30, 1940, by accepting the Mediation Plan presented on separate sheet. **On the basis of that spirit and being**

desirous of avoiding all kinds of a conflict between Third Powers, the Government of France hereby declare that they have no intention of entering into any agreement or understanding with a third Power or Powers regarding French Indo-China envisaging political economic or military cooperation aimed either directly or indirectly against Japan (emphasis added). Moreover, it is expected by the Government of France that the Government of Japan will assure the strict observance of the agreement of the 30th of August, 1940, and the subsequent military arrangements.

I avail myself of this opportunity to renew to Your Excellency the assurance of my highest consideration.

CHARLES ARSÈNE-HENRY

Acting Secretary Of State Sumner Welles' Statement On Japanese-French Collaboration In Indochina

July 24, 1941

It will be recalled that in 1940 the Japanese Government gave expression on several occasions to its desire that conditions of disturbance should not spread to the region of the Pacific, with special references to the Netherlands East Indies and French Indochina. This desire was expressly concurred in by many other governments, including the Government of the United

States. In statements by this Government, it was made clear that any alteration in the existing status of such areas by other than peaceful processes could not but be prejudicial to the security and peace of the entire Pacific area and that this conclusion was based on a doctrine which has universal application.

On September 23, 1940, referring to the events then rapidly happening in the Indochina situation, the Secretary of State stated that it seemed obvious that the existing situation was being upset and that the changes were being achieved under duress. Present developments relating to Indochina provide clear indication that further changes are now being effected under duress.

The present unfortunate situation in which the French Government of Vichy and the French Government of Indochina find themselves is, of course, well known. It is only too clear that they are in no position to resist the pressure exercised upon them (emphasis added).

There is no doubt as to the attitude of the Government and people of the United States toward acts of aggression carried out by use or threat of armed force. That attitude has been made abundantly clear.

By the course which it has followed and is following in regard to Indochina, the Japanese Government is giving clear indication that it is determined to pursue an objective of expansion by force or threat of force.

There is not apparent to the Government

of the United States any valid ground upon which the Japanese Government would be warranted in occupying Indochina or establishing bases in that area as measures of self-defense.

There is not the slightest ground for belief on the part of even the most credulous that the Governments of the United States, of Great Britain, or of the Netherlands have any territorial ambitions in Indochina or have been planning any moves which could have been regarded as threats to Japan. This Government can, therefore, only conclude that the action of Japan is undertaken because of the estimated value to Japan of bases in that region primarily for purposes of further and more obvious movements of conquest in adjacent areas.

In the light of previous developments, steps such as are now being taken by the Government of Japan endanger the peaceful use by peaceful nations of the Pacific. They tend to jeopardize the procurement by the United States of essential materials such as tin and rubber which are necessary for the normal economy of this country and the consummation of our defense program. The purchase of tin, rubber, oil, or other raw materials in the Pacific area on equal terms with other nations requiring these materials has never been denied to Japan. The steps which the Japanese Government has taken also endanger the safety of other areas of the Pacific, including the Philippine Islands.

The Government and people of this

country fully realize that such developments bear directly upon the vital problem of our national security[404].

Agreement Between Japan And France Pledging Military Co-Operation In Defense Of Indo-China

Tokyo, July 29, 1941

Imperial Japanese Government and the Government of France,

Taking into consideration the present international situation, And recognizing as the result, that there exist reasons for Japan to consider that, in case the security of French Indo-China should be threatened, general tranquillity in East Asia and her own security would be exposed to danger,

And renewing at this opportunity the promise made by Japan, on the one hand, to respect the rights and interests of France in East Asia, especially the territorial integrity of French Indo-China and the French sovereignty over the whole of the Union of French Indo-China; and **the promise made by France, on the other hand, not to conclude with any third Power or Powers any agreement or understanding regarding Indo-China envisaging political, economic or military co-operation which is directly or indirectly aimed against Japan** (emphasis added).

Have agreed upon the following provisions:

(1)The two Governments mutually promise military co-operation for joint defence (sic.) of French Indo-China.

(2)Measures to be taken for such co-operation shall be the object of special arrangements.

(3) The above stipulations shall be valid only so long as the situation which has motivated their adoption exists[405].

This agreement to cooperate put the local resistance fighters such as the Viet Minh in the precarious position that their continued resistance against the western colonialist NOW became resistance against the new Japanese colonialists. Consequently, the truism which states, "the friend of my enemy becomes my enemy," dictated that the Viet Minh would fight the Japanese. So the opposing truism, "The enemy of our enemy becomes our friend" dictated that at least during World War II the Viet Minh become at least in theory the "friend" of the Allies.

Statement By Japanese Board Of Information On "Reinforcing Japanese Forces In Indo-China"

Tokyo, August 1, 1941

"Since the arrival of a Japanese army force in French Indo-China on September 23 of last year, the object of cutting off the Chiang Kai-shek regime from supply routes across the Indo-China-Yunnan border has been completely achieved. On the other hand, the strict discipline and high morale of the Japanese troops have impressed the local populace favourably (sic.), with the result that the Japancse-French Indo-China relations have continued to improve rapidly as is borne out by the conclusion, sometime ago, of an economic agreement between Japan and French Indo-China, by which the latter has definitely come to share the responsibility for **the co-prosperity sphere of East Asia** (emphasis added). The international situation, however, has recently undergone radical changes in such a way as to aggravate the situation in which French Indo-China is placed. The French colony has come to find itself in an embarrassing position as was Syria in the current European War. In view of this situation, additional Japanese forces have been dispatched to this part of the Asiatic continent in accordance with the provisions of the Protocol for Joint Defence (sic.) of French Indo-China, concluded between Japan and France on July 29, which stipulates that "the two Governments mutually promise military cooperation for joint defence (sic.) of French Indo-China." In this connection, the recent situation of French Indo-China, both internal and external, is surveyed below primarily from a military point of view.

The political situation in French Indo-China has for some time remained complicated and chaotic with Governor-General (sic.) Vice-Admiral Jean Decoux and the leading officials of the Hanoi Government favouring (sic.) cooperation with Japan under instructions from the Vichy Government; while in Southern French Indo-China, a group of de Gaullists has apparently been endeavouring (sic.) to defend its ground in league with certain financiers and Chinese residents, with the support of third Powers.

According to information now available, General Catroux, former Governor-General of French Indo-China, was appointed representative of the de Gaulle regime for the Near East and the Orient in general in January, 1941, and has since been manoeuvring (sic.) to disturb and obstruct the constructive policy now being followed by the authorities of French Indo-China under Governor-General Vice-Admiral Decoux. The activities of General Catroux rapidly extend from his headquarters at Cairo to India, the Netherlands East Indies, French Indo-China and the Oceanic islands. During the recent negotiations between Thailand and French Indo-China concerning the border dispute and also during the Japanese-French Indo-China economic negotiations, the de Gaullists' machinations are known to have stood considerably in the way of the progress of the said parleys.

Further, attempts have been made by the

Chungking regime of China in cooperation with a third Power to disturb peace and order in French Indo-China to such an extent that, if left alone, the safety of the French colony would have been seriously menaced and the maintenance of peace and order made extremely difficult.

Since the arrival of the Japanese troops in French Indo-China, the Chungking regime has made desperate efforts to counteract the influence from this direction. For instance, its 5th Army, which had been stationed in the vicinity of Kweiyang, started operations in the early part of July and was recently reported to be moving toward French Indo-China by way of Kunming in Yunnan Province, apparently in anticipation of advancing into the French territory as soon as an opportunity offers itself.

Meanwhile, political agitators affiliated with the Chungking faction of the Kuomintang have infiltrated into various parts of the French colony with the view of fanning anti-Japanese feelings among the Chinese population there, which total approximately 320,000. These agitators were enabled to carry on an increasingly widespread anti-Japanese movement in the southern districts of French Indo-China with the aid of the de Gaullist agents, although they found little room for their activities in the northern part of the colony garrisoned by Japanese troops. On July 7, the fourth anniversary of the outbreak of the China Affair, the entire Chinese community numbering some 60,000 of Cholon, four kilometres (sic.) west of Saigon, observed a holiday and participated in an anti-Japanese programme (sic.) including a popular meeting held in commemoration of the said anniversary.

Further, according to later information, there are indications of a significantly closer relationship being effected between Great Britain and the Chiang Kai-shek regime, while the charges of some form of cooperation between Great Britain, the United States, China and the Netherlands, which form what is known as a democratic front are being substantiated. Thus, **French Indo-China, which as a member of the East Asia co-prosperity bloc** (emphasis added), has vital economic relations with Japan, has now come to sense a direct danger from the Chungking regime, British Malaya, Burma and the Dutch East Indies, which now constitute a ring of hostile nations around the French colony, jeopardizing its self-preservation and defence (sic.).

In view of this situation, the recent reinforcement of the Japanese garrison in French Indo-China was no more than an action calculated to remove the menace mentioned above and strengthen the defence (sic.) of French Indo-China so as to forestall any possible disquieting situation. In accordance with the agreement for joint defence (sic.) between Japan and France, therefore, the Japanese forces began landing in the vicinity of Saigon in perfect order on July 29, and the newly-arrived troops are now braving the tropical heat and the malaria plague in mounting guard for the safety of this part of French colony[406]."

Winston Churchill's "Iron Curtain" Speech

March 5, 1946
Westminster College, Fulton, Missouri

I am glad to come to Westminster College this afternoon, and am complimented that you should give me a degree. The name "Westminster" is somehow familiar to me.

I seem to have heard of it before. Indeed, it was at Westminster that I received a very large part of my education in politics, dialectic, rhetoric, and one or two other things. In fact we have both been educated at the same, or similar, or, at any rate, kindred establishments.

It is also an honour (sic.), perhaps almost unique, for a private visitor to be introduced to an academic audience by the President of the United States. Amid his heavy burdens, duties, and responsibilities-unsought but not recoiled from-the President has travelled (sic.) a thousand miles to dignify and magnify our meeting here to-day and to give me an opportunity of addressing this kindred nation, as well as my own countrymen across the ocean, and perhaps some other countries too. The President has told you that it is his wish, as I am sure it is yours, that I should have full liberty to give my true and faithful counsel in these anxious and baffling times. I shall certainly avail myself of this freedom, and feel the more right to do so because any private ambitions I may have cherished in my younger days have been satisfied beyond my wildest dreams. Let me, however, make it clear that I have no official mission or status of any kind, and that I speak only for myself. There is nothing here but what you see.

I can therefore allow my mind, with the experience of a lifetime, to play over the problems which beset us on the morrow of our absolute victory in arms, and to try to make sure with what strength I have that what has been gained with so much sacrifice and suffering shall be preserved for the future glory and safety of mankind.

The United States stands at this time at the pinnacle of world power. It is a solemn moment for the American Democracy. For with primacy in power is also joined an awe inspiring accountability to the future. If you look around you, you must feel not only the sense of duty done but also you must feel anxiety lest you fall below the level of achievement. Opportunity is here now, clear and shining for both our countries. To reject it or ignore it or fritter it away will bring upon us all the long reproaches of the after-time. It is necessary that constancy of mind, persistency of purpose, and the grand simplicity of decision shall guide and rule the conduct of the English-speaking peoples in peace as they did in war. We must, and I believe we shall, prove ourselves equal to this severe requirement.

When American military men approach some serious situation they are wont to write at the head of their directive the words "over-all strategic concept." There is wisdom in this, as it leads to clarity of thought. What then is the over-all strategic concept which we should inscribe today? It is nothing less than the safety and welfare, the freedom and progress, of all the homes and families of all the men and women in all the lands. And here I speak particularly of the myriad cottage or apartment homes where the wage-earner strives amid the accidents and difficulties of life to guard his wife and children from privation and bring the family up in the fear of the Lord, or upon ethical conceptions which often play their potent part.

To give security to these countless homes, they must be shielded from the two giant marauders, war and tyranny. We all know the frightful disturbances in which the ordinary family is plunged when the curse of war swoops down upon the bread-winner and those for whom he works and contrives. The awful ruin of Europe, with all its vanished glories, and of large parts of Asia glares us in the eyes. When the designs of wicked men or the aggressive urge of mighty States dissolve over large areas the frame of civilised (sic.) society, humble folk are confronted with difficulties with which they cannot cope. For them all is distorted, all is broken, even ground to pulp.

When I stand here this quiet afternoon I shudder to visualise (sic.) what is actually happening to millions now and what is going to happen in this period when famine stalks the earth. None can compute what has been called "the unestimated (sic.) sum of human pain." Our supreme task and duty is to guard the homes of the common people from the horrors and miseries of another war. We are all agreed on that.

Our American military colleagues, after having proclaimed their "over-all strategic concept" and computed available resources, always proceed to the next step-namely, the method. Here again there is widespread agreement. A world organisation (sic.) has already been erected for the prime purpose of preventing war, UNO (United Nations Organization), the successor of the League of Nations, with the decisive addition of the United States and all that that means, is already at work. We must make sure that its work is fruitful, that it is a reality and not a sham, that it is a force for action, and not merely a frothing of words, that it is a true temple of peace in which the shields of many nations can someday be hung up, and not merely a cockpit in a Tower of Babel. Before we cast away the solid assurances of national armaments for self-preservation we must be certain that our temple is built, not upon shifting sands or quagmires, but upon the rock. Anyone can see with his eyes open that our path will be difficult and also long, but if we persevere together as we did in the two world wars-though not, alas, in the interval between them-I cannot doubt that we shall achieve our common purpose in the end.

I have, however, a definite and practical proposal to make for action. Courts and magistrates may be set up but they cannot function without sheriffs and constables. The United Nations Organisation (sic.) must immediately begin to be equipped with an international armed force. In such a matter we can only go step by step, but we must begin now. I propose that each of the Powers and States should be invited to delegate a certain number of air squadrons to the service of the world organisation (sic.). These squadrons would be trained and prepared in their own countries, but would move around in rotation from one country to another. They would wear the uniform of their own countries but with different badges. They would not be required to act against their own nation, but in other respects they would be directed by the world organisation (sic.). This might be started on a modest scale and would grow as confidence grew. I wished to see this done after the First World War, and I devoutly trust it may be done forthwith.

It would nevertheless be wrong and imprudent to entrust the secret knowledge or experience of the atomic bomb, which the United States, Great Britain, and Canada now share, to the world organisation (sic.), while it is still in its infancy. It would be criminal madness to cast it adrift in this still agitated and un-united (sic.) world. No one in any country has slept less well in their beds because this knowledge and the method and the raw materials to apply it, are at present largely retained in American hands. I do not believe we should all have slept so soundly had the positions been reversed and if some Communist or neo-Fascist State monopolised (sic.) for the time being these dread agencies. The fear of them alone might easily have been used to enforce totalitarian systems upon the free democratic world, with consequences appalling to human imagination. God has willed that this shall not be and we have at least a breathing space to set our house in order before this peril has to be encountered: and even then, if no effort is spared, we should still possess So formidable a superiority as to impose effective deterrents upon its employment, or threat of employment, by others. Ultimately, when the essential brotherhood of man is truly embodied and expressed in a world organisation (sic.) with all the necessary practical safeguards to make it effective, these powers would naturally be confided to that world organisation (sic.).

Now I come to the second danger of these two marauders which threatens the cottage, the home, and the ordinary people-namely, tyranny. We cannot be blind to the fact that the liberties enjoyed by individual citizens throughout the British Empire are not valid in a considerable number of countries, some of which are very powerful. In these States control is enforced upon the common people by various kinds of all-embracing police governments. The power of the State is exercised without restraint, either by dictators or by compact oligarchies operating through a privileged party and a political police. It is not our duty at this time when difficulties are so numerous to interfere forcibly in the internal affairs of countries which we have not conquered in war. But we must never cease to proclaim in fearless tones the great principles of freedom and the rights of man which are the joint inheritance of the English-speaking world and which through Magna Carta, the Bill of Rights, the Habeas Corpus, trial by jury, and the English common law find their most famous expression in the American Declaration of Independence.

All this means that the people of any country have the right, and should have the power by constitutional action, by free unfettered elections, with secret ballot, to choose or change the character or form of government under which they dwell; that freedom of speech and thought should reign; that courts of justice, independent of the executive, unbiased by any party, should administer laws which have received the broad assent of large majorities or are consecrated by time and custom. Here are the title deeds of freedom which should lie in every cottage home. Here is the message of the British and American peoples to mankind. Let us preach what we practise (sic.) - let us practise (sic.)

what we preach.

I have now stated the two great dangers which menace the homes of the people: War and Tyranny. I have not yet spoken of poverty and privation which are in many cases the prevailing anxiety. But if the dangers of war and tyranny are removed, there is no doubt that science and co-operation can bring in the next few years to the world, certainly in the next few decades newly taught in the sharpening school of war, an expansion of material well-being beyond anything that has yet occurred in human experience. Now, at this sad and breathless moment, we are plunged in the hunger and distress which are the aftermath of our stupendous struggle; but this will pass and may pass quickly, and there is no reason except human folly or sub-human crime which should deny to all the nations the inauguration and enjoyment of an age of plenty. I have often used words which I learned fifty years ago from a great Irish-American orator, a friend of mine, Mr. Bourke Cockran. "There is enough for all. The earth is a generous mother; she will provide in plentiful abundance food for all her children if they will but cultivate her soil in justice and in peace." So far I feel that we are in full agreement.

Now, while still pursuing the method of realising (sic.) our overall strategic concept, I come to the crux of what I have travelled (sic.) here to Say. Neither the sure prevention of war, nor the continuous rise of world organisation (sic.) will be gained without what I have called the fraternal association of the English-speaking peoples. This means a special relationship between the British Commonwealth and Empire and the United States. This is no time for generalities, and I will venture to be precise. Fraternal association requires not only the growing friendship and mutual understanding between our two vast but kindred Systems of society, but the continuance of the intimate relationship between our military advisers, leading to common study of potential dangers, the similarity of weapons and manuals of instructions, and to the interchange of officers and cadets at technical colleges. It should carry with it the continuance of the present facilities for mutual security by the joint use of all Naval and Air Force bases in the possession of either country all over the world. This would perhaps double the mobility of the American Navy and Air Force. It would greatly expand that of the British Empire Forces and it might well lead, if and as the world calms down, to important financial savings. Already we use together a large number of islands; more may well be entrusted to our joint care in the near future.

The United States has already a Permanent Defence (sic.) Agreement with the Do-minion of Canada, which is so devotedly attached to the British Commonwealth and Empire. This Agreement is more effective than many of those which have often been made under formal alliances. This principle should be extended to all British Commonwealths with full reciprocity. Thus, whatever happens, and thus only, shall we be secure ourselves and able to work together for the high and simple causes that are dear to us and bode no ill to any. Eventually there may come-I feel eventually there will come-the principle of common citizenship, but that we may be content to leave to destiny, whose outstretched arm many of us can already clearly see.

There is however an important question we must ask ourselves. Would a special relationship between the United States and the British Commonwealth be inconsistent with our over-riding loyalties to the World Organisation (sic.)? I reply that, on the contrary, it is probably the only means by which that organisation (sic.) will achieve its full stature and strength. There are already the special United States relations with Canada which I have just mentioned, and there are the special relations between the United States and the South American Republics. We British have our twenty years Treaty of Collaboration and Mutual Assistance with Soviet Russia. I agree with Mr. Bevin, the Foreign Secretary of Great Britain, that it might well be a fifty years Treaty so far as we are concerned. We aim at nothing but mutual assistance and collaboration. The British have an alliance with Portugal unbroken since 1384, and which produced fruitful results at critical moments in the late war. None of these clash with the general interest of a world agreement, or a world organisation (sic.); on the contrary they help it. "In my father's house are many mansions." Special associations between members of the United Nations which have no aggressive point against any other country, which harbour (sic.) no design incompatible with the Charter of the United Nations, far from being harmful, are beneficial and, as I believe, indispensable.

I spoke earlier of the Temple of Peace. Workmen from all countries must build that temple. If two of the workmen know each other particularly well and are old friends, if their families are inter-mingled, and if they have "faith in each other's purpose, hope in each other's future and charity towards each other's shortcomings"-to quote some good words I read here the other day-why cannot they work together at the common task as friends and partners? Why cannot they share their tools and thus increase each other's working powers? Indeed they must do so or else the temple may not be built, or, being built, it may collapse, and we shall all be proved again unteachable (sic.) and have to go and try to learn again for a third time in a school of war, incomparably more rigorous than that from which we have just been released. The dark ages may return, the Stone Age may return on the gleaming wings of science, and what might now shower immeasurable material blessings upon mankind, may even bring about its total destruction. Beware, I say; time may be short. Do not let us take the course of allowing events to drift along until it is too late. If there is to be a fraternal association of the kind I have described, with all the extra strength and security which both our countries can derive from it, let us make sure that that great fact is known to the world, and that it plays its part in steadying and stabilising (sic.) the foundations of peace. There is the path of wisdom. Prevention is better than cure.

A shadow has fallen upon the scenes so lately lighted by the Allied victory. Nobody knows what Soviet Russia and its Communist international organisation (sic.) intends to do in the immediate future, or what are the limits, if any, to their expansive and proselytising (sic.) tendencies. I have a strong admiration and regard for the valiant Russian people and for my wartime comrade, Marshal Stalin. There is deep sympathy and goodwill in Britain-and I doubt not here also-towards the peoples of all the Russias (sic.) and a resolve to persevere through many differences and rebuffs in establishing lasting friendships. We understand the Russian need to be secure on her western frontiers by the removal of all possibility of German aggression. We welcome Russia to her rightful place among the leading nations of the world. We welcome her flag upon the seas. Above all, we welcome constant, frequent and growing contacts between the Russian people and our own people on both sides of the Atlantic. It is my duty however, for I am sure you would wish me to state the facts as I see them to you, to place before you certain facts about the present position in Europe.

From Stettin in the Baltic to Trieste in the Adriatic, an iron curtain has descended across the Continent. (Emphasis added.) Behind that line lie all the capitals of the ancient states of Central and Eastern Europe. Warsaw, Berlin, Prague, Vienna, Budapest, Belgrade, Bucharest and Sofia, all these famous cities and the populations around them lie in what I must call the Soviet sphere, and all are subject in one form or another, not only to Soviet influence but to a very high and, in many cases, increasing measure of control from Moscow. Athens alone-Greece with its immortal glories-is free to decide its future at an election under British, American and French observation. The Russian-dominated Polish Government has been encouraged to make enormous and wrongful inroads upon Germany, and mass expulsions of millions of Germans on a scale grievous and undreamed-of are now taking place. The Communist parties, which were very small in all these Eastern States of Europe, have been raised to pre-eminence and power far beyond their numbers and are seeking everywhere to obtain totalitarian control. Police governments are prevailing in nearly every case, and so far, except in Czechoslovakia, there is no true democracy.

Turkey and Persia are both profoundly alarmed and disturbed at the claims which are being made upon them and at the pressure being exerted by the Moscow Government. An attempt is being made by the Russians in Berlin to build up a quasi-Communist party in their zone of Occupied Germany by showing special favours (sic.) to groups of left-wing German leaders. At the end of the fighting last June, the American and British Armies withdrew westwards, in accordance with an earlier agreement, to a depth at some points of 150 miles upon a front of nearly four hundred miles, in order to allow our Russian allies to occupy this vast expanse of territory which the Western Democracies had conquered.

If now the Soviet Government tries, by separate action, to build up a pro-Communist Germany in their areas, this will cause new serious difficulties in the British and American zones, and will give the defeated Germans the power of putting themselves up to auction between the Soviets and the Western Democracies. Whatever conclusions may be drawn from these facts-and facts they are-this is certainly not the Liberated Europe we fought to build up. Nor is it one which contains the essentials of permanent peace.

The safety of the world requires a new unity in Europe, from which no nation should be permanently outcast. It is from the quarrels of the strong parent races in Europe that the world wars we have witnessed, or which occurred in former times, have sprung. Twice in our own lifetime we have seen the United States, against their wishes and their traditions, against arguments, the force of which it is impossible not to comprehend, drawn by irresistible forces, into these wars in time to secure the victory of the good cause, but only after frightful slaughter and devastation had occurred. Twice the United States has had to send several millions of its young men across the Atlantic to find the war; but now war can find any nation, wherever it may dwell between dusk and dawn. Surely we should work with conscious purpose for a grand pacification of Europe, within the structure of the United Nations and in accordance with its Charter. That I feel is an open cause of policy of very great importance.

In front of the iron curtain which lies across Europe are other causes for anxiety. In Italy the Communist Party is seriously hampered by having to Support the Communist-trained Marshal Tito's claims to former Italian territory at the head of the Adriatic. Nevertheless the future of Italy hangs in the balance. Again one cannot imagine a regenerated Europe without a strong France. All my public life I have worked for a Strong France and I never lost faith in her destiny, even in the darkest hours. I will not lose faith now. However, in a great number of countries, far from the Russian frontiers and throughout the world, Communist fifth columns are established and work in complete unity and absolute obedience to the directions they receive from the Communist centre (sic.). Except in the British Commonwealth and in the United

States where Communism is in its infancy, the Communist parties or fifth columns constitute a growing challenge and peril to Christian civilisation (sic.). These are sombre (sic.) facts for anyone to have to recite on the morrow of a victory gained by so much splendid comradeship in arms and in the cause of freedom and democracy; but we should be most unwise not to face them squarely while time remains.

The outlook is also anxious in the Far East and especially in Manchuria. The Agreement which was made at Yalta, to which I was a party, was extremely favourable (sic.) to Soviet Russia, but it was made at a time when no one could say that the German war might not extend all through the summer and autumn of 1945 and when the Japanese war was expected to last for a further 18 months from the end of the German war. In this country you are all so well-informed about the Far East, and such devoted friends of China, that I do not need to expatiate on the situation there.

I have felt bound to portray the shadow which, alike in the west and in the east, falls upon the world. I was a high minister at the time of the Versailles Treaty and a close friend of Mr. Lloyd-George, who was the head of the British delegation at Versailles. I did not myself agree with many things that were done, but I have a very Strong impression in my mind of that situation, and I find it painful to contrast it with that which prevails now. In those days there were high hopes and unbounded confidence that the wars were over, and that the League of Nations would become all-powerful. I do not see or feel that same confidence or even the same hopes in the haggard world at the present time.

On the other hand I repulse the idea that a new war is inevitable; still more that it is imminent. It is because I am sure that our fortunes are still in our own hands and that we hold the power to save the future, that I feel the duty to speak out now that I have the occasion and the opportunity to do so. I do not believe that Soviet Russia desires war. What they desire is the fruits of war and the indefinite expansion of their power and doctrines. But what we have to consider here to-day while time remains, is the permanent prevention of war and the establishment of conditions of freedom and democracy as rapidly as possible in all countries. Our difficulties and dangers will not be removed by closing our eyes to them. They will not be removed by mere waiting to see what happens; nor will they be removed by a policy of appeasement. What is needed is a settlement, and the longer this is delayed, the more difficult it will be and the greater our dangers will become.

From what I have seen of our Russian friends and Allies during the war, I am convinced that there is nothing they admire so much as strength, and there is nothing for which they have less respect than for weakness, especially military weakness. For that reason the old doctrine of a balance of power is unsound. We cannot afford, if we can help it, to work on narrow margins, offering temptations to a trial of strength. If the Western Democracies stand together in strict adherence to the principles of the United Nations Charter, their influence for furthering those principles will be immense and no one is likely to molest them. If however they become divided or falter in their duty and if these all-important years are allowed to slip away then indeed catastrophe may overwhelm us all.

Last time I saw it all coming and cried aloud to my own fellow-countrymen and to the world, but no one paid any attention. Up till the year 1933 or even 1935, Germany might have been saved from the awful fate which has overtaken her and we might all have been spared the miseries Hitler let loose upon mankind. There never was a war in all history easier to prevent by timely action than the one which has just desolated such great areas of the globe. It could have been prevented in my belief without the firing of a single shot, and Germany might be powerful, prosperous and honoured (sic.) to-day; but no one would listen and one by one we were all sucked into the awful whirlpool. We surely must not let that happen again. This can only be achieved by reaching now, in 1946, a good understanding on all points with Russia under the general authority of the United Nations Organisation (sic.) and by the maintenance of that good understanding through many peaceful years, by the world instrument, supported by the whole strength of the English-speaking world and all its connections. There is the solution which I respectfully offer to you in this Address to which I have given the title "The Sinews of Peace."

Let no man underrate the abiding power of the British Empire and Commonwealth. Because you see the 46 millions in our island harassed about their food supply, of which they only grow one half, even in war-time, or because we have difficulty in restarting our industries and export trade after six years of passionate war effort, do not suppose that we shall not come through these dark years of privation as we have come through the glorious years of agony, or that half a century from now, you will not see 70 or 80 millions of Britons spread about the world and united in defence (sic.) of our traditions, our way of life, and of the world causes which you and we espouse. If the population of the English-speaking Commonwealths be added to that of the United States with all that such co-operation implies in the air, on the sea, all over the globe and in science and in industry, and in moral force, there will be no quivering, precarious balance of power to offer its temptation to ambition or adventure. On the contrary, there will be an overwhelming assurance of security. If we adhere faithfully to the Charter of the United Nations and walk forward in sedate and sober strength seeking no one's land or treasure, seeking to lay no arbitrary control upon the thoughts of men; if all British moral and material forces

> and convictions are joined with your own in fraternal association, the high-roads of the future will be clear, not only for us but for all, not only for our time, but for a century to come.[407]

Truman Doctrine

PRESIDENT HARRY S. TRUMAN'S ADDRESS BEFORE A JOINT SESSION OF CONGRESS, MARCH 12, 1947

Mr. President, Mr. Speaker, Members of the Congress of the United States:

The gravity of the situation which confronts the world today necessitates my appearance before a joint session of the Congress. The foreign policy and the national security of this country are involved.

One aspect of the present situation, which I wish to present to you at this time for your consideration and decision, concerns Greece and Turkey.

The United States has received from the Greek Government an urgent appeal for financial and economic assistance. Preliminary reports from the American Economic Mission now in Greece and reports from the American Ambassador in Greece corroborate the statement of the Greek Government that assistance is imperative if Greece is to survive as a free nation.

I do not believe that the American people and the Congress wish to turn a deaf ear to the appeal of the Greek Government.

Greece is not a rich country. Lack of sufficient natural resources has always forced the Greek people to work hard to make both ends meet. Since 1940, this industrious and peace loving country has suffered invasion, four years of cruel enemy occupation, and bitter internal strife.

When forces of liberation entered Greece they found that the retreating Germans had destroyed virtually all the railways, roads, port facilities, communications, and merchant marine. More than a thousand villages had been burned. Eighty-five per cent of the children were tubercular. Livestock, poultry, and draft animals had almost disappeared. Inflation had wiped out practically all savings.

As a result of these tragic conditions, a militant minority, exploiting human want and misery, was able to create political chaos which, until now, has made economic recovery impossible.

Greece is today without funds to finance the importation of those goods which are essential to bare subsistence. Under these circumstances the people of Greece cannot make progress in solving their problems of reconstruction. Greece is in desperate need of financial and economic assistance to enable it to resume purchases of food, clothing, fuel and seeds. These are indispensable for the subsistence of its people and are obtainable only from abroad. Greece must have help to import the goods necessary to restore internal order and security, so essential for economic and political recovery.

The Greek Government has also asked for the assistance of experienced American administrators, economists and technicians to insure that the financial and other aid given to Greece shall be used effectively in creating a stable and self-sustaining economy and in improving its public administration.

The very existence of the Greek state is today threatened by the terrorist activities of several thousand armed men, led by Communists, who defy the government's authority at a number of points, particularly along the northern boundaries. A Commission appointed by the United Nations security Council is at present investigating disturbed conditions in northern Greece and alleged border violations along the frontier between Greece on the one hand and Albania, Bulgaria, and Yugoslavia on the other.

Meanwhile, the Greek Government is unable to cope with the situation. The Greek army is small and poorly equipped. It needs supplies and equipment if it is to restore the authority of the government throughout Greek territory. Greece must have assistance if it is to become a self-supporting and self-respecting democracy.

The United States must supply that assistance. We have already extended to Greece certain types of relief and economic aid but these are inadequate.

There is no other country to which democratic Greece can turn.

No other nation is willing and able to provide the necessary support for a democratic Greek government.

The British Government, which has been helping Greece, can give no further financial or economic aid after March 31. Great Britain finds itself under the necessity of reducing or liquidating its commitments in several parts of the world, including Greece.

We have considered how the United Nations might assist in this crisis. But the situation is an urgent one requiring immediate action and the United Nations and its related organizations are not in a position to extend help of the kind that is required.

It is important to note that the Greek Government has asked for our aid in utilizing effectively the financial and other assistance we may give to Greece, and in improving its public administration. It is of the utmost importance that we supervise the use of any funds made available to Greece; in such a manner that each dollar spent will count toward making Greece self-supporting, and will help to build an economy in which a healthy democracy can flourish.

No government is perfect. One of the chief virtues of a democracy, however, is that its defects are always visible and under democratic processes can be pointed out and corrected. The Government of Greece is not perfect. Nevertheless it represents eighty-five per cent of the members of the Greek Parliament who were chosen in an election last year. Foreign observers, including 692 Americans, considered this election to be a fair expression of the views of the Greek people.

The Greek Government has been operating in an atmosphere of chaos and extremism. It has made mistakes. The extension of aid by this country does not mean that the United States condones everything that the Greek Government has done or will do. We have condemned in the past, and we condemn now, extremist measures of the right or the left. We have in the past advised tolerance, and we advise tolerance now.

Greece's neighbor, Turkey, also deserves our attention.

The future of Turkey as an independent and economically sound state is clearly no less important to the freedom-loving peoples of the world than the future of Greece. The circumstances in which Turkey finds itself today are considerably different from those of Greece. Turkey has been spared the disasters that have beset Greece. And during the war, the United States and Great Britain furnished Turkey with material aid.

Nevertheless, Turkey now needs our support.

Since the war Turkey has sought financial assistance from Great Britain and the United States for the purpose of effecting that modernization necessary for the maintenance of its national integrity.

That integrity is essential to the preservation of order in the Middle East.

The British government has informed us that, owing to its own difficulties can no longer extend financial or economic aid to Turkey.

As in the case of Greece, if Turkey is to have the assistance it needs, the United States must supply it. We are the only country able to provide that help.

I am fully aware of the broad implications involved if the United States extends assistance to Greece and Turkey, and I shall discuss these implications with you at this time.

One of the primary objectives of the foreign policy of the United States is the creation of conditions in which we and other nations will be able to work out a way of life free from coercion. This was a fundamental issue in the war with Germany and Japan. Our victory was won over countries which sought to impose their will, and their way of life, upon other nations.

To ensure the peaceful development of nations, free from coercion, the United States has taken a leading part in establishing the United Nations, The United Nations is designed to make possible lasting freedom and independence for all its members. We shall not realize our objectives, however, unless we are willing to help free peoples to maintain their free institutions and their national integrity against aggressive movements that seek to impose upon them totalitarian regimes. This is no more than a frank recognition that totalitarian regimes imposed on free peoples, by direct or indirect aggression, undermine the foundations of international peace and hence the security of the United States.

The peoples of a number of countries of the world have recently had totalitarian regimes forced upon them against their will. The Government of the United States has made frequent protests against coercion and intimidation, in violation of the Yalta Agreement, in Poland, Rumania, and Bulgaria. I must also state that in a number of other countries there have been similar developments.

At the present moment in world history nearly every

nation must choose between alternative ways of life. The choice is too often not a free one.

One way of life is based upon the will of the majority, and is distinguished by free institutions, representative government, free elections, guarantees of individual liberty, freedom of speech and religion, and freedom from political oppression.

The second way of life is based upon the will of a minority forcibly imposed upon the majority. It relies upon terror and oppression, a controlled press and radio; fixed elections, and the suppression of personal freedoms.

I believe that it must be the policy of the United States to support free peoples who are resisting attempted subjugation by armed minorities or by outside pressures.

I believe that we must assist free peoples to work out their own destinies in their own way.

I believe that our help should be primarily through economic and financial aid which is essential to economic stability and orderly political processes.

The world is not static, and the status quo is not sacred. But we cannot allow changes in the status quo in violation of the Charter of the United Nations by such methods as coercion, or by such subterfuges as political infiltration. In helping free and independent nations to maintain their freedom, the United States will be giving effect to the principles of the Charter of the United Nations.

It is necessary only to glance at a map to realize that the survival and integrity of the Greek nation are of grave importance in a much wider situation. If Greece should fall under the control of an armed minority, the effect upon its neighbor, Turkey, would be immediate and serious. Confusion and disorder might well spread throughout the entire Middle East.

Moreover, the disappearance of Greece as an independent state would have a profound effect upon those countries in Europe whose peoples are struggling against great difficulties to maintain their freedoms and their independence while they repair the damages of war.

It would be an unspeakable tragedy if these countries, which have struggled so long against overwhelming odds, should lose that victory for which they sacrificed so much. Collapse of free institutions and loss of independence would be disastrous not only for them but for the world. Discouragement and possibly failure would quickly be the lot of neighboring peoples striving to maintain their freedom and independence.

Should we fail to aid Greece and Turkey in this fateful hour, the effect will be far reaching to the West as well as to the East.

We must take immediate and resolute action.

I therefore ask the Congress to provide authority for assistance to Greece and Turkey in the amount of $400,000,000 for the period ending June 30, 1948. In requesting these funds, I have taken into consideration the maximum amount of relief assistance which would be furnished to Greece out of the $350,000,000 which I recently requested that the Congress authorize for the prevention of starvation and suffering in countries devastated by the war.

In addition to funds, I ask the Congress to authorize the detail of American civilian and military personnel to Greece and Turkey, at the request of those countries, to assist in the tasks of reconstruction, and for the purpose of supervising the use of such financial and material assistance as may be furnished. I recommend that authority also be provided for the instruction and training of selected Greek and Turkish personnel.

Finally, I ask that the Congress provide authority which will permit the speediest and most effective use, in terms of needed commodities, supplies, and equipment, of such funds as may be authorized.

If further funds, or further authority, should be needed for purposes indicated in this message, I shall not hesitate to bring the situation before the Congress. On this subject the Executive and Legislative branches of the Government must work together.

This is a serious course upon which we embark.

I would not recommend it except that the alternative is much more serious. The United States contributed $341,000,000,000 toward winning World War II. This is an investment in world freedom and world peace.

The assistance that I am recommending for Greece and Turkey amounts to little more than 1 tenth of 1 per cent of this investment. It is only common sense that we should safeguard this investment and make sure that it was not in vain.

The seeds of totalitarian regimes are nurtured by misery and want. They spread and grow in the evil soil of poverty and strife. They reach their full growth when the hope of a people for a better life has died. We must keep that hope alive.

The free peoples of the world look to us for support in maintaining their freedoms.

If we falter in our leadership, we may endanger the peace of the world — and we shall surely endanger the welfare of our own nation.

Great responsibilities have been placed upon us by the swift movement of events.

I am confident that the Congress will face these responsibilities squarely.[408]

Indochina - Additional United States Aid for France and Indochina: Joint Franco-American Communiqué, September 30, 1953

The forces of France and the Associated States in Indochina have for 8 years been engaged in a bitter struggle to prevent the engulfment of Southeast Asia by the forces of international communism. The heroic efforts and sacrifices of these French Union allies in assuring the liberty of the new and independent states of Cambodia, Laos and Vietnam has earned the admiration and support of the free world. In recognition of the French Union effort the United States Government has in the past furnished aid of various kinds to the Governments of France and the Associated States to assist in bringing the long struggle to an early and victorious conclusion.

The French Government is firmly resolved to carry out in full its declaration of July 3, 1953, by which is announced its intention of perfecting the independence of the three Associated States in Indochina, through negotiations with the Associated States.

The Governments of France and the United States have now agreed that, in support of plans of the French Government for the intensified prosecution of the war against the Viet Minh, the United States will make available to the French Government prior to December 31, 1954 additional financial resources not to exceed $385 million. This aid is in addition to funds already earmarked by the United States for aid to France and the Associated States.

The French Government is determined to make every effort to break up and destroy the regular enemy forces in Indochina.

Toward this end the government intends to carry through, in close cooperation with the Cambodian, Laotian, and Vietnamese Governments, the plans for increasing the Associated States forces while increasing temporarily French forces to levels considered necessary to assure the success of existing military plans. The additional United States aid is designed to help make it possible to achieve these objectives with maximum speed and effectiveness.

The increased French effort in Indochina will not entail any basic or permanent alteration of the French Government's plans and programs for its NATO forces. [409]

The Final Declaration of The Geneva Conference: On Restoring Peace in Indochina, July 21, 1954

Final declaration, dated July 21, 1954, of the Geneva Conference on the problem of restoring peace in Indochina, in which the representatives of Cambodia, the Democratic Republic of Viet-Nam (sic.), France, Laos, the People's Republic of China, the State of Viet-Nam (sic.), the Union of Soviet Socialist Republics, the United Kingdom and the United States of America took part.

1. The Conference takes note of the agreements ending hostilities in Cambodia, Laos, and Viet-Nam (sic.) and organizing international control and the supervision of the execution of the provisions of these agreements.

2. The Conference expresses satisfaction at the

ending of hostilities in Cambodia, Laos, and Viet-Nam (sic.). The Conference expresses its conviction that the execution of the provisions set out in the present declaration and in the agreements on the cessation of hostilities will permit Cambodia, Laos, and Viet-Nam henceforth to play their part, in full independence and sovereignty, in the peaceful community of nations.

3. The Conference takes note of the declarations made by the Governments of Cambodia and of Laos of their intention to adopt measures permitting all citizens to take their place in the national community, in particular by participating in the next general elections, which, in conformity with the constitution of each of these countries, shall take place in the course of the year 1955, by secret ballot and in conditions of respect for fundamental freedoms.

4. The Conference takes note of the clauses in the agreement on the cessation of hostilities in Viet-Nam (sic.) prohibiting the introduction into Viet Nam (sic.) of foreign troops and military personnel as well as of all kinds of arms and munitions. The Conference also takes note of the declarations made by the Governments of Cambodia and Laos of their resolution not to request foreign aid, whether in war material, in personnel, or in instructors except for the purpose of effective defense of their territory and, in the case of Laos, to the extent defined by the agreements on the cessation of hostilities in Laos.

5. The Conference takes note of the clauses in the agreement on the cessation of hostilities in Viet-Nam (sic.) to the effect that no military base at the disposition of a foreign state may be established in the regrouping zones of the two parties, the latter having the obligation to see that the zones allotted to them

shall not constitute part of any military alliance and shall not be utilized for the resumption of hostilities or in the service of an aggressive policy. The Conference also takes note of the declarations of the Governments of Cambodia and Laos to the effect that they will not join in any agreement with other states if this agreement includes the obligation to participate in a military alliance not in conformity with the principles of the charter of the United Nations or, in the case of Laos, with the principles of the agreement on the cessation of hostilities in Laos or, so long as their security is not threatened, the obligation to establish bases on Cambodian or Laotian territory for the military forces of foreign powers.

6. The Conference recognizes that the essential purpose of the agreement relating to Viet-Nam (sic.) is to settle military questions with a view to ending hostilities and that the military demarcation line should not in any way be interpreted as constituting a political or territorial boundary. The Conference expresses its conviction that the execution of the provisions set out in the present declaration and in the agreement on the cessation of hostilities creates the necessary basis for the achievement in the near future of a political settlement in Viet-Nam (sic.).

7. The Conference declares that, so far as Viet-Nam (sic.) is concerned, the settlement of political problems, effected on the basis of respect for the principles of independence, unity, and territorial integrity, shall permit the Vietnamese people to enjoy the fundamental freedoms, guaranteed by democratic institutions established as a result of free general elections by secret ballot.

In order to insure that sufficient progress in the restoration of peace has been made, and that all the necessary conditions obtain for free expression of the national will, general elections shall be held in July 1956, under the supervision of an international commission composed of representatives of the member states of the International Supervisory Commission referred to in the agreement on the cessation of hostilities. Consultations will be held on this subject between the competent representative authorities of the two zones from April 20, 1955, onwards.

8. The provisions of the agreements on the cessation of hostilities intended to insure the protection of individuals and of property must be most strictly applied and must, in particular, allow everyone in Viet-Nam (sic.) to decide freely in which zone he wishes to live.

9. The competent representative authorities of the northern and southern zones of Viet-Nam (sic.), as well as the authorities of Laos and Cambodia, must not permit any individual or collective reprisals against persons who have collaborated in any way with one of the parties during the war, or against members of such persons' families.

10. The Conference takes note of the declaration of the French Government to the effect that it is ready to withdraw its troops from the territory of Cambodia, Laos, and Viet-Nam (sic.), at the request of the governments concerned and within a period which shall be fixed by agreement between the parties except in the cases where, by agreement between the two parties, a certain number of French troops shall remain at specified points and for a specified time.

11. The Conference takes note of the declaration of the French Government to the effect that for the

settlement of all the problems connected with the reestablishment and consolidation of peace in Cambodia, Laos, and Viet-Nam (sic.), the French Government will proceed from the principle of respect for the independence and sovereignty, unity, and territorial integrity of Cambodia, Laos, and Viet-Nam (sic.).

12. In their relations with Cambodia, Laos, and Viet-Nam (sic.), each member of the Geneva Conference undertakes to respect the sovereignty, the independence, the unity, and the territorial integrity of the above-mentioned states, and to refrain from any interference in their internal affairs.

13. The members of the Conference agree to consult one another on any question which may be referred to them by the International Supervisory Commission, in order to study such measures as may prove necessary to insure that the agreements on the cessation of hostilities in Cambodia, Laos, and Viet-Nam (sic.) are respected.[410]

The American Response to the Geneva Declarations, July 21, 1954.

Declaration

The Government of the United States being resolved to devote its efforts to the strengthening of peace in accordance with the principles and purposes of the United Nations takes note of the agreements concluded at Geneva on July 20 and 21, 1954 between (a) the Franco-Laotian Command and the Command of the Peoples Army of

Viet-Nam (sic.); (b) the Royal Khmer Army Command and the Command of the People's Army of Viet-Nam (sic.); (c) Franco-Vietnamese Command and the Command of the People's Army of Viet-Nam (sic.) and of paragraphs 1 to 12 inclusive of the declaration presented to the Geneva Conference on July 21, 1954 declares with regard to the aforesaid agreements and paragraphs that (i) it will refrain from the threat or the use of force to disturb them, in accordance with Article 2(4) of the Charter of the United Nations dealing with the obligation of members to refrain in their international relations from the threat or use of force; and (ii) it would view any renewal of the aggression in violation of the aforesaid agreements with grave concern and as seriously threatening international peace and security.

In connection with the statement in the declaration concerning free elections in Viet-Nam (sic.) my Government wishes to make clear its position which it has expressed in a declaration made in Washington on June 29, 1954, as follows:

In the case of nations now divided against their will, we shall continue to seek to achieve unity through free elections supervised by the United Nations to insure that they are conducted fairly.

With respect to the statement made by the representative of the State of Viet-Nam (sic.), the United States reiterates its traditional position that peoples are entitled to determine their own future and that it will not join in an arrangement which would hinder this. Nothing in its declaration just made is intended to or does indicate any departure from this traditional position.

We share the hope that the agreements will permit Cambodia, Laos and Viet-Nam (sic.) to play their part, in full independence and sovereignty, in the peaceful community of nations, and will enable the peoples of that area to determine their own future.[411]

Presidential Press Conference April 7, 1954

Question by Robert Richards, Copley Press: Mr. President, would you mind commenting on the strategic importance of Indochina for the free world (emphasis added)? I think there has been, across the country, some lack of understanding on just what it means to us.

The President. You have, of course, both the specific and the general when you talk about such things. First of all, you have the specific value of a locality in its production of materials that the world needs.

Then you have the possibility that many human beings pass under a dictatorship that is inimical to the free world.

Finally, you have broader considerations that might follow what you would call the "falling domino" principle. You have a row of dominoes set up, you knock over the first one, and what will happen to

the last one is the certainty that it will go over very quickly. So you could have a beginning of a disintegration that would have the most profound influences (emphasis added).

Now, with respect to the first one, two of the items from this particular area that the world uses are tin and tungsten. They are very important. There are others, of course, the rubber plantations and so on.

Then with respect to more people passing under this domination, Asia, after all, has already lost some 450 million of its peoples to the Communist dictatorship, and we simply can't afford greater losses.

But **when we come to the possible sequence of events, the loss of Indochina, of Burma, of Thailand, of the Peninsula, and Indonesia following** (emphasis added), now you begin to talk about areas that not only multiply the disadvantages that you would suffer through the loss of materials, sources of materials, but now you are talking about millions and millions of people.

Finally, the geographical position achieved thereby does many things. It turns the so-called island defensive chain of Japan, Formosa, of the Philippines and to the southward; it moves in to threaten Australia and New Zealand.

It takes away, in its economic aspects, that region that Japan must have as a trading area or Japan, in turn, will have only one place in the world to go—that is, toward the Communist areas in order to live.

So, **the possible consequences of the loss are just incalculable to the free world** (emphasis added).

Q. Mr. President, what response has Secretary Dulles and the administration got to the request for united action in Indochina?

So far as I know, there are no positive reactions as yet, because the time element would almost forbid. The suggestions we have, have been communicated; and we will have communications on them in due course, I should say.

Q. Mr. President, do you agree with Senator Kennedy (emphasis added) that independence must be guaranteed the people of Indochina in order to justify an all-out effort there?

Well, I don't know, of course, exactly in what way a Senator was talking about this thing. I will say this: for many years, in talking to different countries, different governments, I have tried to insist on this principle: no outside country can come in and be really helpful unless it is doing something that the local people want.

Now, let me call your attention to this independence theory. Senator Lodge, on my instructions, stood up in the United Nations and offered one country independence if they would just simply pass a resolution saying they wanted it, or at least said, "I would work for it." They didn't accept it. So I can't say that the associated states want independence in the sense that the United States is independent. I do not know what they want.

I do say this: the aspirations of those people must be met, otherwise there is in the long run no final answer to the problem.

Q. Do you favor bringing this Indochina situation before the United Nations?

I really can't say. I wouldn't want to comment at too great a length at this moment, but I do believe this: this is the kind of thing that must not be handled by one nation trying to act alone. We must have a concert of opinion, and a concert of readiness to react in whatever way is necessary. Of course, the hope is always that it is peaceful conciliation and accommodation of these problems.[412]

Eisenhower's Letter of Support to Ngo Dinh Diem, October 23, 1954.

Dear Mr. President: I have been following with great interest the course of developments in Viet-Nam, (sic.) particularly since the conclusion of the conference at Geneva. The implications of the agreement concerning Viet-Nam (sic.) have caused grave concern regarding the future of a country temporarily divided by an artificial military grouping, weakened by a long and exhausting war and faced with enemies without and by their subversive collaborations within. Your recent requests for aid to assist in the formidable project of the movement of several hundred thousand loyal Vietnamese citizens away from areas which are passing under a de facto rule and political ideology which they abhor, are being fulfilled. I am glad that the United States is able to assist in this humanitarian effort. We have been exploring ways and means to permit our aid to Viet-Nam (sic.) to be more effective and to make a greater contribution to the welfare and stability of the government of Viet-Nam (sic.). I am, accordingly, instructing the American Ambassador to Viet-Nam (sic.) to examine with you in your capacity as Chief of Government, how an intelligent program of American aid given directly to your government can serve to assist Viet-Nam (sic.) in its present hour of trial, provided that your Government is prepared to give assurances as to the standards of performance it would be able to maintain in the event such aid were supplied. **The purpose of this offer is to assist the Government of Viet-Nam (sic.) in developing and maintaining a strong, viable state, capable of resisting attempted subversion or aggression through military means** (emphasis added). The Government of the United States expects that this aid will be met by performance on the part of the Government of Viet-Nam (sic.) in undertaking needed reforms. It hopes that such aid, combined with your own continuing efforts, will contribute effectively toward an independent Viet-Nam (sic.) endowed with a strong government. Such a government would, I hope, be so responsive to the nationalist aspirations of its people, so enlightened in purpose and effective in performance, that it will be respected both at home and abroad and discourage any who might wish to impose a foreign ideology on your free people.

Sincerely,
Dwight D. Eisenhower[413]

Memorandum of Conference on January 19, 1961 between President Eisenhower and President-elect Kennedy on the Subject of Laos December 29, 1960/ Prepared by Clark Clifford

The meeting was held in the Cabinet Room with the following men present: President Eisenhower, Secretary of State Christian Herter, Secretary of Defense Thomas Gates, Secretary of Treasury Robert Anderson, and General Wilton B. Persons.

With President-elect Kennedy were the new Secretary of State Dean Rusk, the new Secretary of Defense Robert McNamara, the new Secretary of Treasury Douglas Dillon, and Clark M. Clifford.

An agenda for the meeting had been prepared by Persons and Clifford. The subjects on the agenda had been recommended by the parties present at the conference and were arranged under the headings of "State," "Defense," and "Treasury." The first subject under the heading of "State" was Laos.

President Eisenhower opened the discussion

on Laos by stating that the United States was determined to preserve the independence of Laos. It was his opinion that if Laos should fall to the Communists, then it would be just a question of time until South Vietnam, Cambodia, Thailand and Burma would collapse. He felt that the Communists had designs on all of Southeast Asia, and that it would be a tragedy to permit Laos to fall.

President Eisenhower gave a brief review of the various moves and coups that had taken place in Laos involving the Pathet Lao, Souvanna Phouma, Boun Oum, and Kong Le. He said that the evidence was clear that Communist China and North Vietnam were determined to destroy the independence of Laos. He also added that the Russians were sending in substantial supplies in support of the Pathet Lao in an effort to overturn the government.

President Eisenhower said it would be fatal for us to permit Communists to insert themselves in the Laotian government. He recalled that our experience had clearly demonstrated that under such circumstances the Communists always ended up in control. He cited China as an illustration.

At this point, Secretary of State Herter intervened to state that if the present government of Laos were to apply to SEATO (Southeast Asia Treaty Organization, information added) for aid under the Pact, Herter was of the positive opinion that the signatories to the SEATO Pact were bound. President Eisenhower agreed with this and in his statement gave the impression that the request for aid had already come from the government of Laos. He corroborated the binding nature of the obligation of the United States under the SEATO Pact.

President Eisenhower stated that the British and the French did not want SEATO to intervene in Laos, and he indicated that they would probably continue to maintain that attitude. President Eisenhower said that if it were not appropriate for SEATO to intervene in Laos, that his next preference would be the International Control Commission. He was sure, however, that the Soviet Union did not want the ICC to go into Laos. President Eisenhower stated that if this country had a choice as to whether the task should be assumed by SEATO or the ICC, that he personally would prefer SEATO.

Secretary Herter stated that we possibly could work out some agreement with the British, if they could be persuaded to recognize the present government in Laos. The chances of accomplishing this, however, appeared to be remote.

Secretary Herter stated, with President Eisenhower's approval, that we should continue every effort to make a political settlement in Laos. He added, however, that if such efforts were fruitless, then the United States must intervene in concert with our allies. If we were unable to persuade our allies, then we must go it alone.

At this point, President Eisenhower said with considerable emotion that Laos was the key to the entire area of Southeast Asia. He said that if we permitted Laos to fall, then we would have to write off all the area. He stated that we must not permit a Communist take-over. He reiterated that we should make every effort to persuade member nations of SEATO or the ICC to accept the burden with us to defend the freedom of Laos.

As he concluded these remarks, President Eisenhower stated it was imperative that Laos be defended. He said that the United States should accept this task with our allies, if we could persuade them, and alone if we could not. He added that "our unilateral intervention would be our last desperate hope" in the event we were unable to prevail upon the other signatories to join us.

At one time it was hoped that perhaps some type of arrangement could be made with Kong Le. This had proved fruitless, however, and President Eisenhower said "he was a lost soul and wholly irretrievable."

Commenting upon President Eisenhower's statement that we would have to go to the support of Laos alone if we could not persuade others to proceed with us, President-elect Kennedy asked the question as to how long it would take to put an American division into Laos. Secretary Gates replied that it would take from twelve to seventeen days but that some of that time could be saved if American forces, then in the Pacific, could be utilized. Secretary Gates added that the American forces were in excellent shape and that modernization of the Army was making good progress.

President-elect Kennedy commented upon the seriousness of the situation in Laos and in Southeast Asia and asked if the situation seemed to be approaching a climax. General Eisenhower stated that the entire proceeding was extremely confused but that it was clear that this country was obligated to support the existing government in Laos.

The discussion of Laos led to some concluding general statements regarding Southeast Asia. It was agreed that Thailand was a valuable ally of the United States, and that one of the dangers of a Communist take-over in Laos would be to expose Thailand's borders. In this regard, it was suggested that the military training under French supervision in Thailand was very poor and that it would be a good idea to get American military instructors there as soon as possible so the level of military capability could be raised.

President Eisenhower said there was some

> indication that Russia was concerned over Communist pressures in Laos and in Southeast Asia emanating from China and North Vietnam. It was felt that this attitude could possibly lead to some difficulty between Russia and China.

This phase of the discussion was concluded by President Eisenhower in commenting philosophically upon the fact that the morale existing in the democratic forces in Laos appeared to be disappointing. He wondered aloud why, in interventions of this kind, we always seem to find that the morale of the Communist forces was better than that of the democratic forces. His explanation was that the Communist philosophy appeared to produce a sense of dedication on the part of its adherents, while there was not the same sense of dedication on the part of those supporting the free forces. He stated that the entire problem of morale was a serious one and would have to be taken into consideration as we became more deeply involved.[414]

Kennedy Presidential News Conference March 24, 1961

> The President's opening statement:
>
> "My fellow Americans, Laos is far away from America, but the world is small. Its 2,000,000 people live in a country three times the size of Austria in real neutrality. The security of all Southeast Asia will be endangered if Laos loses its neutral independence. Its own safety runs with the safety of us all observed by all.

"I want to make it clear to the American people and to all of the world that all we want in Laos is peace and not war, a truly neutral government and not a cold war pawn, a settlement concluded at the conference table and not on the battlefield."

Q. Mr. President, there appears to be some national unawareness of the importance of a free Laos to the security of the United States and to the individual American. Could you spell out your views on that a little further?"

A. Well, quite obviously geographically Laos borders on Thailand, which is, to which the United States has treaty obligations under the SEATO agreement of 1954, it borders on South Vietnam—it borders on Vietnam—to which the United States has very close ties, and also which is a signatory of the SEATO pact.

The aggression against Laos itself was referred to in the SEATO agreement, so that given this, the nature of the geography, its location the commitments which the United States and obligations which the United States has assumed towards Laos as well as the surrounding countries—as well as other signatories of the SEATO pact—it's quite obvious that if the Communists were able to move in and dominate this country, it would endanger the security of all, and the peace of all of Southeast Asia.

And as a member of the United Nations and as a signatory to the SEATO pact, and as a country which is concerned with the strength of the cause of freedom around the world, that quite obviously affects the security of the United States.[415]

Excerpts from Rusk-McNamara Report to Kennedy, November 11, 1961

1. United States National Interests in South Viet-Nam (sic.).

The deteriorating situation in South Viet-Nam (sic.) requires attention to the nature and scope of United States national interests in that country. The loss of South Viet-Nam (sic.) to Communism would involve the transfer of a nation of 20 million people from the free world to the Communism bloc. **The loss of South Viet-Nam (sic.) would make pointless any further discussion about the importance of Southeast Asia to the free world; we would have to face the near certainty that the remainder of Southeast Asia and Indonesia would move to a complete accommodation with Communism, if not formal incorporation with the Communist bloc** (emphasis added). The United States, as a member of SEATO, has commitments with respect to South Viet-Nam (sic.) under the Protocol to the SEATO Treaty. Additionally, in a formal statement at the conclusion session of the 1954 Geneva Conference, the United States representative stated that the United States "would view any renewal of the aggression . . . with grave concern and seriously threatening international peace and security."

The loss of South Viet-Nam (sic.) to Communism would not only destroy SEATO but would undermine the credibility of American commitments elsewhere. Further, loss of South Viet-Nam (sic.) would stimulate bitter domestic controversies in the United States and would be seized upon by extreme elements to divide the country and harass the Administration...

3. The United States' Objective in South Viet-Nam (sic.)

The United States should commit itself to the clear objective of preventing the fall of South Viet-Nam (sic.) *to Communist* (sic.). The basic means for accomplishing this objective must be to put the Government of South Viet-Nam (sic.) into a position to win its own war against the Guerrillas. We must insist that that Government itself take the measures necessary for that purpose in exchange for large-scale United States assistance in the military, economic and political fields. At the same time we must recognize that it will probably not be possible for the GVN to win this war as long as the flow of men and supplies from North Viet-Nam (sic.) continues unchecked and the guerrillas enjoy a safe sanctuary in neighboring territory.

We should be prepared to introduce United States combat forces if that should become necessary for success. Dependent upon the circumstances, it may also be necessary for United States forces to strike at the source of the aggression in North Viet-Nam (sic.).

4. The Use of United States Forces in South Viet-Nam (sic.).

The commitment of United States forces to South Viet-Nam (sic.) involves two different catgories (sic.): (A) Units of modest size required for the direct support of South Viet-Namese (sic.) military effort, such as communications, helicopter and other forms of airlift, reconnaissance aircraft, naval patrols, intelligence units, etc., and (B) larger organized units with actual or potential direct military mission. *Category (A) should be introduced as speedily as possible.* Category (B) units pose a more serious problem in that they are much more significant from the point of view of domestic and international political factors and greatly increase the probabilities of Communist bloc escalation. Further, the employment of United States combat forces (in the absence of Communist bloc escalation) involves a certain dilemma: if there is a strong South Viet Namese (sic.) effort, they may not be needed; if there is not such an effort, United States forces could not accomplish their mission in the midst of an apathetic or hostile population. Under present circumstances, therefore, the question of injecting United States and SEATO combat forces should in large part be considered as a contribution to the morale of the South Viet Namese (sic.) in their own effort to do the principal job themselves....

In the light of the foregoing, the Secretary of State and the Secretary of Defense recommend that:

1. We now take the decision to commit ourselves to the objective of preventing the fall of South Viet-Nam (sic.) to Communism and that, in doing so, we recognize that the introduction of United States and other SEATO forces may be necessary to achieve this objective. (However, if it is necessary to commit outside forces to achieve the foregoing objective, our decision to introduce United States forces should not be contingent upon unanimous SEATO agreement thereto.)

2. The Department of Defense be prepared with plans for the use of United States forces in South Viet Nam (sic.) under one or more of the following purposes:

(a) Use of a significant number of United States forces to signify United States determination to defend Viet-Nam (sic.) and to boost South Viet-Nam (sic.) morale.

(b) Use of substantial United States forces to assist in suppressing Viet Cong insurgency short of engaging in detailed counter-guerrilla operations but including relevant operations in North Viet-Nam (sic.).

(c) Use of United States forces to deal with the situation if there is organized Communist military intervention.

3. We immediately undertake the follow-

ing actions in support of the GVN:

> . . . **(d)** Provide the GVN with small craft, including such United States uniformed advisers and operating personnel as may be necessary for quick and effective operations in effecting surveillance and control over coastal waters and inland waterways....
>
> **(e)** Provide such personnel and equipment as may be necessary to prove the military-political intelligence system beginning at the provincial level and extending upward through the Government and the armed forces to the Central Intelligence Organization.
>
> **(f)** Provide such new terms of reference, reorganization and additional personnel for United States military forces as are required for increased United States participation in the direction and control of GVN military operations and to carry out the other increased responsibilities which accrue to MAAG under these recommendations....
>
> **(i)** Provide individual administrators and advisers for insertion into the Governmental machinery of South VietNam (sic.) in types and numbers to be agreed upon by the two Governments....[416]

President Kennedy's News Conference, March 6, 1963

Q: "Mr. President, the Mansfield committee,

sent at your suggestion to the Far East and Europe, has recommended a thorough security reassessment in the Far East and a clamp down, if not a reduction in our aid to that part of the world. Would you have any comment on this, sir?"

A: "I don't see how we are going to be able, unless we are going to pull out of Southeast Asia and turn it over to the Communists, how we are going to be able to reduce very much our economic programs and military programs in South Viet-Nam (sic.), in Cambodia, in Thailand.

"I think that unless you want to withdraw from the field and decide that it is in the national interest to permit that area to collapse, I would think that it would be impossible to substantially change it particularly, as we are in a very intensive struggle in those areas.

"So I think we ought to judge the economic burden it places upon us as opposed to having the Communists control all of Southeast Asia with the inevitable effect that this would have on the security of India and, therefore, really begin to run perhaps all the way toward the Middle East. So I think that while we would all like to lighten the burden, I don't see any real prospect of the burden being lightened for the U.S. in Southeast Asia in the next year if we are going to do the job and meet what I think are very clear national needs."[417]

President Kennedy's NBC Interview, September 9, 1963

Mr. Huntley: "Mr. President, in respect to our difficulties in South Viet-Nam (sic.), could it be that our Government tends occasionally to get locked into a policy or an attitude and then finds it difficult to alter or shift that policy?"

***THE PRESIDENT*:** "Yes, that is true. I think in the case of South Vietnam we have been dealing with a Government which is in control, has been in control for 10 years. In addition, we have felt for the last 2 years that the struggle against the Communists was going better. Since June, however—the difficulties with the Buddhists—we have been concerned about a deterioration, particularly in the Saigon area, which hasn't been felt greatly in the outlying areas but may spread. So we are faced with the problem of wanting to protect the area against the Communists. On the other hand, we have to deal with the Government there. That produces a kind of ambivalence in our efforts which exposes us to some criticism. We are using our influence to persuade the Government there to take those steps which will win back support. That takes some time, and we must be patient, we must persist."

Mr. Huntley: "Are we likely to reduce our

aid to South Viet-Nam (sic.) now?"

***THE PRESIDENT*:** "I don't think we think that would be helpful at this time. If you reduce your aid, it is possible you could have some effect upon the government structure there. On the other hand, you might have a situation which could bring about a collapse. Strongly in our mind is what happened in the case of China at the end of World War II, where China was lost—a weak government became increasingly unable to control events. We don't want that."

Mr. Brinkley: "Mr. President, have you had any reason to doubt this so-called 'domino theory,' (emphasis added) that if South Viet-Nam (sic.) falls, the rest of Southeast Asia will go behind it?"

***THE PRESIDENT*: "No, I believe it. I believe it** (emphasis added). I think that the struggle is close enough. China is so large, looms so high just beyond the frontiers, that if South Viet-Nam went, it would not only give them an improved geographic position for a guerrilla assault on Malaya but would also give the impression that the wave of the future in Southeast Asia was China and the Communists. **So I believe it** (emphasis added)."[418]

Excerpts from McGeorge Bundy's Memo to President Johnson,

February 7, 1965

I. Introductory
We believe that the best available way of increasing our chance of success in Vietnam is the development and execution of a policy of sustained reprisal against North Vietnam a policy in which air and naval action against the North is justified by and related to the whole Viet Cong campaign of violence and terror in the South.

While we believe that the risks of such a policy are acceptable, we emphasize that its costs are real. It implies significant U.S. air losses even if no full air war is joined, and it seems likely that it would eventually require an extensive and costly effort against the whole air defense system of North Vietnam. U.S. casualties would be higher and more visible to American feelings than those sustained in the struggle of South Vietnam.... And even if it fails to turn the tide as it may the value of the effort seems to us to exceed its costs....

3. Once a program of reprisals is clearly underway, it should not be necessary to connect each specific act against North Vietnam to a particular outrage in the South. It should be possible, for example, to publish weekly lists of outrages in the South and to have it clearly understood that these outrages are the cause of such action against the North as may be occurring in the current period. Such a more generalized pattern of reprisal would remove much of the difficulty involved in finding precisely matching targets in response to specific atrocities. Even in such a more general pattern, however, it would be important to insure that the general level of reprisal action remained in close correspondence with the level of outrages in the South. We must keep it clear at every stage both to Hanoi and to the world, that our reprisals will be reduced or stopped when outrages in the South are reduced or stopped and that **we are *not* attempting to destroy or conquer North Vietnam** (Emphasis added).

4. In the early stages of such a course, we should take the appropriate occasion to make clear our firm intent to undertake reprisals on any further acts, major or minor, that appear to us and the GVN as indicating Hanoi's support. We would announce that our two governments have been patient and fore-bearing (sic.) in the hope that Hanoi would come to its senses without the necessity of our having to take further action; but the outrages continue and now we must react against those who are responsible; we will not provoke; we will not use our force indis-criminately; but we can no longer sit by in the face of repeated acts of terror and violence for which the DRV is responsible.

9. We are convinced that the political values of reprisal require a *continuous* operation. Episodic responses geared on a one-for-one basis to "spectacu-lar" outrages would lack the persuasive force of sustained pressure. More important still, they would leave it open to the Communists to avoid reprisals entirely by giving up only a small element of their own program. The Gulf of Tonkin affair produced a sharp upturn in morale in South Vietnam. When it remained an isolated episode, however, there was a severe relapse. It is the great merit of the proposed scheme that to stop it the Communists would have to stop enough of their activity in the South to permit the probable success of a determined pacification effort....

We emphasize that our primary target in advocating a reprisal policy is the improvement of the situation in South Vietnam. Action against the North is usually urged as a means of affecting the will of Hanoi to direct and support the VC. We consider this an important but longer-range purpose. The immediate and critical targets are in the South in the minds of the South Vietnamese and in the minds of the Viet Cong cadres....

The Vietnamese increase in hope could well increase the readiness of Vietnamese factions themselves to join together in forming a more effective government...

We think it plausible that effective and sustained reprisals, even in a low key, would have a sustained depressing effect upon the morale of Viet Cong cadres in South Vietnam. This is the strong opinion of CIA Saigon. It is based upon reliable reports of the initial Viet Cong reaction to the Gulf of Tonkin episode, and also upon the solid general assessment that the determination of Hanoi and the apparent timidity of the mighty United States are both major items in Viet Cong confidence....

While emphasizing the importance of reprisals in the South, we do not exclude the impact on Hanoi. We believe, indeed, that it is of great importance that the level of reprisal be adjusted rapidly and visibly to both upward and downward shifts in the level of

Viet Cong offenses. We want to keep before Hanoi the carrot of our desisting as well as the stick of continued pressure. We also need to conduct the application of force so that there is always a prospect of worse to come.

We cannot assert that a policy of sustained reprisal will succeed in changing the course of the contest in Vietnam. It may fail, and we cannot estimate the odds of success with any accuracy they may be somewhere between 25% and 75%. What we can say is that even if it fails, the policy will be worth it. **At a minimum it will damp down the charge that we did not do all that we could have done, and this charge will be important in many countries, including our own** (emphasis showing the domestic political considerations added). Beyond that, a reprisal policy to the extent that it demonstrates **U.S. willingness to employ this new norm in counterinsurgency will set a higher price for the future upon all adventures of guerrilla warfare, and it should therefore somewhat increase our ability to deter such adventures** (emphasis highlighting the wider applications sought from the policies in Vietnam added). We must recognize, however, that that ability will be gravely weakened if there is failure for any reason in Vietnam....[419]

Excerpts from Speech Given by President Johnson at Johns Hopkins University, April 7,1965

Viet Nam (sic.) is far away from this quiet campus. We have no territory there, nor do we seek any. The war is dirty and brutal and difficult. And some 400 young men, born into an America that is bursting with opportunity and promise, have ended their lives, on Viet-Nam's (sic.) steaming soil.

Why must we take this painful road?

Why must this Nation hazard its ease, and its interest, and its power for the sake of a people so far away?

We fight because we must fight if we are to live in a world where every country can shape its own destiny. And only in such a world will our own freedom be finally secure....

The first reality is that North VietNam (sic.) has attacked the independent nation of South Viet-Nam (sic.). Its object is total conquest.

Of course, some of the people of South Viet-Nam (sic.) are participating in attack on their own government. But trained men and supplies, orders and arms, flow in a constant stream from north to south....

Over this war and all Asia is another reality: the deepening shadow of Communist China (emphasis added). The rulers in Hanoi are urged on by Peking. This is a regime which has destroyed freedom in Tibet, which has attacked India, and has been condemned by the United Nations for aggression in Korea.

Why are these realities our concern? Why are we in South Vietnam?

We are there because we have a promise to keep. Since 1954 every American President has offered support to the people of South Viet-Nam (sic.). We have helped to build, and we have helped to defend. Thus, over many years, we have made a national pledge to help South Viet-Nam (sic.) defend its independence. And I intend to keep that promise...

We are also there to strengthen world order. **Around the globe, from Berlin to Thailand, are people whose well being rests, in part, on the belief that they can count on us if they are attacked** (Emphasis added). To leave Viet-Nam (sic) to its fate would shake the confidence of all these people in the value of an American commitment and in the value of America's word. The result would be increased unrest and instability, and even wider war.

We are also there because there are great stakes in the balance. **Let no one think for a moment that retreat from Viet-Nam** (sic.) **would bring an end to conflict. The battle would be renewed in one country and then another. The central lesson of our time is that the appetite of aggression is never satisfied. To withdraw from one battlefield means only to prepare for the next** (emphasis added). We must say in Southeast Asia as we did in Europe in the words of the

Bible: "Hitherto shalt thou come, but no further."...

Our objective is the independence of South Viet-Nam, (sic.) **and its freedom from attack** (emphasis added). We want nothing for ourselves only that the people of South Viet-Nam (sic.) be allowed to guide their own country in their own way. We will do everything necessary to reach that objective. And we will do only what is absolutely necessary.

In recent months attacks on South Viet Nam (sic.) were stepped up. Thus, it became necessary for us to increase our response and to make attacks by air. This is not a change of purpose. It is a change in which we believe that purpose requires...

These countries of southeast Asia are homes for millions of impoverished people. Each day these people rise at dawn and struggle through until the night to wrestle existence from the soil. They are often wracked by disease, plagued by hunger, and death comes at the early age of 40.

For our part I will ask the Congress to join in a billion dollar American investment in this effort as soon as it is underway.

The task is nothing less than to enrich the hopes and the existence of more than a hundred million people. And there is much to be done.

The vast Mekong River can provide food and water and power on a scale to dwarf even our own TVA.... [420]

President Nixon's Report On Vietnam May 14, 1969

We can have honest debate about whether we should have entered the war. We can have honest debate about the past conduct of the war. But the urgent question today is what to do now that we are there, not whether we should have entered on this course, but what is required of us today.

Against that background, let me discuss, first, what we have rejected, and second, what we are prepared to accept.

We have ruled out attempting to impose a purely military solution on the battlefield.

We have also ruled out either a one-sided withdrawal from South Vietnam or the acceptance in Paris of terms that would amount to a disguised defeat.

When we assumed the burden of helping South Vietnam, millions of South Vietnamese men, women, and children placed their trust in us. To abandon them now would risk a massacre that would shock and dismay everyone in the world who values human life.

Abandoning the South Vietnam people, however, would jeopardize more than lives in South Vietnam. It would threaten our longer term hopes for peace in the world. A great nation cannot renege on its pledges, A great nation must be worthy of trust.

When it comes to maintaining peace, "prestige" is not an empty word. I am not speaking of false pride or bravado - they should have no place in our policies. I speak rather of the respect that one nation has for another's integrity in defending its principles and meeting its obligations.

If we simply abandoned our efforts in South Vietnam, the cause of peace might not survive the damage that would be done to other nations' confidence in our reliability.

Another reason stems from debates within the communist world between those who argue for a policy of confrontation with the United States and those who argue against it. **If Hanoi were to succeed in taking over South Vietnam by force- even after the power of the United States had been engaged - it would greatly strengthen those leaders who scorn negotiation, who advocate aggression, who minimize the risks of confrontation. It would bring peace now, but it would enormously increase the danger of a bigger war later** (emphasis added).

If we are to move successfully from an era of confrontation to an era of negotiation, then we have to demonstrate - at the point at which confrontation is being tested - that confrontation with the United States is costly and unrewarding.

Almost without exception, the leaders of non-communist Asia have told me that they would consider a one-sided American withdrawal from South Vietnam to be a threat to the security of their own nations.

In determining what choices would be acceptable, we have to understand our essential objective: We seek the opportunity for the South Vietnam people to determine their own political future without outside interference.

Let me put is plainly: What the United States wants for South Vietnam is not the important thing. What North Vietnam wants for South Vietnam is not the important thing. What is important is what the people of South Vietnam want for themselves.

The United States has suffered over one million casualties in four wars in this century. Whatever faults we may have as a nation, we have asked nothing for ourselves in return for these sacrifices. We have been generous toward those who we have fought, helping former foes as well as friends in the task of reconstruction. We are proud of this record, and we bring the same attitude to our search for a settlement in South Vietnam.

In this spirit, let me be explicit about several points:

> We seek not bases in South Vietnam.
>
> We insist on no military ties.
>
> We are willing to agree to neutrality if that is what the South Vietnam people freely choose.
>
> We believe there should be an opportunity for full participation in the political life of South Vietnam by all political elements that are prepared to do so without the use of force or intimidation.
>
> We are prepared to accept any

> government in South Vietnam that results from the free choice of the South Vietnam people themselves.
>
> We have no intention of imposing any form of govt upon the people of South Vietnam, nor will we be a party to such coercion.
>
> We have no objection to reunification, if that turns out to be what the people of South Vietnam and the people of North Vietnamese want; we ask only that the decision reflect the free choice of the people concerned.

In pursuing our limited objective, we insist on no rigid diplomatic formula. Peace could be achieved by a formal negotiated settlement. Peace could be achieved by an informal understanding, provided that the understanding is clear and that there were adequate assurance that it would be observed. Peace on paper is not as important as peace in fact.

This brings us, then, to the matter of negotiations.

We must recognize that peace in South Vietnam cannot be achieved overnight. A war which has raged for so many years will require detailed negotiations and cannot be settled at a single stroke.

What kind of settlement will permit the South Vietnam people to determine freely their own political future? Such a settlement will require the withdrawal of all non-South Vietnam forces from South Vietnam and procedures for political choice that give each significant group in South Vietnam a real opportunity to participate in the political life of the nation.

To implement these principles, I reaffirm now our willingness to withdraw our forces on a specified timetable. We ask only that North Vietnamese withdraw its forces from South Vietnam, Cambodia, and Laos into North Vietnam, also in accordance with a timetable.

We include Cambodia and Laos to ensure that these countries would not be used as bases for a renewed war. The Cambodian border is only 35 miles from Saigon; the Laotian border is only 25 miles from Hue.

Our offer provides for a simultaneous start on withdrawal by both sides; agreement on a mutually acceptable timetable; and for the withdrawal to be accomplished quickly.

If North Vietnamese wants to insist that it has no forces in South Vietnam, we will no longer debate the point - provided that its forces cease to be there and that we have reliable assurances that they will not return.

The North Vietnamese delegates have been saying in Paris that political issues should be discussed along with military issues and that there must be a political settlement in the south. We do not dispute this, but the military withdrawal involves outside forces and can therefore be properly negotiated by North Vietnamese and the United States, with the concurrence of its allies. The political settlement is an internal matter which ought to be decided among the

South Vietnam people themselves and not imposed by outside powers. However, if our presence at these political negotiations would be helpful, and if the South Vietnam people concerned agreed, we would be willing to participate, along with the representatives of Hanoi if that were also desired.

Recent statement by President Thieu have gone far forward opening the way to a political settlement. He has publicly declared his govts willingness to discuss a political solution with the NLF and has offered free elections. This was dramatic step forward, a reasonable offer that could lead to a settlement. The South Vietnam govt has offered to talk without preconditions. I believe that the other side should also be willing to talk without preconditions.

The South Vietnam govt recognizes, as we do, that a settlement must permit all persons and groups that are prepared to renounce the use of force to participate freely in the political life of South Vietnam. To be effective, such a settlement would require two things: first, a process that would allow the South Vietnam people to express their choice; and second, a guarantee that this process would be a fair one.

We do not insist on a particular form of guarantee. The important thing is that the guarantees should have the confidence of the South Vietnam people and that they should be broad enough and strong enough to protect the interests of all major South Vietnam groups.

This, then, is the outline of the settlement that we seek to negotiate in Paris. Its basic terms are very simple: mutual withdrawal of non-South Vietnam forces from South Vietnam and free choice for the people of South Vietnam. I believe that the long-term interests of peace required that we insist on no less and that the realities of the situation require that we seek no more.

To make very concrete what I have said, I propose the following measures, which seem to me consistent with the principles of all parties. These proposals are made on the basis of full consultation with President Thieu.

> As soon as agreement can be reached, all non-South Vietnam forces would begin withdrawals from South Vietnam.
>
> Over a period of twelve months, by agreed-upon stages, the major portions of all United States Allied, and other non-South Vietnam forces would be withdrawn. At the end of this 12-month period, the remaining US, Allied, and other non-South Vietnam forces would move into designated base area and would not engage in combat operations.
>
> The remaining United States and Allied forces would move to complete their withdrawals as the remaining North Vietnamese forces were withdrawn and returned to North Vietnam.

> An international supervisory body, acceptable to both sides, would be created for the purpose agreed upon between the two sides.
>
> This international body would begin operating in accordance with an agreed timetable and would participate in arranging supervised cease-fires.
>
> As soon as possible after the international body was functioning, elections would be held under agreed procedures and under the supervision of the international body.
>
> Arrangements would be made for the earliest possible release of prisoners of war on both sides.
>
> All parties would agree to observe the GA of '54 regarding Vietnam and Cambodia, and the Laos accords of '62.

I believe this proposal for peace is realistic and takes account of the legitimate interests of all concerned. It is consistent with President Thieu's six points. It can accommodate the various programs put forth by the other side. We and the govt of South Vietnam are prepared to discuss its details with the other side. Secretary Rogers is now in Saigon and will be discussing with President Thieu how, together, we may put forward these proposed measures most usefully in Paris. He will, as well, be consulting with our other Asian allies on these measures while on his Asian trip. However, I would stress that these proposals are not offered on a take-it-or-leave-it basis. We are quite willing to consider other approaches consistent with our principles.

We are willing to talk about anybody's program - Hanoi's four points, the NLF's ten points - provided it can be made consistent with the few basic principles I have set forth here. Despite our disagreement with several of its points, we welcome the fact that the NLF has put forward its first comprehensive program. We are continuing to study it carefully. However, we cannot ignore the fact that immediately after the offer, the scale of enemy attacks stepped up and American casualties increased.

Let me make one point very clear. If the enemy wants peace with the United States, that is not the way to get it.

I have set forth a peace program tonight which is generous in its terms. I have indicated our willingness to consider other proposals. No greater mistake could be made than to confuse flexibility with weakness or being reasonable with lack of resolution. I must make clear, in all candor, that if the needless suffering continues, this will affect other decisions. Nobody has anything to gain by delay.

Reports from Hanoi indicate that the enemy has given up hope for a military victory in South Vietnam but is counting on a collapse of American will in the United States. They could make no greater error in judgment.

Let me be quite blunt. Our fighting men are not going to be worn down; our negotiators are not going to be talked down; our allies are not going to be let down.

In my campaign for the Presidency, I pledged to end this war in a way that would increase our chances to win true and lasting peace in South Vietnam, in the Pacific, and in the world. I am determined to keep that pledge. If I fail to do so, I expect the American people to hold me accountable for that failure.[421]

Nixon's 'Silent Majority' Speech
November 3, 1969

Good evening, my fellow Americans.

Tonight I want to talk to you on a subject of deep concern to all Americans and to many people in all parts of the world — the war in Vietnam.

I believe that one of the reasons for the deep division about Vietnam is that many Americans have lost confidence in what their Government has told them about our policy. The American people cannot and should not be asked to support a policy which involves the overriding issues of war and peace unless they know the truth about that policy.

Tonight, therefore, I would like to answer some of the questions that I know are on the minds of many of you listening to me. How and why did America get involved in

Vietnam in the first place? How has this administration changed the policy of the previous administration? What has really happened in the negotiations in Paris and on the battlefront in Vietnam? What choices do we have if we are to end the war? What are the prospects for peace? Now, let me begin by describing the situation I found when I was inaugurated on January 20:

The war had been going on for four years. One thousand Americans had been killed in action. The training program for the South Vietnamese was behind schedule; 540,000 Americans were in Vietnam with no plans to reduce the number. No progress had been made at the negotiations in Paris and the United States had not put forth a comprehensive peace proposal. The war was causing deep division at home and criticism from many of our friends as well as our enemies abroad.

In view of these circumstances there were some who urged that I end the war at once by ordering the immediate withdrawal of all American forces. From a political standpoint this would have been a popular and easy course to follow. After all, we became involved in the war while my predecessor was in office. I could blame the defeat which would be the result of my action on him and come out as the peacemaker. Some put it to me quite bluntly: This was the only way to avoid allowing Johnson's war to become Nixon's war.

But I had a greater obligation than to

think only of the years of my administration and of the next election. **I had to think of the effect of my decision on the next generation and on the future of peace and freedom in America and in the world** (emphasis added).

Let us all understand that the question before us is not whether some Americans are for peace and some Americans are against peace. The question at issue is not whether Johnson's war becomes Nixon's war. **The great question is: How can we win America's peace?** (emphasis added)

Well, let us turn now to the fundamental issue. **Why and how did the United States become involved in Vietnam in the first place? Fifteen years ago North Vietnam, with the logistical support of communist China and the Soviet Union, launched a campaign to impose a communist government on South Vietnam by instigating and supporting a revolution** (emphasis added).

In response to the request of the Government of South Vietnam, President Eisenhower sent economic aid and military equipment to assist the people of South Vietnam in their efforts to prevent a communist takeover. Seven years ago, President Kennedy sent 16,000 military personnel to Vietnam as combat advisers. Four years ago, President Johnson sent American combat forces to South Vietnam.

Now, many believe that President Johnson's decision to send American combat forces to South Vietnam was wrong. And many others — I among them — have been strongly critical of the way the war has been conducted.

But the question facing us today is: Now that we are in the war, what is the best way to end it? (emphasis added)

In January I could only conclude that the precipitate withdrawal of American forces from Vietnam would be a disaster not only for South Vietnam but for the United States and for the cause of peace.

For the South Vietnamese, our precipitate withdrawal would inevitably allow the Communists to repeat the massacres which followed their takeover in the North 15 years before; They then murdered more than 50,000 people and hundreds of thousands more died in slave labor camps.

We saw a prelude of what would happen in South Vietnam when the Communists entered the city of Hue last year. During their brief rule there, there was a bloody reign of terror in which 3,000 civilians were clubbed, shot to death, and buried in mass graves.

With the sudden collapse of our support, these atrocities of Hue would become the nightmare of the entire nation — and particularly for the million and a half Catholic refugees who fled to South Vietnam when the Communists took over in the North.

For the United States, this first defeat in our nation's history would result in a collapse of confidence in American leadership, **not only in Asia but throughout the world** (emphasis added).

Three American presidents have recognized the great stakes involved in Vietnam and understood what had to be done.

In 1963, President Kennedy, with his characteristic eloquence and clarity, said:

> ... we want to see a stable government there, carrying on a struggle to maintain its national independence. We believe strongly in that. We are not going to withdraw from that effort. **In my opinion, for us to withdraw from that effort would mean a collapse not only of South Vietnam, but Southeast Asia** (emphasis added). So we are going to stay there.

President Eisenhower and President Johnson expressed the same conclusion during their terms of office.

For the future of peace, precipitate withdrawal would thus be a disaster of immense magnitude. A nation cannot remain great if it betrays its allies and lets down its friends. Our defeat and humiliation in South Vietnam without question would promote recklessness in the councils of **those great powers who have not yet abandoned their goals of world conquest (emphasis added).** This would spark violence wherever our commitments help maintain the peace — in the Middle East, in Berlin, eventually even in the Western Hemisphere. Ultimately, this would cost more lives. It would not bring peace; it would bring more war.

For these reasons, I rejected the recommendation that I should end the war by immediately withdrawing all of our forces. I chose instead to change American policy on both the negotiating front and battlefront. In order to end a war fought on many fronts, I initiated a pursuit for peace on many fronts. In a television speech on May 14, in a speech before the United Nations, and on a number of other occasions I set forth our peace proposals in great detail.

We have offered the complete withdrawal of all outside forces within one year.

We have proposed a cease-fire under international supervision.

We have offered free elections under international supervision with the Communists participating in the organization and conduct of the elections as an organized political force. And the Saigon Government has pledged to accept the result of the elections.

We have not put forth our proposals on a take-it-or-leave-it basis. We have indicated that we are willing to discuss the proposals that have been put forth by the other side. We have declared that **anything is negotiable except the right of the people of South Vietnam to determine their own future** (emphasis added). At the Paris peace conference, Ambassador Lodge has demonstrated our flexibility and good faith in 40 public meetings.

Hanoi has refused even to discuss our proposals. They demand our unconditional acceptance of their terms, which are that we withdraw all American forces immediately and unconditionally and that we overthrow the Government of South Vietnam as we leave.

We have not limited our peace initiatives to public forums and public statements. I recognized, in January, that a long and bitter war like this usually cannot be settled in a public forum. That is why in addition to the public statements and negotiation I have explored every possible private avenue that might lead to a settlement.

Tonight I am taking the unprecedented step of disclosing to you some of our other initiatives for peace — initiatives we undertook privately and secretly because we thought we thereby might open a door which publicly would be closed.

I did not wait for my inauguration to begin my quest for peace.

Soon after my election, through an individual who is directly in contact on a personal basis with the leaders of North Vietnam, I made two private offers for a rapid, comprehensive settlement. Hanoi's replies called in effect for our surrender before negotiations.

Since the Soviet Union furnishes most of the military equipment for North Vietnam, Secretary of State Rogers, my Assistant for National Security Affairs, Dr. Kissinger, Ambassador Lodge, and I, personally, have met on a number of occasions with representatives of the Soviet Government to enlist their assistance in getting meaningful negotiations started. In addition, we have had extended discussions directed toward that same end with representatives of other governments which have diplomatic relations with North Vietnam. None of these initiatives have to date produced results.

In mid-July, I became convinced that it was necessary to make a major move to break the deadlock in the Paris talks. I spoke directly in this office, where I am now sitting, with an individual who had known Ho Chi Minh on a personal basis for 25 years. Through him I sent a letter to Ho Chi Minh. I did this outside of the usual diplomatic channels with the hope that with the necessity of making statements for propaganda removed, there might be constructive progress toward bringing the war to an end. Let me read from that letter to you now:

> Dear Mr. President:
> I realize that it is difficult to communicate meaningfully across the gulf of four years of war. But precisely because of this gulf, I wanted to take this opportunity to reaffirm in all solemnity my desire to work for a just peace. I deeply believe that the war in Vietnam has gone on too long and delay in bringing it to an end can benefit no one — least of all the people of Vietnam. ... The time has come to move forward at the conference table toward an early resolution

> of this tragic war. You will find us forthcoming and open-minded in a common effort to bring the blessings of peace to the brave people of Vietnam. Let history record that at this critical juncture, both sides turned their face toward peace rather than toward conflict and war.

I received Ho Chi Minh's reply on August 30, three days before his death. It simply reiterated the public position North Vietnam had taken at Paris and flatly rejected my initiative.

The full text of both letters is being released to the press.

In addition to the public meetings that I have referred to, Ambassador Lodge has met with Vietnam's chief negotiator in Paris in 11 private sessions.

We have taken other significant initiatives which must remain secret to keep open some channels of communication which may still prove to be productive.

But the effect of all the public, private and secret negotiations which have been undertaken since the bombing halt a year ago and since this administration came into office on January 20 can be summed up in one sentence: No progress whatever has been made except agreement on the shape of the bargaining table.

Well now, who is at fault?

It has become clear that the obstacle in negotiating an end to the war is not the

President of the United States. It is not the South Vietnamese Government.

The obstacle is the other side's absolute refusal to show the least willingness to join us in seeking a just peace. And it will not do so while it is convinced that all it has to do is to wait for our next concession, and our next concession after that one, until it gets everything it wants.

There can now be no longer any question that progress in negotiation depends only on Hanoi's deciding to negotiate, to negotiate seriously.

I realize that this report on our efforts on the diplomatic front is discouraging to the American people, but the American people are entitled to know the truth — the bad news as well as the good news — where the lives of our young men are involved.

Now let me turn, however, to a more encouraging report on another front.

At the time we launched our search for peace I recognized we might not succeed in bringing an end to the war through negotiation. I, therefore, put into effect another plan to bring peace — a plan which will bring the war to an end regardless of what happens on the negotiating front.

It is in line with a major shift in U.S. foreign policy which I described in my press conference at Guam on July 25. Let me briefly explain what has been described as the Nixon Doctrine — policy which not only will help end the war in Vietnam, but which is an essential element of our program to prevent future Vietnams.

We Americans are a do-it-yourself people. We are an impatient people. Instead of teaching someone else to do a job, we like to do it ourselves. And this trait has been carried over into our foreign policy. In Korea and again in Vietnam, the United States furnished most of the money, most of the arms, and most of the men to **help the people of those countries defend their freedom against Communist aggression** (emphasis added).

Before any American troops were committed to Vietnam, a leader of another Asian country expressed this opinion to me when I was traveling in Asia as a private citizen. He said: "When you are trying to assist another nation defend its freedom, U.S. policy should be to help them fight the war but not to fight the war for them."

Well, in accordance with this wise counsel, I laid down in Guam three principles as guidelines for future American policy toward Asia:

> First, the United States will keep all of its treaty commitments.
>
> Second, we shall provide a shield if a nuclear power threatens the freedom of a nation allied with us or of a nation whose survival we consider vital to our security.
>
> Third, in cases involving other types of aggression, we shall furnish military and economic assistance

> when requested in accordance with our treaty commitments. But we shall look to the nation directly threatened to assume the primary responsibility of providing the manpower for its defense.

After I announced this policy, I found that the leaders of the Philippines, Thailand, Vietnam, South Korea, and other nations which might be **threatened by Communist aggression** (emphasis added) welcomed this new direction in American foreign policy.

The defense of freedom is everybody's business — not just America's business. And it is particularly the responsibility of the people whose freedom is threatened. In the previous administration, we Americanized the war in Vietnam. In this administration, we are Vietnamizing the search for peace.

The policy of the previous administration not only resulted in our assuming the primary responsibility for fighting the war, but even more significantly did not adequately stress the goal of strengthening the South Vietnamese so that they could defend themselves when we left.

The Vietnamization plan was launched following Secretary Laird's visit to Vietnam in March. Under the plan, I ordered first a substantial increase in the training and equipment of South Vietnamese forces.

In July, on my visit to Vietnam, I changed General Abrams' orders so that they were consistent with the objectives of our new policies. Under the new orders, the primary mission of our troops is to enable the South Vietnamese forces to assume the full responsibility for the security of South Vietnam.

Our air operations have been reduced by over 20 percent.

And now we have begun to see the results of this long overdue change in American policy in Vietnam.

After five years of Americans going into Vietnam, we are finally bringing American men home. By December 15, over 60,000 men will have been withdrawn from South Vietnam, including 20 percent of all of our combat forces.

The South Vietnamese have continued to gain in strength. As a result they have been able to take over combat responsibilities from our American troops.

Two other significant developments have occurred since this administration took office.

Enemy infiltration (emphasis added), infiltration which is essential if they are to launch a major attack, over the last three months is less than 20 percent of what it was over the same period last year. Most important — United States casualties have declined during the last two months to the lowest point in three years.

Let me now turn to our program for the future.

We have adopted a plan which we have worked out in cooperation with the South

Vietnamese for the complete withdrawal of all U.S. combat ground forces and their replacement by South Vietnamese forces on an orderly scheduled timetable. This withdrawal will be made from strength and not from weakness. As South Vietnamese forces become stronger, the rate of American withdrawal can become greater.

I have not and do not intend to announce the timetable for our program. And there are obvious reasons for this decision which I am sure you will understand. As I have indicated on several occasions, the rate of withdrawal will depend on developments on three fronts.

One of these is the progress which can be or might be made in a Paris talks. An announcement of a fixed timetable for our withdrawal would completely remove any incentive for the enemy to negotiate an agreement. They would simply wait until our forces had withdrawn and then move in.

The other two factors on which we will base our withdrawal decisions are the level of enemy activity and the progress of the training programs of the South Vietnamese forces. And I am glad to be able to report tonight progress on both of these fronts has been greater than we anticipated when we started the program in June for withdrawal. As a result, our timetable for withdrawal is more optimistic now than when we made our first estimates in June. Now, this clearly demonstrates why it is not wise to be frozen in on a fixed timetable.

We must retain the flexibility to base

each withdrawal decision on the situation as it is at that time rather than on estimates that are no longer valid.

Along with this optimistic estimate, I must — in all candor — leave one note of caution. If the level of enemy activity significantly increases we might have to adjust our timetable accordingly.

However, I want the record to be completely clear on one point.

At the time of the bombing halt just a year ago, there was some confusion as to whether there was an understanding on the part of the enemy that if we stopped the bombing of North Vietnam they would stop the shelling of cities in South Vietnam. I want to be sure that there is no misunderstanding on the part of the enemy with regard to our withdrawal program.

We have noted the reduced level of infiltration, the reduction of our casualties, and are basing our withdrawal decisions partially on those factors. If the level of infiltration or our casualties increase while we are trying to scale down the fighting, it will be the result of a conscious decision by the enemy.

Hanoi could make no greater mistake than to assume that an increase in violence will be to its advantage. If I conclude that increased enemy action jeopardizes our remaining forces in Vietnam, I shall not hesitate to take strong and effective measures to deal with that situation.

This is not a threat. This is a statement of policy, which as commander in chief of our armed forces, I am making in meeting my responsibility for the protection of American fighting men wherever they may be.

My fellow Americans, I am sure you can recognize from what I have said that we really only have two choices open to us if we want to end this war.

I can order an immediate, precipitate withdrawal of all Americans from Vietnam without regard to the effects of that action. Or we can persist in our search for a just peace through a negotiated settlement if possible, or through continued implementation of our plan for Vietnamization if necessary, a plan in which we will withdraw all of our forces from Vietnam on a schedule in accordance with our program, as the South Vietnamese become strong enough to defend their own freedom.

I have chosen this second course. It is not the easy way. It is the right way.

It is a plan which will end the war and serve the cause of peace — **not just in Vietnam but in the Pacific and in the world** (emphasis added).

In speaking of the consequences of a precipitate withdrawal, I mentioned that our allies would lose confidence in America.

Far more dangerous, we would lose confidence in ourselves. Oh, the immediate reaction would be a sense of relief that our men were coming home. But as we saw the consequences of what we had done, inevitable remorse and divisive recrimination would scar our spirit as a people.

We have faced other crises in our history and have become stronger by rejecting the easy way out and taking the right way in meeting our challenges. Our greatness as a nation has been our capacity to do what had to be done when we knew our course was right.

I recognize that some of my fellow citizens disagree with the plan for peace I have chosen. Honest and patriotic Americans have reached different conclusions as to how peace should be achieved.

In San Francisco a few weeks ago, I saw demonstrators carrying signs reading: "Lose in Vietnam, bring the boys home."

Well, one of the strengths of our free society is that any American has a right to reach that conclusion and to advocate that point of view. But as president of the United States, I would be untrue to my oath of office if I allowed the policy of this nation to be dictated by the minority who hold that point of view and who try to impose it on the nation by mounting demonstrations in the street.

For almost 200 years, the policy of this nation has been made under our Constitution by those leaders in the Congress and the White House elected by all of the people. If a vocal minority, however fervent its cause, prevails over reason and the will of the majority, this nation has no future as a free society.

And now I would like to address a word, if I may, to the young people of this nation who are particularly concerned, and I understand why they are concerned, about this war.

I respect your idealism. I share your concern for peace. I want peace as much as you do. There are powerful personal reasons I want to end this war. This week I will have to sign 83 letters to mothers, fathers, wives and loved ones of men who have given their lives for America in Vietnam. It is very little satisfaction to me that this is only one-third as many letters as I signed the first week in office. There is nothing I want more than to see the day come when I do not have to write any of those letters.

I want to end the war to save the lives of those brave young men in Vietnam.

But I want to end it in a way which will increase the chance that their younger brothers and their sons will not have to fight in some future Vietnam someplace in the world (emphasis added).

And I want to end the war for another reason. I want to end it so that the energy and dedication of you, our young people, now too often directed into bitter hatred against those responsible for the war, can be turned to the great challenges of peace, a better life for all Americans, a better life for all people on this Earth.

I have chosen a plan for peace. I believe it will succeed. If it does succeed, what the critics say now won't matter. If it does not succeed, anything I say then won't matter.

I know it may not be fashionable to speak of patriotism or national destiny these days. But I feel it is appropriate to do so on this occasion.

Two hundred years ago this nation was weak and poor. But even then, America was the hope of millions in the world. Today we have become the strongest and richest nation in the world. And the wheel of destiny has turned so that **any hope the world has for the survival of peace and freedom will be determined by whether the American people have the moral stamina and the courage to meet the challenge of free world leadership** (emphasis added).

Let historians not record that when America was the most powerful nation in the world we passed on the other side of the road and **allowed the last hopes for peace and freedom of millions of people to be suffocated by the forces of totalitarianism** (emphasis added).

And so tonight — to you, the great silent majority of my fellow Americans — I ask for your support.

I pledged in my campaign for the presidency to end the war in a way that we could **win the peace** (emphasis added). I have initiated a plan of action which will enable me to keep that pledge.

The more support I can have from the American people, the sooner that pledge can be redeemed; for the more divided we are at home, the less likely the enemy is to negotiate at Paris.

Let us be united for peace. Let us also be united against defeat. Because let us understand: North Vietnam cannot defeat or humiliate the United States. Only Americans can do that.

Fifty years ago, in this room and at this very desk, President Woodrow Wilson spoke words which caught the imagination of a war-weary world. He said: "This is the war to end war." His dream for peace after World War I was shattered on the hard realities of great power politics, and Woodrow Wilson died a broken man.

Tonight I do not tell you that the war in Vietnam is the war to end wars. But I do say this: I have initiated a plan which will end this war in a way that will bring us closer to that great goal to which Woodrow Wilson and every American president in our history has been dedicated — the goal of a just and lasting peace.

As president I hold the responsibility for choosing the best path to that goal and then leading the nation along it. I pledge to you tonight that I shall meet this responsibility with all of the strength and wisdom I can command in accordance with our hopes, mindful of your concerns, sustained by your prayers.

Thank you and good night.[422]

President Nixon: Cambodian Invasion May, 1970

Good evening, my fellow Americans. Ten days ago, in my report to the Nation on Vietnam, I announced a decision to withdraw an additional 150,000 Americans from Vietnam over the next year. I said then that I was making that decision despite our concern over increased enemy activity in Laos, in Cambodia, and in South Vietnam.

At that time, I warned that if I concluded that increased enemy activity in any of these areas endangered the lives of Americans remaining in Vietnam, I would not hesitate to take strong and effective measures to deal with that situation.

Despite that warning, North Vietnam has increased its military aggression in all these areas, and particularly in Cambodia. After full consultation with the National Security Council, Ambassador Bunker, General Abrams, and my other advisers, I have concluded that the actions of the enemy in the last 10 days clearly endanger the lives of Americans who are in Vietnam now and would constitute an unacceptable risk to those who will be there after withdrawal of another 150,000. To protect our men who are in Vietnam and to guarantee the continued success of our withdrawal and Vietnamization programs, I have concluded that the time has come for action. Tonight I shall describe the actions of the enemy, the actions I have ordered to deal with that situation, and the reasons for my decision.

Cambodia, a small country of seven million people, has been a neutral nation since the Geneva agreement of 1954 an agreement, incidentally, which was signed by the Government of North Vietnam.

American policy since then has been to scrupulously respect the neutrality of the Cambodian people. We have maintained a skeleton diplomatic mission of fewer than 15 in Cambodia's capital, and that only since last August. For the previous four years, from 1965 to 1969, we did not have any diplomatic mission whatever in Cambodia. And for the past five years, we have provided no military assistance whatever and no economic assistance to Cambodia. North Vietnam, however, has not respected that neutrality. For the past five years, as indicated on this map that you see here, North Vietnam has occupied military sanctuaries all along the Cambodian frontier with South Vietnam. Some of these extend up to 20 miles into Cambodia. The sanctuaries are in red, and as you note, they are on both sides of the border. They are used for hit-and-run attacks on American and South Vietnamese forces in South Vietnam. These Communist-occupied territories contain major base camps, training sites, logistics facilities, weapons and ammunition factories, airstrips, and prisoner of war compounds. For five years neither the United States nor South Vietnam has moved against these enemy sanctuaries, because we did not wish to violate the territory of a neutral nation. Even after the Vietnamese Communists began to expand these sanctuaries four weeks ago, we counseled patience to our South Vietnamese allies and imposed restraints on our own commanders. In contrast to our policy, the enemy in the past two weeks has stepped up his guerrilla actions, and he is concentrating his main forces in these sanctuaries that you see on this map, where they are building up to launch massive attacks on our forces and those of South Vietnam. North Vietnam in the last two weeks has stripped away all pretense of respecting the sovereignty or the neutrality of Cambodia. Thousands of their soldiers are invading the country from the sanctuary from the sanctuaries; they are encircling the Capital of Phnom Penh. Coming from these sanctuaries, as you see here, they have moved into Cambodia and are encircling the Capital. **Cambodia, as a result of this, has sent out a call to the United States, to a number of other nations, for assistance** (emphasis added). Because if this enemy effort succeeds, Cambodia would become a vast enemy staging area and a springboard for attacks on South Vietnam along 600 miles of frontier, a refuge where enemy troops could return from combat without fear of retaliation. **North Vietnamese men and supplies could then be poured into that country** (emphasis added), jeopardizing not only the lives of our own men but the people of South Vietnam as well.

Now, confronted with this situation, we have three options. First, we can do nothing. Well, the ultimate result of that course of action is clear. Unless we indulge in wishful thinking, the lives of Americans remaining in Vietnam after our next withdrawal of

150,000 would be gravely threatened.

Let us go to the map again. Here is South Vietnam. Here is North Vietnam. North Vietnam already occupies this part of Laos. If North Vietnam also occupied this whole band in Cambodia, or the entire country, it would mean that South Vietnam was completely outflanked and the forces of Americans in this area, as well as the South Vietnamese, would be in an untenable military position. Our second choice is to provide massive military assistance to Cambodia itself. Now, unfortunately, while we deeply sympathize with the plight of seven million Cambodians, whose country is being invaded, massive amounts of military assistance could not be rapidly and effectively utilized by the small Cambodian Army against the immediate threat. With other nations, we shall do our best to provide the small arms and other equipment which the Cambodian Army of 40,000 needs and can use for its defense. But the aid we will provide will be limited to the purpose of enabling Cambodia to defend its neutrality and not for the purpose of making it an active belligerent on one side or the other. Our third choice is to go to the heart of the trouble. That means cleaning out major North Vietnamese and Viet Cong occupied territories and sanctuaries which serve as bases for attacks on both Cambodia and American and South Vietnamese forces in South Vietnam. Some of these, incidentally, are as close to Saigon as Baltimore is to Washington.

Now, faced with these three options, this is the decision I have made.

In cooperation with the armed forces of South Vietnam, attacks are being launched this week to clean out major enemy sanctuaries on the Cambodian-Vietnam border.

A major responsibility for the ground operations is being assumed by South Vietnamese forces. For example, the attacks in several areas, including the Parrots Beak that I referred to a moment ago, are exclusively South Vietnamese ground operations under South Vietnamese command, with the United States providing air and logistical support. There is one area, however, immediately above Parrot's Beak, where I have concluded that a combined American and South Vietnamese operation is necessary.

Tonight American and South Vietnamese units will attack the headquarters for the entire Communist military operation in South Vietnam. This key control center has been occupied by the North Vietnamese and Viet Cong for five years in blatant violation of Cambodia's neutrality.

This is not an invasion of Cambodia (emphasis added). The areas in which these attacks will be launched are completely occupied and controlled by North Vietnamese forces. **Our purpose is not to occupy the areas** (emphasis added). Once enemy forces are driven out of these sanctuaries and once their military supplies are destroyed, we will withdraw. These actions are in no way directed at the security interests of any nation.

Any government that chooses to use these actions as a pretext for harming relations with the United States will be doing so on its own responsibility and on its own initiative, and we will draw the appropriate conclusions. Now, let me give you the reasons for my decision. A majority of the American people, a majority of you listening to me, are for the withdrawal of our forces from Vietnam. The action I have taken tonight is indispensable for the continuing success of the continuing success of that withdrawal program. A majority of the American people want to end this war rather than to have it drag on interminably. The action: have taken tonight will serve that purpose.

A majority of the American people want to keep the casualties of our brave men in Vietnam at an absolute minimum. The action I take tonight is essential if we are to accomplish that goal. We take this action not for the purpose of expanding the war into Cambodia, but for the purpose of ending the war in Vietnam and **winning the just peace we all desire** (emphasis added). We have made and we will continue to make every possible effort to end this war through negotiation at the conference table rather than through more fighting on the battlefield.

Let us look again at the record. We have stopped the bombing of North Vietnam. We have cut air operations by over 20 percent. We have announced withdrawal of over 250,000 of our men. We have offered to withdraw all of our men if they will withdraw theirs. **We have offered to negotiate all issues with only one condition and that is that the future of South Vietnam be determined not by North Vietnam, not by the United States, but by the people of South Vietnam themselves** (emphasis added). The answer of the enemy has been intransigence at the conference table, belligerence in Hanoi, massive military aggression in Laos and Cambodia, and stepped-up attacks in South Vietnam designed to increase American casualties.

This attitude has become intolerable. **We will not react to this threat to American lives merely by plaintive diplomatic protests. If we did, the credibility of the United States would be destroyed in every area of the world where only the power of the United States deters aggression** (emphasis added). Tonight I again warn the North Vietnamese that if they continue to escalate the fighting when the United States is withdrawing its forces, I shall meet my responsibility as Commander in Chief of our Armed Forces to take the action I consider necessary to defend the security of our American men. **The action that I have announced tonight puts the leaders of North Vietnam on notice that we will be patient in working for peace, we will be conciliatory at the conference table, but we will not be humiliated. We will not be defeated. We will not allow American men by the thousands to be killed by an enemy from privileged sanctuaries** (emphasis added). The time came long ago to end this war through peaceful negotiations. We stand ready for those negotiations. We have made major efforts, many of which must remain secret. I say tonight that all the offers and approaches made previously remain on the conference table whenever Hanoi is ready to negotiate seriously. But if the enemy response to our most conciliatory offers for peaceful negotiation continues to be to increase its attacks and humiliate and defeat us, we shall react accordingly. My fellow Americans, **we live in an age of anarchy, both abroad and at home. We see mindless attacks on all the great institutions which have been created by free civilizations in the last 500 years. Even here in the United States, great universities are being systematically destroyed. Small nations all over the world find themselves under attack from within and from without** (emphasis added).

If, when the chips are down, the world's most powerful nation, the United States of America, acts like a pitiful, helpless giant, the forces of totalitarianism and anarchy will threaten free nations and free institutions throughout the world. It is not our power but our will and character that is being tested tonight. The question all Americans must ask and answer tonight is this: Does the richest and strongest nation in the history of the world have the character to meet a direct challenge by a group which rejects every effort to win a just peace, ignores our warning, tramples on solemn agreements, violates the neutrality of an unarmed people, and uses our prisoners as hostages?

If we fail to meet this challenge, all other nations will be on notice that despite its overwhelming power the United States, when a real crisis comes, will be found wanting. During my campaign for the Presidency, I pledged to bring Americans home from Vietnam. They are coming home. I promised to end this war. I shall keep that promise. I promised to win a just peace. I shall keep that pace. I shall keep that promise. We shall avoid a wider war. But we are also determined to put an end to this war... I have rejected all political considerations in making this decision. Whether my party gains in November is nothing compared to the lives of 400,000 brave Americans fighting for our country and for the cause of peace and freedom in Vietnam.

Whether I may be a one-term President is insignificant compared to whether by our failure to act in this crisis the United States proves itself to be unworthy to lead the forces of freedom **in this critical period in world history** (emphasis added). I would rather be a one-term President and do what I believe is right than to be a two-term President at the cost of seeing America become a second-rate power and to see this nation accept the first defeat in its proud 190-year history.[423]

Paris Peace Accords

The Agreement on Ending
the War and Restoring Peace in Vietnam

The Parties participating in the Paris Conference on Viet-Nam (sic.), With a view to ending the war and restoring peace in Viet-Nam (sic.) on the basis of respect for the Vietnamese people's fundamental national rights and the South Vietnamese people's right to self- determination, and to contributing to the consolidation of peace in Asia and the world, Have agreed on the following provisions and undertake to respect and to implement them:

Chapter I THE VIETNAMESE PEOPLE'S FUNDAMENTAL NATIONAL RIGHTS

Article 1 The United States and all other countries respect the independence, sovereignty, unity, and territorial integrity of Viet-Nam (sic.) as recognized by the 1954 Geneva Agreements on Viet- Nam (sic.).

Chapter II CESSATION OF HOSTILITIES - WITHDRAWAL OF TROOPS,

Article 2 A cease-fire shall be observed throughout South Viet-Nam (sic.) as of 2400 hours G.M.T. [Greenwich Mean Time], on January 27, 1973. At the same hour, the United States will stop all its military activities against the territory of the Democratic Republic of Viet-Nam by ground, air and naval forces, wherever they may be based, and end the mining of the territorial waters, ports, harbors, and waterways of the Democratic Republic of Viet-Nam (sic.). The United States will remove, permanently deactivate or destroy all the mines in the territorial waters, ports, harbors, and waterways of North Viet-Nam (sic.) as soon as this Agreement goes into effect. The complete cessation of hostilities mentioned in this Article shall be durable and without limit of time.

Article 3 The parties undertake to maintain the cease-fire and to ensure a lasting and stable peace. As soon as the cease-fire goes into effect: (a) The United States forces and those of the other foreign countries allied with the United States and the Republic of Viet-Nam (sic.) shall remain in-place pending the implementation of the plan of troop withdrawal. The Four-Party Joint Military Commission described in Article 16 shall determine the modalities. (b) The armed forces of the two South Vietnamese parties shall remain in-place. The Two-Party Joint Military Commission described in Article 17 shall determine the areas controlled by each party and the modalities of stationing. (c) The regular forces of all services and arms and the irregular forces of the parties in South Viet-Nam (sic.) shall stop all offensive activities against each other and shall strictly abide by the following stipulations: - All acts of force on the ground, in the air, and on the sea shall be prohibited; - All hostile acts, terrorism and reprisals by both sides will be banned.

Article 4 The United States will not continue its military involvement or intervene in the internal affairs of South Viet-Nam (sic.).

Article 5 Within sixty days of the signing of this Agreement, there will be a total withdrawal from South Viet-Nam (sic.) of troops, military advisers, and military personnel, including technical military personnel and military personnel associated with the pacification program, armaments, munitions, and war material of the United States and those of the other foreign countries mentioned in Article 3 (a). Advisers from the above-mentioned countries to all paramilitary organizations and the police force will also be withdrawn within the same period of time.

Article 6 The dismantlement (sic.) of all military bases in South Viet-Nam (sic.) of the United States and of the other foreign countries mentioned in Article 3 (a) shall be completed within sixty days of the signing of this agreement.

Article 7 From the enforcement of the cease-fire to the formation of the government provided for in Article 9 (b) and 14 of this Agreement, the two South Vietnamese parties shall not accept the introduction of troops, military advisers, and military personnel including technical military personnel, armaments, munitions, and war material into South Viet-Nam (sic.). The two South Vietnamese parties shall be permitted to make periodic replacement of armaments, munitions and war material which have been destroyed, damaged, worn out or used up after the cease-fire, on the basis of piece-for-piece, of the same characteristics and properties, under the supervision of the Joint Military Commission of the two South Vietnamese parties and of the International Commission of Control and Supervision.

Chapter III THE RETURN OF CAPTURED MILITARY PERSONNEL AND FOREIGN CIVILIANS AND CAPTURED AND DETAINED VIETNAMESE CIVILIAN PERSONNEL

Article 8 (a) The return of captured military personnel and foreign civilians of the parties shall be carried out simultaneously with and completed not later than the same day as the troop withdrawal mentioned in Article 5. The parties shall exchange complete lists of the above-mentioned captured military personnel and foreign civilians on the day of the signing of this Agreement. (b) The parties shall help each other to get information about those military personnel and foreign civilians of the parties missing in action, to determine the location and take care of the graves of the dead so as to facilitate the exhumation and repatriation of the remains, and to take any such other measures as may be required to get information about those still considered missing in action. (c) The question of the return of Vietnamese civilian personnel captured and detained in South Viet-Nam (sic.) will be resolved by the two South Vietnamese parties on the basis of the principles of Article 21 (b) of the Agreement on the Cessation of Hostilities in Viet-Nam (sic.) of July 20, 1954. The two South Vietnamese parties will do so in a spirit of national reconciliation and concord, with a view to ending hatred and enmity, in order to ease suffering and to reunite families. The two South Vietnamese parties will do their utmost to resolve this question within ninety days after the cease-fire comes into effect.

Chapter IV THE EXERCISE OF THE SOUTH VIETNAMESE PEOPLE'S RIGHT TO SELF- DETERMINATION

Article 9 The Government of the United States of America and the Government of the Democratic Republic of Viet-Nam (sic.) undertake to respect the following principles for the exercise of the South Vietnamese people's right to self-determination: (a) The South Vietnamese people's right to self-determination is sacred, inalienable, and shall be respected by all countries. (b) The South Vietnamese people shall decide themselves the political future of South Viet-Nam (sic.) through genuinely free and democratic general elections under international supervision. (c) Foreign countries shall not impose any political tendency or personality on the South Vietnamese people.

Article 10 The two South Vietnamese parties undertake to respect the cease- fire and maintain peace in South Viet-Nam (sic.), settle all matters of contention through negotiations, and avoid all armed conflict.

Article 11 Immediately after the cease-fire, the two South Vietnamese parties will: - achieve national reconciliation and concord, end hatred and enmity, prohibit all acts of reprisal and discrimination against individuals or organizations that have collaborated with one side or the other; - ensure the democratic liberties of the people: personal freedom, freedom of speech, freedom of the press, freedom of meeting, freedom of organization, freedom of political activities, freedom of belief, freedom of movement, freedom of residence, freedom of work, right to property ownership, and right to free enterprise.

Article l2 (a) Immediately after the cease-fire, the two South Vietnamese parties shall hold consultations in a spirit of national reconciliation and concord, mutual respect, and mutual non- elimination to set up a National Council of National Reconciliation and Concord of three equal segments. The Council shall operate on the principle of unanimity, After the National Council of National Reconciliation and Concord has assumed its functions, the two South Vietnamese parties will consult about the formation of councils at lower levels. The two South Vietnamese parties shall sign an agreement on the internal matters of South Viet-Nam (sic.) as soon as possible and do their utmost to accomplish this within ninety days after the cease- fire comes into effect, in keeping with the South Vietnamese people's aspirations for peace, independence and democracy. (b) The National Council of National Reconciliation and Concord shall have the task of promoting the two South Vietnamese parties' implementation of this Agreement, achievement of national reconciliation and concord and ensurance (sic.) of democratic liberties. The National Council of National Reconciliation and Concord will organize the free and democratic general elections provided for in Article 9 (b) and decide the procedures and modalities of these general elections. The institutions for which the general elections are to be held will be agreed upon through consultations between the two South Vietnamese parties. The National Council of National Reconciliation and Concord will also decide the procedures and modalities of such local elections as the two South Vietnamese parties agree upon.

Article 13 The question of Vietnamese armed forces in South Viet-Nam (sic.) shall be settled by the two South Vietnamese parties in a spirit of national reconciliation and concord, equality and mutual respect, without foreign interference, in accordance with the postwar situation. Among the questions to be discussed by the two South Vietnamese parties are steps to reduce their military effectives (sic.) and to demobilize the troops being reduced. The two South Vietnamese parties will accomplish this as soon as possible.

Article 14 South Viet-Nam (sic.) will pursue a foreign policy of peace and independence. It will be prepared to establish relations with all countries irrespective of their political and social systems on the basis of mutual respect for independence and sovereignty and accept economic and technical aid from any country with no political conditions attached. The acceptance of military aid by South Viet-Nam (sic.) in the future shall come under the authority of the government set up after the general elections in South Viet- Nam (sic.) provided for in Article 9 (b).

Chapter V THE REUNIFICATION OF VIET-NAM (sic.) AND THE RELATIONSHIP BETWEEN NORTH AND SOUTH VIET-NAM (sic.)

Article 15 The reunification of Viet-Nam (sic.) shall be carried out step by step through peaceful means on the basis of discussions and agreements between North and South Viet-Nam (sic.), without coercion or annexation by either party, and without foreign interference. The time for reunification will be agreed upon by North and South Viet-Nam (sic.) - Pending reunification: (a) The military demarcation line between the two zones at the 17th parallel is only provisional and not a political or territorial boundary, as provided for in paragraph 6 of the Final Declaration of the 1954 Geneva Conference. (b) North and South Viet-Nam (sic.) shall respect the Demilitarized Zone on either side of the Provisional Military Demarcation Line. (c) North and South Viet-Nam (sic.) shall promptly start negotiations with a view to reestablishing-normal relations in various fields. Among the questions to be negotiated are the modalities of civilian movement across the Provisional Military Demarcation Line, (d) North and South Viet-Nam (sic.) shall not join any military alliance or military bloc and shall not allow foreign powers to maintain military bases, troops; military advisers, and military personnel on their respective territories, as stipulated in the 1954 Geneva Agreements on Viet-Nam (sic.).

Chapter VI THE JOINT MILITARY COMMISSIONS, THE INTERNATIONAL COMMISSION OF CONTROL AND SUPERVISION, THE INTERNATIONAL CONFERENCE

Article 16 (a) The Parties participating in the

Paris Conference on Viet- Nam (sic.) shall immediately designate representatives to form a Four- Party Joint Military Commission with the task of ensuring joint action by the parties in implementing the following provisions of this Agreement: - The first paragraph of Article 2, regarding the enforcement of the cease-fire throughout South Viet-Nam (sic.); - Article 3 (a), regarding the cease-fire by U.S. forces and those of the other foreign countries referred to in that Article; - Article 3 (c), regarding the cease-fire between all parties in South Viet-Nam (sic.); - Article 5, regarding the withdrawal from South Viet-Nam (sic.) of U.S. troops and those of the other foreign countries mentioned in Article 3 (a); - Article 6, regarding the dismantlement (sic.) of military bases in South Viet-Nam of the United States and those of the other foreign countries mentioned in Article 3 (a); - Article 8 (a), regarding the return of captured military personnel and foreign civilians of the parties; - Article 8 (b), regarding the mutual assistance of the parties in getting information about those military personnel and foreign civilians of the parties missing in action. (b) The Four-Party Joint Military Commission shall operate in accordance with the principle of consultations and unanimity. Disagreements shall be referred to the International Commission of Control and Supervision. (c) The Four-Party Joint Military Commission shall begin operating immediately after the signing of this Agreement and end its activities in sixty days, after the completion of the withdrawal of U.S.

troops and those of the other foreign countries mentioned in Article 3 (a) and the completion of the return of captured military personnel and foreign civilians of the parties. (d) The four parties shall agree immediately on the organization, the working procedure, means of activity, and expenditures of the Four-Party Joint Military Commission.

Article 1 7 (a) The two South Vietnamese parties shall immediately designate representatives to form a Two-Party Joint Military Commission with the task of ensuring joint action by the two South Vietnamese parties in implementing the following provisions of this Agreement: - The first paragraph of Article 2, regarding the enforcement of the cease-fire throughout South Viet-Nam (sic.), when the Four-Party Joint Military Commission has ended its activities; - Article 3 (b), regarding the cease-fire between the two South Vietnamese parties; - Article 3 (c), regarding the cease-fire between all parties in South Viet-Nam (sic.), when the Four-Party Joint Military Commission has ended its activities; - Article 7, regarding the prohibition of the introduction of troops into South Viet-Nam (sic.) and all other provisions of this Article; - Article 8 (c), regarding the question of the return of Vietnamese civilian personnel captured and detained in South Viet-Nam (sic.); - Article 1 3, regarding the reduction of the military effectives (sic.) of the two South Vietnamese parties and the demobilization of the troops being reduced. (b) Disagreements shall be referred to the International Commission of Control and Supervision. (c) After the signing of this Agreement, the Two-Party Joint Military Commission shall agree immediately on the measures and organization aimed at enforcing the cease-fire and preserving peace in South Viet-Nam (sic.),

Article 18 (a) After the signing of this Agreement, an International Commission of Control and Supervision shall be established immediately. (b) Until the International Conference provided for in Article 19 makes definitive arrangements, the International Commission of Control and Supervision will report to the four parties on matters concerning the control and supervision of the implementation of the following provisions of this Agreement: - The first paragraph of Article 2, regarding the enforcement of the cease-fire throughout South Viet-Nam (sic.); - Article 3 (a), regarding the cease-fire by U.S. forces and those of the other foreign countries referred to in that Article; - Article 3 (c), regarding the cease-fire between all the parties in South Viet-Nam (sic.); - Article 5, regarding the withdrawal from South Viet-Nam (sic.) of U.S. troops and those of the other foreign countries mentioned in Article 3 (a); - Article 6, regarding the dismantlement (sic.) of military bases in South Viet-Nam (sic.) of the United States and those of the other foreign countries mentioned in Article 3 (a); - Article 8 (a), regarding the return of captured military personnel and foreign civilians of the parties. The International Commission of Control and Supervision shall form control teams for carrying out its tasks. The four parties shall agree immediately on the location and operation of these teams. The parties will facilitate their operation. (c) Until the International Conference makes definitive arrangements, the International Commission of Control and Supervision will report to the two South Vietnamese parties on matters concerning the control and supervision of the implementation of the following provisions of this Agreement: - The first paragraph of Article 2, regarding the enforcement of the cease-fire throughout South Viet-Nam (sic.), when the Four-Party Joint Military Commission has ended its activities; - Article 3 (b), regarding the cease-fire between the two South Vietnamese parties; - Article 3 (c), regarding the cease-fire between all parties in South Viet-Nam (sic.), when the Four-Party Joint Military Commission has ended its activities; - Article 7, regarding the prohibition of the introduction of troops into South Viet-Nam (sic.) and all other provisions of this Article; - Article 8 (c), regarding the question of the return of Vietnamese civilian personnel captured and detained in South Viet-Nam (sic.); - Article 9 (b), regarding the free and democratic general elections in South Viet-Nam (sic.); - Article 13, regarding the reduction of the military effectives (sic.) of the two South Vietnamese parties and the demobilization of the troops being reduced. The International Commission of Control and

Supervision shall form control teams for carrying out its tasks. The two South Vietnamese parties shall agree immediately on the location and operation of these teams. The two South Vietnamese parties will facilitate their operation. (d) The International Commission of Control and Supervision shall be composed of representatives of four countries: Canada, Hungary, Indonesia and Poland. The chairmanship of this Commission will rotate among the members for specific periods to be determined by the Commission. (e) The International Commission of Control and Supervision shall carry out its tasks in accordance with the principle of respect for the sovereignty of South Viet-Nam (sic.). (f) The International Commission of Control and Supervision shall operate in accordance with the principle of consultations and unanimity. (g) The International Commission of Control and Supervision shall begin operating when a cease-fire comes into force in Viet-Nam (sic.). As regards the provisions in Article 18 (b) concerning the four parties, the International Commission of Control and Supervision shall end its activities when the Commission's tasks of control and supervision regarding these provisions have been fulfilled. As regards the provisions in Article 18 (c) concerning the two South Vietnamese parties, the International Commission of Control and Supervision shall end its activities on the request of the government formed after the general elections in South Viet-Nam (sic.) provided for in Article 9 (b). (h) The four parties shall agree immediately on the organization, means of activity, and expenditures of the International Commission of Control and Supervision. The relationship between the International Commission and the International Conference will be agreed upon by the International Commission and the International Conference.

Article 19 The parties agree on the convening of an International Conference within thirty days of the signing of this Agreement to acknowledge the signed agreements; to guarantee the ending of the war, the maintenance of peace in Viet-Nam (sic.), the respect of the Vietnamese people's fundamental national rights, and the South Vietnamese people's right to self-determination; and to contribute to and guarantee peace in Indochina. The United States and the Democratic Republic of Viet-Nam (sic.), on behalf of the parties participating in the Paris Conference on Viet-Nam (sic.) will propose to the following parties that they participate in this International Conference: the People's Republic of China, the Republic of France, the Union of Soviet Socialist Republics, the United Kingdom, the four countries of the International Commission of Control and Supervision, and the Secretary General of the United Nations, together with the parties participating in the Paris Conference on Viet-Nam (sic.).

Chapter VII REGARDING CAMBODIA AND LAOS

Article 20 (a) The parties participating in the Paris Conference on Viet- Nam (sic.) shall strictly respect the 1954 Geneva Agreements on Cambodia's and the 1954 Geneva Agreements on Laos, which recognized the Cambodian and the Lao peoples' fundamental national rights, i.e., the independence, sovereignty, unity, and territorial integrity of these countries. The parties shall respect the neutrality of Cambodia and Laos. The parties participating in the Paris Conference on Viet-Nam (sic.) undertake to refrain from using the territory of Cambodia and the territory of Laos to encroach on the sovereignty and security of one another and of other countries. (b) Foreign countries shall put an end to all military activities in Cambodia and Laos, totally withdraw from and refrain from reintroducing into these two countries troops, military advisers and military personnel, armaments, munitions and war material. (c) The internal affairs of Cambodia and Laos shall be settled by the people of each of these countries without foreign interference. (d) The problems existing between the Indochinese countries shall be settled by the Indochinese parties on the basis of respect for each other's independence, sovereignty, and territorial integrity, and non-interference in each other's internal affairs.

Chapter VIII THE RELATIONSHIP

BETWEEN THE UNITED STATES AND THE DEMOCRATIC REPUBLIC OF VIET-NAM (sic.)

Article 21 The United States anticipates that this Agreement will usher in an era of reconciliation with the Democratic Republic of Viet- Nam (sic.) as with all the peoples of Indochina. In pursuance of its traditional policy, the United States will contribute to healing the wounds of war and to postwar reconstruction of the Democratic Republic of Viet-Nam (sic.) and throughout Indochina.

Article 22 The ending of the war, the restoration of peace in Viet-Nam (sic.), and the strict implementation of this Agreement will create conditions for establishing a new, equal and mutually beneficial relationship between the United States and the Democratic Republic of Viet-Nam (sic.) on the basis of respect for each other's independence and sovereignty, and non-interference in each other's internal affairs. At the same time this will ensure stable peace in Viet-Nam (sic.) and contribute to the preservation of lasting peace in Indochina and Southeast Asia.

Chapter IX OTHER PROVISIONS

Article 23 This Agreement shall enter into force upon signature by plenipotentiary representatives of the parties participating in the Paris Conference on Viet-Nam (sic.). All the parties concerned shall strictly implement this Agreement and its Protocols. Done in Paris this twenty-seventh day of January, one thousand nine hundred and seventy-three, in English and Vietnamese. The English and Vietnamese texts are official and equally authentic. FOR THE GOVERNMENT OF THE FOR THE GOVERNMENT OF THE UNITED STATES OF AMERICA: REPUBLIC OF VIET-NAM (sic.): (Signed): (Signed): William P. Rogers Tran Van Lam Secretary of State Minister for Foreign Affairs FOR THE GOVERNMENT OF THE FOR THE PROVISIONAL DEMOCRATIC REPUBLIC REVOLUTIONARY GOVERNMENT OF VIET-NAM (sic.): OF THE REPUBLIC OF SOUTH VIET-NAM (sic.): (Signed): (Signed): Nguyen Duy Trinh Nguyen Thi Binh Minister for Foreign Affairs Minister for Foreign Affairs [424]

President Nixon's "Peace With Honor": Radio-television broadcast, 23 Jan. 1973

Good evening. I have asked for this radio and television time tonight for the purpose of announcing that we today have concluded an agreement to end the war and bring **peace with honor** (emphasis added) in Vietnam and in Southeast Asia.

The following statement is being issued at this moment in Washington and Hanoi:

At 12:30 Paris time today [Tuesday],

January 23, 1973, **the Agreement on Ending the War and Restoring Peace in Vietnam** (emphasis added) was initialed by Dr. Henry Kissinger on behalf of the United States, and Special Adviser Le Duc Tho on behalf of the Democratic Republic of Vietnam.

The agreement will be formally signed by the parties participating in the Paris Conference on Vietnam on January 27, 1973, at the International Conference Center in Paris.

The cease-fire will take effect at 2400 Greenwich Mean Time, January 27, 1973. The United States and the Democratic Republic of Vietnam express the hope that this agreement will insure stable peace in Vietnam and contribute to the preservation of lasting peace in Indochina and Southeast Asia.

That concludes the formal statement.

Throughout the years of negotiations, we have insisted on **peace with honor** (emphasis added). **In my addresses to the Nation from this room of January 25 and May 8, [1972] I set forth the goals that we considered essential for peace with honor** (emphasis added).

In the settlement that has now been agreed to, **all the conditions that I laid down then have been met** (emphasis added). A cease-fire, internationally supervised, will begin at 7 p.m., this Saturday, January 27, Washington time. Within 60 days from this Saturday, all Americans held prisoners of war throughout Indochina will be released. There will be the fullest possible accounting for all of those who are missing in action.

During the same 60-day period, all American forces will be withdrawn from South Vietnam.

The people of South Vietnam have been guaranteed the right to determine their own future, without outside interference (emphasis added).

By joint agreement, the full text of the agreement and the protocols to carry it out, will be issued tomorrow.

Throughout these negotiations we have been in the closest consultation with President Thieu and other representatives of the Republic of Vietnam. **This settlement meets the goals** (emphasis added) and has the full support of President Thieu and the Government of the Republic of Vietnam, as well as that of our other allies who are affected.

The United States will continue to recognize the Government of the Republic of Vietnam as the sole legitimate government of South Vietnam (emphasis added).

We shall continue to aid South Vietnam within the terms of the agreement and we shall support efforts by the people of South Vietnam to settle their problems peacefully among themselves (emphasis added).

We must recognize that ending the war is only the first step toward building the peace (emphasis added). All parties must now see to it that this is a peace that lasts, and also a peace that heals, and a peace that not only ends the war in Southeast Asia, but contributes to the prospects of peace in the whole world.

This will mean that the terms of the agreement must be scrupulously adhered to (emphasis added). **We shall do everything the agreement requires of us and we shall expect the other parties to do everything it requires of them** (emphasis added). We shall also expect other interested nations to help insure that the agreement is carried out and peace is maintained.

As this long and very difficult war ends, I would like to address a few special words to each of those who have been parties in the conflict.

First, to the people and Government of South Vietnam: By your courage, by your sacrifice, you have won the precious right to determine your own future and you have developed the strength to defend that right. **We look forward to working with you in the future, friends in peace as we have been allies in war** (emphasis added).

To the leaders of North Vietnam: As we have ended the war through negotiations, let us now build a peace of reconciliation. For our part; we are prepared to make a major effort to help achieve that goal. But just as reciprocity was needed to end the war, so, too, will it be needed to build and strengthen the peace.

To the other major powers that have been

involved even indirectly: Now is the time for mutual restraint so that the peace we have achieved can last.

And finally, to all of you who are listening, the American people: Your steadfastness in supporting our insistence on peace with honor has made peace with honor possible. I know that you would not have wanted that peace jeopardized. With our secret negotiations at the sensitive stage they were in during this recent period, for me to have discussed publicly our efforts to secure peace would not only have violated our understanding with North Vietnam, it would have seriously harmed and possibly destroyed the chances for peace. Therefore, I know that you now can understand why, during these past several weeks, I have not made any public statements about those efforts.

The important thing was not to talk about peace, but to get peace and to get the right kind of peace. This we have done (emphasis added).

Now that we have achieved an honorable agreement, let us be proud that America did not settle for a peace that would have betrayed our allies, that would have abandoned our prisoners of war, or that would have ended the war for us but would have continued the war for the 50 million people of Indochina. Let us be proud of the 2 1/2 million young Americans who served in Vietnam, who served with honor and distinction in one of the most selfless enterprises in the history of nations.

And let us be proud of those who sacrificed, who gave their lives so that the people of South Vietnam might live in freedom (emphasis added) and so that the world might live in peace.

In particular, I would like to say a word to some of the bravest people I have ever met-the wives, the children, the families of our prisoners of war and the missing in action. When others called on us to settle on any terms, you had the courage to stand for **the right kind of peace** (emphasis added) so that those who died and those who suffered would not have died and suffered in vain, and so that, where this generation knew war, the next generation would know peace. Nothing means more to me at this moment than the fact that your long vigil is coming to an end.

Just yesterday, a great American, who once occupied this office, died. In his life President [Lyndon B.] Johnson endured the vilification of those who sought to portray him as a man of war. But there was nothing he cared about more deeply than achieving a lasting peace in the world.

I remember the last time I talked with him. It was just the day after New Year's. He spoke then of his concern with bringing peace, with making it **the right kind of peace** (emphasis added), and I was grateful that he once again expressed his support for my efforts to gain such a peace. No one would have welcomed this peace more than he.

And I know he would join me in asking

for those who died and for those who live, **let us consecrate this moment by resolving together to make the peace we have achieved a peace that will last** (emphasis added).

Thank you and good evening.[425]

---

[402] http://www.ibiblio.org/pha/policy/1941/410207a.html (11-20-03). Tokyo Gazette, Vol. IV, no. 9, p. 384-5.

[403] http://www.ibiblio.org/pha/policy/1941/410311b.html (11-20-03). Tokyo Gazette, IV, p. 417, 422 ff.

[404]Department of State Bulletin, July 26, 1941 http://www.ibiblio.org/pha/policy/1941/410724a.html /9-23-03

[405]Unofficial translation, Contemporary Japan, October, 1941.] http://www.ibiblio.org/pha/policy/1941/410729a.html 9/23/03

[406] Tokyo Gazette, Vol. V, no. 3, p. 129-131. http://www.ibiblio.org/pha/policy/1941/410801a.html (9/23/03)

[407] http://www.fordham.edu/halsall/mod/churchill-iron.html (11-19-03).

[408] http://www.yale.edu/lawweb/avalon/trudoc.htm (11-19-03).

[409] http://www.yale.edu/lawweb/avalon/intdip/indoch/inch017.htm (11-20-03). Department of State Bulletin, Oct. 12, 1953, pp. 486-487.

[410] http://www.fordham.edu/halsall/mod/1954-geneva-indochina.html (11-20-03). Modern History Source Book: The Department of State Bulletin, XXXI, No. 788 (August 2, 1954), p. 164: The Final Declaration of The Geneva Conference: On Restoring Peace in Indochina, July 21, 1954.

[411] The Pentagon Papers, pp. 52-53.

[412] http://www.uiowa.edu/~c030162/Common/Handouts/POTUS/IKE.html (11-20-03). The Row of Dominos: Presidential Press Conference April 7, 1954.

[413] http://www.fordham.edu/halsall/mod/1954-eisenhower-vietnam1.html (11-20-03). Modern History Source Book: Department of State Bulletin. November 15, 1954, pp.735-736: President Eisenhower: Letter to Ngo Dinh Diem, October 23, 1954.

414 The Pentagon Papers, Gravel Edition, Volume 2, pp. 635-637.

415 http://www.mtholyoke.edu/acad/intrel/pentagon2/ps5.htm (11-20-03). Kennedy Presidential News Conference as Quoted in the *New York Times*, March 24, 1961. News Conference of March 23, 1961: Statement by President Kennedy on the Importance of Laos: Source: The Pentagon Papers, Gravel Edition, Volume 2, pp. 799-800.

416 Sheehan and others (eds.), *Pentagon Papers*, Crown Publishing Group, 1971, pp. 150-153.

417 http://www.mtholyoke.edu/acad/intrel/pentagon2/ps29.htm (11-20-03). Public Papers of the Presidents, Kennedy, 1963, p. 243: President Kennedy's News Conference, March 6, 1963: Source: The Pentagon Papers, Gravel Edition, Volume 2, pp. 816-817.

418 http://www.mtholyoke.edu/acad/intrel/pentagon2/ps38.htm (11-20-03). President Kennedy's NBC Interview, September 9, 1963, Department of State Bulletin, September 30, 1963, p. 499: Source: The Pentagon Papers, Gravel Edition, Volume 2, pp. 827-828.

419 The Pentagon Papers, pp. 423-427.

420 http://oll.temple.edu/hist249/course/Documents/excerpts_from_speech_given_by_pr.htm (11-20-03) & http://vietnam.vassar.edu/doc12.html (11-20-03). Public Papers of the Presidents of the United States: Lyndon B. Johnson, 1965, pp. 394-397. Excerpts from Speech Given by President Johnson at Johns Hopkins University, on April 7,1965.

421 http://www.usconstitution.com/PresidentNixon'sReportOnVietnam.htm (11-19-03). U. S. Constitution: President Nixon's Report on Vietnam.

422 http://www.nixonfoundation.org/Research_Center/1969_pdf_files/1969_0425.pdf (10-6-03). Nixon Foundation: Research Center.

423 http://www.usconstitution.com/PresidentNixonCambodianInvasion.htm (10-10-03). U. S. Constitution: President Nixon Cambodian Invasion Speech.

424 http://www.aiipowmia.com/sea/ppa1973.html (11-19-03).

425 http://www.usconstitution.com/PeaceWithHonorRichardNixonVietnamWarAgreement.htm (10-8-03) (Text from PRESIDENTIAL DOCUMENTS, vol. 9 (1973), pp. 43-5).

Bibliography

New times call for new methods. The Internet provided the majority of the research assets for this work. Therefore, to provide full disclosure and easy access to source materials I have devised a new manner of bibliographic citation. Instead of listing sources in separate categories such as books, magazines, etc. in alphabetical order sources appear in this bibliography based upon chronology of use. Web-address followed by date of access and site name identifies all Internet sources. A traditional manner cites textual sources. The sources for all documents reproduced in Appendix are listed in this bibliography under that heading.

PREFACE

Berra, Yogi, The Yogi Book: "I Didn't Really Say Everything I Said!" Workman Publishing: New York, NY, 1998

http://gi.grolier.com/presidents/ea/side/mcgovern.html (11-25-03) Informational. Grolier Presents: The American Presidency.

INTRODUCTION

Herrington, Stuart A.. Peace With Honor?. Presido: Novato, CA., 1983.

CHAPTER ONE

Clausewitz, Carl von,. On War. Michael Howard and Peter Paret edition, Princeton: Princeton University Press, 1984.

http://www.newadvent.org/cathen/07765a.htm New Advent (11-19-03).

http://art-hanoi.com/toda/19.html (11-26-03). The Tay-son Rebellion. 1764-1801.

http://www.geocities.com/olmightykhan/Vietnamese.html (11-26-03). Nguyen Hue.

http://www.geocities.com/imperialvietnam/gialong.html (11-26-03). Emperor Gia Long of Vietnam.

http://www.richmond.edu/~ebolt/history398/EmperorMinhMang.html (11-26-03). Emperor Minh Mang

Karnow, Stanley. Vietnam: A History. The Viking Press: New York, 1983.

http://www.newadvent.org/cathen/10699a.htm (11-26-03). New Advent: Napoleon III.

http://www.historyguy.com/wars_of_vietnam.htm (11-25-03). Informational. The History Guy.

http://www.britannica.com/eb/article?eu=65304 (11-17-03).

Informational. Encyclopedia Britanica.

http://www.onwar.com/aced/data/india/indochina1882.htm (11-17-03). OnWar.com

http://www.geocities.com/imperialvietnam/tuduc.html (11-17-03). Informational. Emperor Tu Duc of Vietnam.

Hayes, Carlton, J. H. Contemporary Europe Since 1870. The Macmillian Company: New York, 1958.

Clifford, John H. (Managing Ed.). The Standard History of the World. The University Society: New York, 1914, Volume 6: page 3349, 3635-3636; Volume 7: page 3844-3845, 3851-3854; Volume 8: Pages 4636-4637; Volume 10: page 132-138.; Johnson, Rossiter (Editor-in-Chief).

Kenway, Sir Robert Douglas. "France In Annam." The Great Events by Famous Historians. (Volume 19: pages 120-132) by. The National Alumni: New York, 1905.

http://www.guidetothailand.com/thailand-history/indochina.htm (11-5-03) A Guide to Thailand.

http://reference.allrefer.com/encyclopedia/I/Indochin.html (11-5-03) North American Gazetteer.

http://www.netcomuk.co.uk/~dpohara/thai.htm (11-25-03). Informational. Franco-Thai Conflict in World War II.

http://www.bartleby.com/59/10/nationalistc.html (11-25-03). Informational. Barlttelby.com.

http://www.zum.de/whkmla/region/seasia/xfrindochina.html (11-5-03) World History at KMLA.

http://www.netcomuk.co.uk/~dpohara/thai.htm (11-25-03). Informational. Franco-Thai Conflict in World War II.

http://www.spartacus.schoolnet.co.uk/2WWvichy.htm (11-25-03). Informational. Spartacus.schoolnet.co.uk

http://en.wikipedia.org/wiki/French_Indochina (11-5-03) Wikipedia.

CHAPTER TWO

http://www.vietquoc.com/0006vq.htm (11-17-03). Informational. Some Collective Facts About Ho Chi Minh.

http://reference.allrefer.com/encyclopedia/G/Giap-VoN.html (11-17-03). Informational. AllREFER.com.

http://www.cosmicbaseball.com/giap7.html (11-5-03) Cosmic Baseball Association.

http://www.cnn.com/SPECIALS/cold.war/episodes/11/interviews/giap/ (11-5-03) CNN InterActive.

http://www.historyguy.com/wars_of_vietnam.htm (11-5-03) The History Guy.

http://www.ibiblio.org/pha/policy/1941/410207a.html (11-20-03). Yosuke Matsuoka Japan's Foreign Minister's address at opening of Thai-French indo-china border dispute, Mediation Conference. Tokyo Gazette, Vol. IV, no. 9, pp. 384-5.

http://www.historyguy.com/wars_of_vietnam.htm (11-5-03) The History Guy.

http://www.ibiblio.org/pha/policy/1941/410311b.html (11-20-03). Mediation terms of the Thai-French Indo-china border dispute. Tokyo Gazette, IV, p. 417, 422 ff.

http://www.zum.de/whkmla/region/seasia/wwiifrindoch.html (11-5-03) World History at KMLA.

http://wgordon.web.wesleyan.edu/papers/coprospr.htm/ (11-5-03) Bill Gordon.
Keegan, John. The Second World War. Penquin Books:New York, 1989.

http://www.euronet.nl/users/wilfried/ww2/japan-1.htm (11-5-03) War in the Far East.

http://www.msu.edu/~navarro6/srop.html (11-5-03) A Critical Comparison Between Japanese and American Propaganda during World War II. by Anthony V. Navarro.

Fernández-Armesto, Felipe. Millenium. Scribner: New York, 1995.

Cooper, Chester. The Last Crusade. Dodd, Mead & Co.: New York, 1970.

Bemis, Samuel Flagg. A Diplomatic History of the United States. Holt, Rinehart and Winston, Inc.: New York, 1965.

http://www.zum.de/whkmla/region/seasia/wwiithai.html (11-25-03). Informational. World History at KMLA: World War II Thailand.

Weinberg, Gerhard L. A World at War. Cambridge University Press, 1994.

http://www.spartacus.schoolnet.co.uk/2WWvichy.htm (11-25-03). Informational. Spartacus.schoolnet.co.uk: Vichy France.

http://www.geocities.com/imperialvietnam/baodai.html (11-20-03). Informational. Emperor Bao Dai of Vietnam

http://www.vietquoc.com/0007vq.htm (11-7-03) VietNam's Independence and Ho Chi Minh.

http://www.norodomsihanouk.info/biography/king-cv.htm (11-17-03). Informational. Summary Biography Norodom Sihanouk of Cambodia.

http://www.nationmaster.com/encyclopedia/Sisavang-Vong (11-25-03). Informational. NationMaster.com.

http://travel.yahoo.com/p-travelguide-826566-cambodia_independence-i (11-7-03) Yahoo Travel.

http://www.4dw.net/royalark/Laos/laos.htm (11-7-03) Laos Brief History.

http://www.bartleby.com/65/vi/VietMinh.html (11-5-03) Bartleby.com.

CHAPTER THREE

http://www.coldwar.org (11-14-03). Informational. The Cold War Museum.

http://www.winstonchurchill.org/i4a/pages/index.cfm?pageid=1 (11-14-03). Informational. The Churchill Centre.

http://www.trumanlibrary.org/oralhist/acheson.htm (11-

14-03). Informational. The Truman Presidential Museum & Library.

http://www.eh.net/bookreviews/library/0635.shtml (11-25-03). Informational. Britain and the Greek Economic Crisis, 1944-1947: From Liberation to the Truman Doctrine.

http://www.britannica.com/eb/article?eu=32248 (12-17-03) Informational. Encyclopedia Britannica: EAM-ELAS.

http://www.geocities.com/gunsnroseswillreunite/ (11-25-03) Informational. The Greek Civil War.

http://www.pamun.org/Position-Paper-Example-2.php (11-25-03). Informational. PAMUN: Land Rights in the Dardanelle Straits.

http://www.trumanlibrary.org/oralhist/acheson.htm (11-14-03). Informational. Truman Presidential Museum & Library: Oral History Interview with Dean Acheson.

http://en.wikipedia.org/wiki/Domino_Theory (12-17-03). Informational. Wikipedia: Domino Theory.

Truman, Harry S. Memoirs: 1946-1952. Signet Books: New York, 1956.

McCullough, David. Truman. Simon & Schuster: New York, 1992.

Truman, Margeret. Harry S. Truman. William Morrow & Co. Inc., 1972.

Commager, Henry Steele. Documents of American History. Appelton – Century – Crofts: New York, 1963.

Mann, Robert. A Grand Delusion. Basic Books: New York, 2001.

http://www.albanian.com/main/history/hoxha.html (11-14-03). Informational. Albanian.com.

http://www.spartacus.schoolnet.co.uk/2WWtito.htm (11-14-03). Informational. Spartacus.schoolnet.co.uk.

http://www.un.org/aboutun/history.htm (12-17-03). Informational. About the United Nations/History.

http://www.yale.edu/lawweb/avalon/league/league.htm (11-25-03). Informational. The Avalon Project at Yale Law School: The League of Nations.

http://www.philosophypages.com/ph/marx.htm (11-26-03). Philosophy Pages: Karl Marx.

http://www.centurychina.com/history/krwarfaq.html (11-14-03). Informational. Korean War FAQ.

Matloff, Maurice (Ed.) Army Historical Series: American Military History: Office of the Chief of Military History, U. S. Army: Washington, D.C. 1973.

http://www.fdrlibrary.marist.edu (11-14-03). Informational. Franklin D. Roosevelt Presidential Museum & Library.

http://www.marxists.org/reference/archive/stalin (11-14-03). Informational. Joseph Stalin Reference Archive.

http://times.hankooki.com/lpage/opinion/200306/kt2003061614450111410.htm (11-26-03). Informational. The Korean Times: The Nation Becomes a Colony.

http://clinton.cnn.com/SPECIALS/cold.war/kbank/profiles/kim (11-14-03). Informational. CNN Interactive.

http://www.spartacus.schoolnet.co.uk/COLDsyngman.htm (11-14-03). Informational. Spartacus.schoolnet.co.uk.

http://en2.wikipedia.org/wiki/United_Nations_Security_Council (12-17-03). Informational. Wikipedia: The United Nations Security Council.

http://www.tv.cbc.ca/national/pgminfo/korea/korea2.html (12-3-03). The National Features: Korea - The forgotten War.

http://news.findlaw.com/hdocs/docs/korea/kwar-magr072753.html (11-26-03). Informational. FindLaw.com: Legal News and Commentary: Text Of The Korean War Armistice Agreement July 27, 1953.

http://www.sispain.org/english/history/civil.html (11-14-03). Informational. Spanish Civil War.

CHAPTER FOUR

Bernstein, Barton J. & Allen J Matusow (eds.) The Truman Administration: A Documentary History. Harper & Row Publishers: New York, 1966.

Herring, George C. America's Longest War. Alfred A. Knopf: New York, 1986.

Adams, Sherman. Firsthand Report. Popular Library: New York, 1961.

http://www.yale.edu/lawweb/avalon/intdip/indoch/inch017.

htm (11-20-03). Documents on American Foreign Relations, 1958 (New York, 1954), pp. 347-348. Indochina - Additional United States Aid for France and Indochina: Joint Franco-American Communiqué, September 30, 1953. The Avalon Project at Yale Law School. Informational

http://www.dienbienphu.org/english (11-14-03). Informational. Diên Biên Phú.

http://cityhonors.buffalo.k12.ny.us/city/aca/hist/ibhist/ibhiststud/histiur.html (11-14-03). Informational. The Chinese Civil War by Jamie Iuranich

Donovan, Robert J. Nemesis. St. Martin's: New York, 1984.

http://www.time.com/time/time100/leaders/profile/hochiminh.html (11-5-03). Informational. Ho Chi Minh.

CHAPTER FIVE

http://www.indyflicks.com/danielle/papers/paper04.htm (12-5-03). How Domestic Politics and Balance of Power Considerations influenced the Truman and Eisenhower Administrations' Containment Policy.

Holbo, Paul S. and Robert W. Sellen (eds.). The Eisenhower Era. The Dryden Press: Hinsdale, IL., 1974.

http://www.eisenhower.archives.gov (11-14-03). Informational. The Dwight D. Eisenhower Library & Museum.

http://hungngo.web1000.com/NgoDinhDiem.html (11-17-03). Informational. The Republic of Viet Nam President Ngo Dinh Diem.

Chomsky, Noam. Rethinking Camelot. South End Press: Boston, MA, 1993.

http://flagspot.net/flags/vn-vcong.html#vc (11-14-03). Informational. National Liberation Front (Vietcong)

http://www.nato.int (11-14-03). Informational. North Atlantic Treaty Organization.

http://nixonfamily.freeservers.com/art10.html (11-25-03). Informational. The 1960 election. Stephen E. Ambrose

http://www.coldwar.org/articles/50s/missile_gap.php3 (11-25-03). Informational. The Cold War Museum.

CHAPTER SIX

http://www.cs.umb.edu/jfklibrary (11-14-03). Informational. The John F. Kennedy Library and Museum.

http://mcadams.posc.mu.edu/progjfk5.htm (11-14-03). Kennedy and the Cold war.

http://www.bartleby.com/65/ke/KennedyJF.html (11-25-03). Bartleby.com: The Columbia Encyclopedia, Sixth Edition. 2001: Kennedy, John f.

http://www.apl.org/history/mccarthy/biography.html (11-17-03). Informational. Appleton Public Library.

http://mcadams.posc.mu.edu/progjfk2.htm (11-14-03). The Kennedys and McCarthyism

http://www.angelfire.com/nb/protest/viet.html (11-25-03). Informational. Self-Immolation in Vietnam http://mcadams.posc.mu.edu/progjfk5.htm (11-25-03). Informational. Kennedy and the Cold War.

http://www.jfklibrary.org/60-2nd.htm (11-25-03). John F. Kennedy Library and Museum: Vice President Richard M. Nixon and Senator John F. Kennedy
Second Joint Radio-Television Broadcast October 7, 1960.

http://www.mtholyoke.edu/acad/intrel/pentagon2/ps2.htm (11-20-03). Senator John F. Kennedy's Statement on Limited War in Congressional Record, June 14, 1960, p. 11631. Source: The Pentagon Papers, Gravel Edition, Volume 2, p. 798

http://www.mtholyoke.edu/acad/intrel/pentagon2/ps3.htm (11-20-03). Senator John F. Kennedy's Statement on the Dangerous Role of the People's Republic of China, *Washington Daily News*, September 22, 1960. Source: The Pentagon Papers, Gravel Edition, Volume 2, p. 799.

http://mcadams.posc.mu.edu/progjfk5.htm (11-14-03). Kennedy and the Cold war.

http://www.vietnam-war.info/figures/ngo_dinh_nhu.php (11-17-03). Informational. Vietnam War.

McNamara, Robert S. In Retrospect. Times Books: New York, 1995.

http://www.infoplease.com/ipa/A0878607.html / (10-2-03). Infoplease.com.

http://ilovefreedom.com/quotations/Christian_Herter.htm (11-14-03). Informational. Ilovefreedom.com.

http://www.austlii.edu.au/au/other/dfat/treaties/1955/3.html (11-14-03). Informational. Australian Treaty Series

http://www.mtholyoke.edu/acad/intrel/pentagon2/ps5.htm (11-20-03). Statement by President Kennedy on the Importance of Laos. New York Times, March 24, 1961. Source: *The Pentagon Papers*, Gravel Edition, Volume 2, pp. 799-800.

http://www.lbjlib.utexas.edu (11-14-03). Informational. Lyndon Baines Johnson Museum and Library.

http://www.mtholyoke.edu/acad/intrel/pentagon2/ps10.htm (11-20-03). Joint Communique Issued at Saigon by the Vice President of the United States and the President of Viet-Nam, May 13, 1961. Department of State Bulletin, June 19, 1961, p. 956. Source: The Pentagon Papers, Gravel Edition, Volume 2, p. 803

http://www.ourgeorgiahistory.com/chronpop/304 (11-14-03). Our Georgia History.

http://globetrotter.berkeley.edu/McNamara/mcnamarabio.html (11-14-03). Robert S. McNamara

http://www.austlii.edu.au/au/other/dfat/treaties/1955/3.html (11-18-03). Informational. Australian Treaty Series

http://www.mtholyoke.edu/acad/intrel/pentagon2/ps29.htm (11-20-03). Excerpts from President Kennedy's News Conference, March 6, 1963. Public Papers of the Presidents, Kennedy, 1963, p. 243. Source: The Pentagon Papers, Gravel Edition, Volume 2, pp. 816-817.

http://www.mtholyoke.edu/acad/intrel/pentagon2/ps31.htm

(11-20-03). President Kennedy's View of the "Domino Theory," News Conference, April 24, 1963. Public Papers of the Presidents, Kennedy, 1963, p. 343. Source: The Pentagon Papers, Gravel Edition, Volume 2, pp. 818-819.

http://www.museum.tv/archives/etv/H/htmlH/huntleychet/huntleychet.htm (11-14-03). Informational. HUNTLEY, CHET.

http://www.museum.tv/archives/etv/B/htmlB/brinkleydav/brinkleydav.htm (12-17-03). Informational. Brinkley, David.

http://www.mtholyoke.edu/acad/intrel/pentagon2/ps38.htm (11-20-03). President Kennedy's NBC Interview, September 9, 1963. Department of State Bulletin, September 30, 1963, p. 499. Source: The Pentagon Papers, Gravel Edition, Volume 2, pp. 827-828.

http://www.mtholyoke.edu/acad/intrel/pentagon2/ps43.htm (11-20-03). President Kennedy's Remarks Prepared for Delivery at the Trade Mart in Dallas, November 22, 1963. Public Papers of the Presidents, Kennedy, 1963, p. 890. Source: The Pentagon Papers, Gravel Edition, Volume 2, pp. 830-831.

http://www.geocities.com/CapitolHill/9854/nikita.htm (11-14-03). Informational. The Old Soviet Times: Nikita Sergeievich Kruschev.

http://www.airpower.maxwell.af.mil/airchronicles/aureview/1980/sep-oct/little.html (11-25-03). Wars of National Liberation—Insurgency, Colonel Wendell E. Little USAR (Ret.)

http://mcadams.posc.mu.edu/progjfk5.htm (12-3-03).

Kennedy and the Cold War.

http://www.polytechnic.org/faculty/gfeldmeth/chart.Vietnam.html (11-14-03). The Vietnam War.

http://mcadams.posc.mu.edu/stjohn.htm (12-5-03). Informational. St. John, The Liberal. By Eric Paddon.

CHAPTER SEVEN

http://collections.ic.gc.ca/kingcoal/5/pacificrim/afterwar.html (11-26-03). Informational. King Coal: BC's Coal Heritage: Japan After WW II.

http://www.marshallfoundation.org/about_gcm/marshall_plan.htm (11-26-03). Informational. GCMF: The Marshall Plan.

http://coursesa.matrix.msu.edu/~hst306/documents/indust.html (11-14-03). Informational. Military-Industrial Complex Speech, Dwight D. Eisenhower, 1961

http://www.gwu.edu/~nsarchiv/NSAEBB/NSAEBB101 (11-14-03). Informational. National Security Archive: JFK and the Diem Coup.

http://www.gwu.edu/~nsarchiv/NSAEBB/NSAEBB101/ (11-25-03). JFK and the Diem Coup by John Prados.

http://www.cikadenet.dk/vietnam/Nguyen_Van_Thieu.htm (11-14-03). Informational. Former South Vietnam president Thieu dead in Boston

Berman, Larry. Jyndon Johnson's War. W. W. Norton & Co.: New York, 1989.

http://www.fair.org/media-beat/940727.html (11-25-03). 30-Year Anniversary: Tonkin Gulf Lie Launched Vietnam War: By Jeff Cohen and Norman Solomon.

http://www.luminet.net/~tgort/tonkin.htm (11-14-03). Informational. Gulf of Tonkin Resolution

http://www.english.upenn.edu/~afilreis/50s/bundy-obit.html (11-14-03). Informational. A Memory of McGeorge Bundy

http://www.aftermathpictures.com/aftermat/bombing.html (11-25-03). Aftermath: The Remnants of War.

http://www.vietnampix.com/popww.htm (11-25-03). Informational. General William Westmoreland.

http://www.11thcavnam.com/education/myth_body_counts_were_falsified.htm (11-26-03). Informational. Myth Body Counts Were Falsified.

http://hubcap.clemson.edu/~eemoise/viet8.html (11-25-03). Informational. The Tet Offensive and its Aftermath: by Edwin E. Moïse.

http://www.720mpvietnamproject.org/21-communist%20forces/history-vc/vc-history.html (11-25-03). History of the VC.

http://www.seanet.com/~jimxc/Politics/Mistakes/Vietnam_support.html (11-25-03). Support for the Vietnam War.

http://www.pbs.org/ladybird/shattereddreams/shattered-dreams_doc_re_elect.html (11-25-03). The President announces he will not run for re-election March 31, 1968.

CHAPTER EIGHT

http://www.whitehouse.gov/history/presidents/rn37.html (12-17-03). Informational. The White House: Richard M. Nixon - Biography.

Nixon, Richard M. The Memoirs of Richard Nixon. Grosset & Dunlap: New York, 1978.

http://etext.lib.virginia.edu/journals/EH/EH41/Fricdman41.html (11-15-03). Informational. Volume Forty-One 1999 Essays in History, Published by the Corcoran Department of History at the University of Virginia, "Congress, the President, and the Battle of Ideas: Vietnam Policy, 1965-1969" by Michael Jay Friedman.

http://www.nixonlibrary.org/Research_Center/Vietnam/Nixon_Role.shtml (11-26-03). The Richard Nixon Library & Birthplace Online: President Nixon's Role in Vietnam.

http://www.war-stories.com/khesanh-02.htm (11-15-03). Informational. Khe Sanh: Story and Photos by Bruce M. Geiger, 1998.

http://www.pbs.org/wgbh/amex/vietnam/107ts.html (12-5-03). Informational. Vietnam: A Television History - The Tet Offensive (1968), Transcript.

http://people.mnhs.org/authors/biog_detail.cfm?PersonID=McCa281 (11-15-03). Informational. Minnesota Historical Society: Minnesota Author Biographies Project: Eugene McCarthy.

http://www.politicallibrary.org/TallState/1968dem.html (11-25-03). The New Hampshire Political Library: 1968 New

Hampshire Presidential Primary, March 12, 1968 Democratic Results.

http://www.arlingtoncemetery.net/rfk.htm (11-15-03). Informational. Arlington National Cemetery Website: Robert Francis Kennedy, Attorney General of the United States, U. S. Senator, Presidential Candidate.

http://www.spartacus.schoolnet.co.uk/USAhumphreyH.htm (11-15-03). Informational. Spartacus.schoolnet.co.uk.

http://www.yorkdispatch.com/Stories/0,1413,138~27257~1206255,00.html (11-25-03). Informational.

http://www.usatoday.com/news/opinion/e1106.htm (11-26-03). Informational. USA Elections: Beauty contest races boost publicity.

http://www.geocities.com/verisimus101/rfk/assasination.htm (11-25-03). Informational.

http://www.cnn.com/US/9809/14/wallace.obit/ (11-25-03). Informational. George Wallace Dies: Former Alabama governor made 2 strong bids for president.

http://en2.wikipedia.org/wiki/American_Independent_Party (12-5-03). Informational. American Independent Party, From Wikipedia, the free encyclopedia.

Millet, Allan R. & Peter Maslowski. For the Common Defense. The Free Press: New York, 1994.

http://www.vwip.org/mb/public.htm (12-5-03). Informational. Edwin Moïse: Vietnam War Bibliography Public Opinion.

http://www.courseworkbank.co.uk/coursework/american_public_opinion_during_vietnam_584/ (12-5-03). Informational. American Public Opinion During Vietnam

http://www.seanet.com/~jimxc/Politics/Mistakes/Vietnam_support.html (11-25-03). Support for the Vietnam War.

http://www.landscaper.net/draft.htm (12-5-03). Informational. 15th Field Artillery Regiment: 1969 Draft Lottery.

http://history.acusd.edu/gen/20th/RN/page002.html (11-15-03). Informational. Nixon & Vietnamization

http://en.wikipedia.org/wiki/Nixon_Doctrine (11-19-03). Wikpedia.

http://www.washingtonpost.com/wp-srv/style/longterm/books/chap1/endingthevietnamwar.htm (10-13-03). WashingtonPost.com.

Wells, Tom. The War Within. Henry Holt & Co.: New York, 1994.

http://dsausa.org/about/history.html (11-25-03). A Brief History of the American Left.

http://www.pbs.org/wgbh/amex/vietnam/trenches/mylai.html (11-15-03). Informational. Vietnam Online.

http://www.law.umkc.edu/faculty/projects/ftrials/mylai/myl_bcalleyhtml.htm (11-15-03). Informational. William Calley.

http://www.vhcma.org/fact.html (12-17-03). Vietnam

Helicopter Crew Members Association: Facts of the Vietnam War.

http://www.nixonlibrary.org/Research_Center/Vietnam/Nixon_Role.shtml (12-2-03). Richard Nixon Library & Birthplace: President Nixon's Role In Vietnam.

http://www.geocities.com/nixonkissingerpeacemaker/part2/part2ch5.html (11-15-03). Informational. Escalation: The Cambodian Incursion

http://chnm.gmu.edu/hardhats/cambodia.html (12-2-03). Nixon Announces Invasion of Cambodia.

http://www.vcdh.virginia.edu/HIUS316/mbase/docs/hue.html (11-15-03). Informational. The Massacre at Hue

http://www.pbs.org/wgbh/amex/vietnam/107ts.html (11-15-03). Vietnam: A Television History: The Tet Offensive (1968) Transcript.

http://members.aol.com/nrbooks/chronol.htm (11-25-03). The Kent State Shootings: A Chronology.
http://www.nobel.se/peace/laureates/1973/kissinger-bio.html (11-15-03). Informational. Nobel E-Museum.

http://www.mcgovernlibrary.com/george.htm (12-17-03). Informational. George McGovern.

http://watergate.info (12-17-03). Watergate: The Scanadal the Brought Down Richard Nixon.

http://www.cnn.com/SPECIALS/cold.war/kbank/profiles/brezhnev (11-15-03). Informational. CNN Interactive.

CHAPTER NINE

http://web.jjay.cuny.edu/~jobrien/reference/ob66.html (11-26-03). Informational. The Munich Agreement, 1938.

http://www.fordham.edu/halsall/mod/1954-eisenhower-vietnam1.html (11-20-03). Modern History Sourcebook: President Eisenhower: Letter to Ngo Dinh Diem, October 23, 1954
Department of State Bulletin Novembei 15 1954, pp.735-736.

http://www.uiowa.edu/~c030162/Common/Handouts/POTUS/IKE.html (11-20-03). Presidential Press Conference April 7, 1954

http://www.mtholyoke.edu/acad/intrel/pentagon2/ps10.htm (11-20-03). Joint Communique Issued at Saigon by the Vice President of the United States and the President of Viet-Nam, May 13 1961, Department of State Bulletin, June 19 1961, p. 956. Source: The Pentagon Papers, Gravel Edition, Volume 2, p. 803

Sheehan, Neil & E. W. Kenworthy. The Pentagon Papers, Crown Publishing Group, 1971

http://www.mtholyoke.edu/acad/intrel/pentagon2/ps29.htm (11-20-03). Excerpts from President Kennedy's News Conference, March 6, 1963. Public Papers of the Presidents, Kennedy, 1963, p. 243. Source: The Pentagon Papers, Gravel Edition, Volume 2, pp. 816-817

http://www.mtholyoke.edu/acad/intrel/pentagon2/ps31.htm (11-20-03). President Kennedy's View of the "Domino Theory," News Conference, April 24, 1963. Public Papers of the Presidents, Kennedy, 1963, p. 343. Source: *The Pentagon Papers,* Gravel Edition, Volume 2, pp. 818-819.

http://vietnam.vassar.edu/doc12.html (11-20-03). Excerpts from Speech Given by President Johnson at Johns Hopkins University, April 7,1965. Public Papers of the Presidents of the United States: Lyndon B. Johnson, 1965, pp. 394-397.

http://www.wccusd.k12.ca.us/elcerrito/history/span-amer-war.htm (12-5-03). Informational. The Spanish-American War.

http://www.vwip.org/mb/limited.htm (12-5-03). Informational. Edwin Moïse: Vietnam War Bibliography U.S. Theories of Limited War and Counterinsurgency

http://www.vietnam.ttu.edu/vietnamcenter/events/2002_Symposium/2002Papers_files/tilford.htm (11-26-03). Who Won the Vietnam War and Why It Matters by Earl H. Tilford, Jr.

http://www.mtholyoke.edu/acad/intrel/pentagon2/ps43.htm (11-20-03). President Kennedy's Remarks Prepared for Delivery at the Trade Mart in Dallas, November 22, 1963. Public Papers of the Presidents, Kennedy, 1963, p. 890. Source: *The Pentagon Papers,* Gravel Edition, Volume 2, pp. 830-831.

http://www.usconstitution.com/PresidentNixon'sReportOnVietnam.htm (11-19-03). U. S. Constitution: President Nixon's Report on Vietnam.

http://www.english.uiuc.edu/maps/vietnam/causes.htm (11-18-03). Informational. Modern American Poetry: The Causes of the Vietnam War.

http://www.fordham.edu/halsall/mod/1954-eisenhower-vietnam1.html (11-20-03). Modern History Sourcebook: President Eisenhower: Letter to Ngo Dinh Diem, October 23, 1954

Department of State Bulletin. November 15, 1954, pp.735-736.

CHAPTER TEN

http://www.newsargus.com/newsport/edit/0512000.html (11-26-03). Vietnam: After 25 years, history is skewed.

http://www.time.com/time/asia/asia/magazine/1999/990823/pol_pot1.html (11-15-03). Informational. Time: Asia.

http://www.ku.edu/carrie/archives/milhst-l/19990701.mil/msg00139.html (11-18-03). Blacks in Vietnam War.

http://www.nobel.se/peace/laureates/1973 (12-17-03). Nobel Peace Prize 1973.

http://hubcap.clemson.edu/~eemoise/viet8.html (11-18-03). Edwin E. Moïse The Vietnam Wars, Section 8: The Tet Offensive and its Aftermath.

http://www.sftoday.com/enn2/sumdex.htm (12-5-03) THE 1967 SUMMER OF LOVE a web site tour; http://www.hippy.com/php/index.php (12-5-03). Welcome To Hippyland! Informational.

CHAPTER ELEVEN

http://www.ehistory.com/vietnam/essays/theend/0007.cfm (10-13-03). H-bar Enterprises, Inc.: E-History.

http://www.bbc.co.uk/dna/h2g2/A715060 (11-15-03). H2G2: BBC Homepage.

Nixon, Richard. The Memoirs of Richard Nixon. Grosset & Dunlap: New York, NY. 1978, p. 888.

http://www.nixonfoundation.org/Research_Center/1973_pdf_files/1973_0229.pdf (11-15-03). Nixon Foundation.

http://www.gwu.edu/~nsarchiv/coldwar/interviews/episode-16/kissinger3.html (11-15-03). Episode 16: Détente.

http://www.flyarmy.org/panel/battle/75010100.HTM (11-15-03). Informational. Attack on Phuoc Long information.

http://news.bbc.co.uk/2/low/asia-pacific/716609.stm (11-26-03). BBC News Online: Vietnam Revisited.

http://www.ichiban1.org/html/history/1975_present_post-war/nvn_invasion_1975.htm (11-15-03). North Vietnamese Invasion 1975.

http://www.grunt.com/hownorthvietnamwonthewar.htm (12-5-03). Informational. How North Vietnam Won The War.

http://www.britannica.com/eb/article?eu=414860 (11-15-03). Informational. Encyclopedia Britannica.

http://www.dposs.com/k9/buonmethout.htm (11-15-03).

Informational. Ban Me Thout, Republic of Viet Nam.

http://news.bbc.co.uk/onthisday/hi/dates/stories/april/21/newsid_2935000/2935347.stm (12-5-03). On This Day, April 21, 1975: Vietnam's President Thieu resigns

http://www.generalhieu.com/xuanloc-m.htm (11-15-03). Informational. Xuan Loc Battle.

http://hnn.us/articles/1574.html (11-15 03). History News Network.

http://www.encyclopedia.com/html/M/Minh-D1uo.asp (11-15-03). Informational. Encyclopedia.com.

http://www.dposs.com/k9/tansonhut.htm (11-15-03). Informational. Tan Son Nhut Air Base, Republic of Viet Nam.

http://www.fas.org/man/dod-101/ops/frequent_wind.htm (11-15-03). Informational. Military Analysis Network: Operation Frequent Wind.

CHAPTER TWELVE

http://www.sftoday.com/enn2/sumdex.htm (11-15-03). Informational. The 1967 Summer of Love.

http://www.cuba-junky.com/cuba/missile-crisis.html (11-15-03). Cuba-Junky: All About Cuba.

http://www.multied.com/vietnam/RollingThunder.html (11-26-03). History Central: March 2, 1965: Rolling Thunder Begins.

http://johnshadegg.house.gov/index.cfm?fuseaction=News.DisplayArticle&Article_id=15 (12-5-03) Guns and Butter : National Review June 06, 2002 By : Eric Schlecht

http://more.abcnews.go.com/sections/us/camelot (11-18-03). Informational. More on the Peter Jennings Report: Kennedy's Dangerous World.

http://www.washingtonpost.com/wp-srv/style/longterm/books/chap1/endingthevietnamwar.htm
(10-13-03). Washingtonpost.com.

http://www.nixoncenter.org/publications/articles/4_28_00Vietnam.htm (11-17-03). Informational. The Nixon Center: "Vietnam: Setting the Stage."

http://www.bartleby.com/65/pa/PathetLa.html (11-15-03). Informational. Bartleby.com: The Columbia Encyclopedia, Sixth Edition. 2001. Pathet Lao.

http://www.hmongnet.org/hmong-au/refugee.htm (11-26-03). Refugees From Laos: Historical Background And Causes.

http://www.encyclopedia.com/html/k/khmerr1ou.asp (11-15-03). Informational. Encyclopedia.com: Khmer Rouge.

Sorley, Lewis. A Better War. Harcourt Brace & Co. :New York, 1999.

http://www.hmongnet.org (11-15-03). Informational. WWW Hmong Homepage.

APPENDIX

http://www.ibiblio.org/pha/policy/1941/410207a.html (11-20-03). Tokyo Gazette, Vol. IV, no. 9, p. 384-5: Yosuke Matsuoka Japan's Foreign Minister's address at opening of Thai-French Indo-china border dispute, mediation conference.

http://www.ibiblio.org/pha/policy/1941/410311b.html (11-20-03). Tokyo Gazette, IV, p. 417, 422 ff: Mediation Terms of the Thai-French Indo-china border dispute.

http://www.ibiblio.org/pha/policy/1941/410724a.html (9-23-03). Department of State Bulletin, July 26, 1941: Acting Secretary of State Sumner Welles' statement on Japanese-French collaboration in Indochina.

http://www.ibiblio.org/pha/policy/1941/410729a.html (9/23/03). Unofficial translation, Contemporary Japan, October, 1941: Agreement between Japan and France pledging military co-operation in defense of Indo-china

http://www.ibiblio.org/pha/policy/1941/410801a.html (9/23/03). Tokyo Gazette, Vol. V, no. 3, p. 129-131: Statement by Japanese Board of Information on reinforcing Japanese forces in Indo-china.

http://www.fordham.edu/halsall/mod/churchill-iron.html (11-19-03). Modern History Sourcebook: Winston S. Churchill: "Iron Curtain Speech", March 5, 1946.

http://www.yale.edu/lawweb/avalon/trudoc.htm (11-19-03). The Avalon Project at Yale Law School: Truman Doctrine.

http://www.yale.edu/lawweb/avalon/intdip/indoch/inch017.

htm (11-20-03). Department of State Bulletin, Oct. 12, 1953, pp. 486-487: Indochina - Additional United States Aid for France and Indochina: Joint Franco-American Communiqué, September 30, 1953.

http://www.fordham.edu/halsall/mod/1954-genev a-indochina.html (11-20-03). Modern History Source Book: The Department of State Bulletin, XXXI, No. 788 (August 2, 1954), p. 164: The Final Declaration of The Geneva Conference: On Restoring Peace in Indochina, July 21, 1954.

Sheehan, Neil & E. W. Kenworthy. The Pentagon Papers, Crown Publishing Group, 1971pp. 52-53.

http://www.uiowa.edu/~c030162/Common/Handouts/POTUS/IKE.html (11-20-03). The Row of Dominos: Presidential Press Conference April 7, 1954.

http://www.fordham.edu/halsall/mod/1954-eisenhower-vietnam1.html (11-20-03). Modern History Source Book: Department of State Bulletin. November 15, 1954, pp.735-736: President Eisenhower: Letter to Ngo Dinh Diem, October 23, 1954.

http://www.mtholyoke.edu/acad/intrel/pentagon2/doc97.htm (11-20-03). Memorandum of Conference on January 19, 1961 between President Eisenhower and President-Elect Kennedy on the Subject of Laos. The Pentagon Papers, Gravel Edition, Volume 2, pp. 635-637.

http://www.mtholyoke.edu/acad/intrel/pentagon2/ps5.htm (11-20-03). Kennedy Presidential News Conference as Quoted in the *New York Times*, March 24, 1961. News Conference of March 23, 1961: Statement by President

Kennedy on the Importance of Laos: Source: The Pentagon Papers, Gravel Edition, Volume 2, pp. 799-800.

Sheehan, Neil & E. W. Kenworthy. The Pentagon Papers, Crown Publishing Group, 1971pp. 150-153.

http://www.mtholyoke.edu/acad/intrel/pentagon2/ps29.htm (11-20-03). Public Papers of the Presidents, Kennedy, 1963, p. 243: President Kennedy's News Conference, March 6, 1963: Source: The Pentagon Papers, Gravel Edition, Volume 2, pp. 816-817

http://www.mtholyoke.edu/acad/intrel/pentagon2/ps38.htm (11-20-03). President Kennedy's NBC Interview, September 9, 1963, Department of State Bulletin, September 30, 1963, p. 499: Source: The Pentagon Papers, Gravel Edition, Volume 2, pp. 827-828.

Sheehan, Neil & E. W. Kenworthy. The Pentagon Papers, Crown Publishing Group, 1971, pp. 423-427.

http://oll.temple.edu/hist249/course/Documents/excerpts_from_speech_given_by_pr.htm (11-20-03) & http://vietnam.vassar.edu/doc12.html (11-20-03). Public Papers of the Presidents of the United States: Lyndon B. Johnson, 1965, pp. 394-397. Excerpts from Speech Given by President Johnson at Johns Hopkins University, on April 7,1965.

http://www.usconstitution.com/PresidentNixon'sReportOnVietnam.htm (11-19-03). U. S. Constitution: President Nixon's Report on Vietnam.

http://www.nixonfoundation.org/Research_Center/1969_pdf_files/1969_0425.pdf (10-6-03). Nixon Foundation: Research Center.

http://www.usconstitution.com/PresidentNixonCambodianInvasion.htm (10-10-03). U. S. Constitution: President Nixon Cambodian Invasion Speech.

http://www.aiipowmia.com/sea/ppa1973.html (11-19-03). Paris Peace Accords.

http://www.usconstitution.com/PeaceWithHonorRichardNixonVietnamWarAgreement.htm (10-8-03) U. S. Constitution: Peace with Honor. (Text from PRESIDENTIAL DOCUMENTS, vol. 9 1973), pp. 43-5)

70875898R00228

Made in the USA
San Bernardino, CA
08 March 2018